D1074095

Developing and Documenting the Curriculum

Developing and Documenting the Curriculum

DAVID G. ARMSTRONG

Texas A&M University

PROPERTY OF
THE ANTHONY WAYNE LIBRARY
THE DEFIANCE COLLEGE
DEFIANCE, OHIO
WITHDRAWN
PILGRIM LIBRARY

Allyn and Bacon

Boston   London   Sydney   Toronto

Copyright © 1989 by Allyn and Bacon
A Division of Simon & Schuster
160 Gould Street
Needham Heights, MA 02194

All rights reserved. No part of the material protected by this copyright notice may be reproduced or utilized in any form or by any means, electronic or mechanical, including photocopying, recording, or by any information storage and retrieval system, without the written permission of the copyright owner.

Series Editor: Sean W. Wakely
Production Coordinator: Annette Joseph
Editorial-Production Service: The Book Department
Cover Designer: Susan Slovinsky
Manufacturing Buyer: Tamara McCracken

Library of Congress Cataloging-in-Publication Data
Armstrong, David G.
  Developing and documenting the curriculum.

  Includes bibliographies and indexes.
  1. Curriculum planning. 2. Curriculum
evaluation.   I. Title.
LB2806.15.A76   1988   375′.001   88-7873
ISBN 0-205-11852-6

Printed in the United States of America

10 9 8 7 6 5 4 3 2   93 92 91 90 89

LB
2806.15
.A76
1989
MAY - 6 1992

WITHDRAWN
PILGRIM LIBRARY

VBTDL

Overview

Contents

Preface

Two basic emphases characterize most curriculum textbooks. One focuses heavily on historical and philosophical issues and on theoretical underpinnings of the curriculum field. The other is heavily oriented toward how-to-do-it information centered on a rather narrow area of curricular practice—for example, the design of individual courses. This book recognizes the importance both of foundation issues and of specific guidelines for people who will be engaged in the curriculum-development process.

The first several chapters orient individuals to the field and introduce some general issues of interest to curriculum leaders. This material provides a useful context for students as they move on to topics in subsequent chapters that examine curriculum as it operates at several levels within school districts or large corporate training enterprises. These later chapters provide detailed information about curricular planning for different levels and different audiences. For example, specific directions and models of curriculum documents are provided for managing the total instructional program, individual courses, and units taught within courses.

Throughout, the text devotes particular attention to guidelines for preparing documentation for the public expression of curriculum decisions. It also provides detailed information regarding strategies for disseminating, implementing, monitoring, and evaluating new programs of instruction.

Chapter 1 provides a general overview of the curriculum field, introducing philosophical and psychological foundations of the field, and describing the general flow of curriculum development. Social and cultural influences and alternative orientations to curriculum are also introduced.

Chapter 2 focuses on the issue of organizing for curriculum development. It introduces a basic curriculum-development model and addresses the important issue of how people should be organized for curriculum development.

Chapter 3 presents a number of key concepts associated with curriculum design, highlighting distinctions among a number of general curriculum designs and introducing approaches to content selection.

Chapter 4 lays out a number of schemes for sequencing content, discussing how cognitive, psychomotor, and affective taxonomies can be used to establish priorities among content elements.

Chapter 5 introduces a number of common curriculum documents and describes the major characteristics and primary users of each. The general issue of curriculum-document quality is also introduced, along with some guidelines curriculum developers might follow to produce good documents.

Chapters 6, 7, and 8 provide detailed explanations for formatting three important document types: the general scope and sequence document, the grade-level plan or course plan, and the instructional-unit document. Examples of each document type are included, along with comments about what the developer was trying to do in individual document sections.

Chapter 9 introduces several approaches to implementing a new program. It provides examples of change strategies and focuses special attention on the importance of inservice training that truly responds to the needs of potential program users.

Chapter 10 focuses on curriculum evaluation, introducing a number of critical issues faced by those who evaluate programs. In addition, several comprehensive curriculum-evaluation models are described. Among these are approaches suggested by Ralph Tyler, Daniel Stufflebeam, Robert Stake, and Malcolm Provus.

Many individuals made important contributions to the development of this manuscript. The author particularly wishes to extend thanks to Gregory D. Clark, Larry L. Kraus of the University of Texas at Tyler, J. Clovis Mitchell of the University of South Alabama, and Donald J. Reyes of Northern Illinois University, who made suggestions on early versions of chapters of this book. Other useful critiques were provided by Professors James Kracht and John Stansell of Texas A&M University. Special thanks are owed to Mary Turnbull, who did the initial work on the materials that ultimately developed into the sample curriculum documents in Chapters 6, 7, and 8.

Leslie Sogandares and Pamela Romig devoted careful attention to proofreading and to other technical aspects of manuscript preparation. Their help is gratefully acknowledged. Finally, I wish to thank my wife Nancy for her support and tolerance during the time this book was being written.

CHAPTER 1

An Orientation to Curriculum

This chapter introduces information to help the reader

1. **point out implications for curriculum developers of definitions of the word** *curriculum.*
2. **distinguish between microcurriculum and macrocurriculum.**
3. **describe the general flow of curriculum-development activity.**
4. **contrast varying philosophies of education.**
5. **describe basic positions of individuals who see (a) learning as behavior, (b) learning as perception, and (c) learning as development.**
6. **differentiate between direct influences and indirect influences on curriculum development.**
7. **explain several general orientations to curriculum development.**

INTRODUCTION

Individuals' conceptions of curriculum differ and their views are not just of theoretical importance. Actions of curriculum developers go forward within a certain framework of understanding. Not all curriculum workers have articulated a tight, personal definition of the term; nevertheless, their actions reflect a set of assumptions regarding its defining features.

1

Simply stated, what curriculum developers do is importantly influenced by their view of what curriculum is.

Because of the power of a given conception of curriculum to shape behavior, curriculum specialists need some understanding of alternative views of the term. They need, too, to understand philosophical influences, learning theory influences, and governmental and nongovernmental influences that affect curriculum specialists' behavior. For individuals, these forces come together and are interpreted in ways that give rise to a number of recognizable general orientations to curriculum.

DEFINING CURRICULUM

The word *curriculum* derives from an ancient Latin term meaning a "running course." Through time, its meaning evolved to include the idea of a "running" sequence of courses or learning experiences. In recent years, there have been many attempts to provide more specific definitions of curriculum.

Some authorities have viewed the term *curriculum* broadly. For example, Brubaker defined curriculum as "what persons experience in a setting" (Brubaker, 1982; p. 2). Such a definition pushes curriculum beyond its more traditional associations with schools and other instructional environments. It is so wide-ranging that virtually any life happening might be arguably considered to be within curriculum's domain.

Others have defined the term in more restricted ways. Tanner and Tanner (1980) described curriculum as, "that reconstruction of knowledge and experience, systematically developed under the auspices of the school (or university), to enable the learner to increase his or her control of knowledge and experience" (p. 43). This conception restricts the range of curriculum to plans for learning occurring within the school (or university) setting.

Individual definitions of curriculum also reflect different basic orientations. Some emphasize the content of the instructional program, as Phenix wrote: "the curriculum should consist entirely of knowledge which comes from the disciplines" (Phenix, 1962; p. 64).

Another curriculum orientation emphasizes the importance of curriculum as the plan for transmitting content rather than as the content itself. In this vein, Taba described "curriculum [as] . . . a plan for learning" (Taba, 1962; p. 11). Oliva continued this tradition more recently, describing curriculum as "a plan or program for all the experiences which the learner encounters under the direction of the school" (Oliva, 1982; p. 10).

Varying conceptions of curriculum carry with them different expectations about what curriculum developers should do. For example, someone subscribing to Phenix's (1962) definition of curriculum might expect curriculum developers' primary responsibilities to be finished once content elements from the disciplines had been identified. On the other hand, someone committed to Oliva's (1982) view of curriculum might expect curriculum developers to plan for everything that logically could be thought of as the responsibility of the school. For example, developers might be obligated to plan much of the extracurricular program as well as the academic program. Debates as to the proper range of curriculum developers' responsibilities, as the Phenix (1962) and Oliva (1982) definitions of curriculum suggest, have characterized much dialogue in the field. Figure 1-1 enumerates some alternative definitions of curriculum.

Many traditional definitions of curriculum have tended to be *schoolcentric* in their conception. Large numbers of them reference planning for learning in the schools, but education today occurs in many settings. For example, the military services provide many kinds of training experiences in nonschool settings. Public service agencies such as the Red

---

FIGURE 1-1   Alternative Definitions of Curriculum: Their Implications

Through the years, many definitions of curriculum have been proposed. Look at the following samples of definitions. Then respond to the questions at the bottom.

A. *Curriculum* is the school's adopted program of studies.

B. *Curriculum* consists of contents of the various courses taught in the school.

C. *Curriculum* involves planned interactions among instructors, learners, and learning resources in the school or in other appropriate instructional settings.

D. *Curriculum* encompasses all of the experiences offered to learners under the authority of the school or under the authority of other appropriate instructional agencies.

E. *Curriculum* includes all planned and unplanned experiences of learners in the school and in other appropriate instructional settings.

1. What are the limits of curriculum specialists' responsibilities, given each definition?
2. What do you see as strengths and weaknesses of each definition?
3. Which of these definitions is closest to your own view of "curriculum"?

Cross, the Boy Scouts, the Girl Scouts, the YMCA, and the YWCA provide extensive training services for staff members. Human relations operations and training and development arms in industries offer employees many educational opportunities. Hence the term curriculum needs to be thought of in terms of its applicability to many educational settings.

The definition proposed here is consistent with the tradition that views the curriculum as a plan for learning rather than as the content of learning. It is broad enough to encompass a variety of educational settings and to accommodate a number of philosophical and psychological orientations: A *curriculum* is a master plan for selecting content and organizing learning experiences for the purpose of changing and developing learners' behaviors and insights.

While this conception incorporates a number of perspectives, it should not be accepted as *the* correct definition. It reflects some priorities the writer considers to be important. Others, quite properly, may disagree. As Beane, Toepfer, and Alessi (1986) have pointed out, ". . . If one selects one definition to have 'most favored status,' one should still recognize that several definitions do exist and are just as favored by others. Thus, they cannot be rejected lightly since all have advantages and disadvantages" (p. 35).

LEVELS OF CURRICULUM WORK

Curriculum work occurs at many levels. In central school district offices and within large corporate training divisions, highly trained curriculum specialists lay out general designs for programs that may influence hundreds of teachers and instructors and thousands of learners. Written curriculum documents at this very general planning level, sometimes called *general scope and sequence documents*, may be many volumes in length. Large-scale curriculum work of this type is sometimes referred to as *macrocurriculum*.

Not all curriculum work is done on such a grand scale. The effort of individual instructors to lay out instructional units and lesson plans also constitutes legitimate curriculum activity. Instructional unit plans and lesson plans, which often result from this activity, are the written expression of curriculum work that is sometimes called *microcurriculum*.

There is no precise line of demarcation between macrocurriculum and microcurriculum. The more curriculum work focuses on the development of widely applicable guidelines and provides relatively few specific details about how programs are to be implemented, the more it tends toward macrocurriculum. The more it results in the design of instructional programs for a specific group and the greater the degree of specificity provided in terms of what the teacher or instructor should do, the more it tends toward microcurriculum.

Curriculum work does not even need to be directed toward organization of learning in a formal instructional setting. Virtually any activity qualifies that seeks to select and organize content that will later be transmitted to another in a way that influences his or her behaviors or insights. For example, authors of texts and how-to-do-it books must make many content and organization decisions. When they develop their organizational schemes, they are involved in curriculum work.

THE FLOW OF CURRICULUM-DEVELOPMENT ACTIVITY

Curriculum work covers a broad spectrum of activity. Curriculum developers make decisions about basic curriculum sources. They decide how to weigh the importance of competing philosophical and psychological perspectives. They deal with legal requirements, consider ethical constraints, and respond to contextual characteristics of the settings where programs will be implemented. They integrate information from a wide variety of sources as they adopt a general curriculum orientation. This orientation is useful as they design, implement, and evaluate the curriculum.

A diagram showing the general flow of curriculum-development activity is presented in Figure 1-2.

SOURCES OF THE CURRICULUM

Ralph Tyler (1949) identified three primary sources of the curriculum: society, learners, and knowledge. Curriculum developers consider information from each source as a beginning point for their work.

Every society has unique perspectives regarding what is "true" and important. Each has special assumptions that bind members together and differentiate them from members of other societies. Because curriculum specialists cannot disassociate themselves from their society, they study it to assure that curricula will respond to widely recognized social needs.

Information about the nature of learners is another important data source for curriculum workers. Patterns of learners' physiological, emotional, and intellectual development are studied to identify needs that can be addressed by the curriculum.

Subject-matter knowledge represents a fundamental source of information for curriculum activity. One important outcome of curriculum work is the development of programs capable of transmitting knowledge processes and products to learners. Curriculum developers, in planning

6

FIGURE 1-2 The General Flow of Curriculum-development Activity

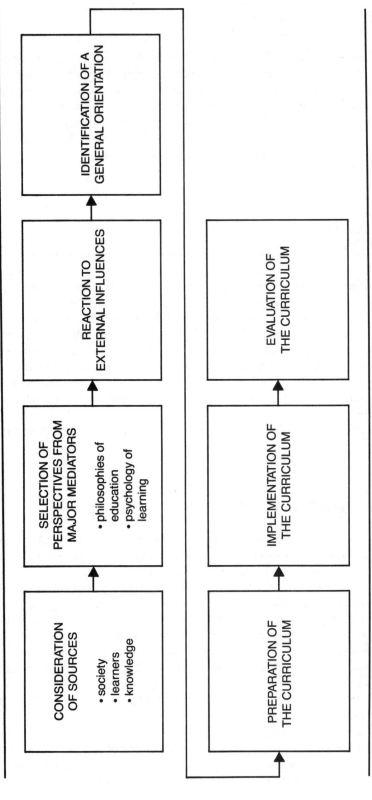

programs, draw on perspectives from academic disciplines and from interdisciplinary efforts. This knowledge forms a key element in curriculum development.

MAJOR MEDIATORS

Once basic decisions have been made about the expectations of society, the nature of learners to be served, and the knowledge to be transmitted, curriculum developers make judgments that reflect their commitments to alternative philosophies of education and psychologies of learning. These decisions help them establish priorities regarding contents to be transmitted. They also suggest general approaches to teaching content to learners.

Decisions reflecting educational philosophy and psychology of learning act as filters to help curriculum workers identify what will be included in new programs. They try to include content and processes that are consistent with adopted philosophical and psychological perspectives.

EXTERNAL INFLUENCES

Curriculum developers must think about a number of influences on the curriculum that are external to their own work. These are varied in nature. They include legal requirements imposed by legislatures, certain ethical constraints, limited availability of learning materials, and interest-group pressures.

GENERAL ORIENTATIONS

There are many ways for curriculum developers to proceed once they have selected information and considered the major mediators and external influences. For example, the relative importance assigned to content from the academic disciplines will vary. The importance of technology and systems' approaches to instructional design will not always be the same.

Additionally, the relative attention paid to learners' personal interests and needs will vary. The degree to which social problems and concerns affect decisions will reflect circumstances peculiar to the setting in which the curriculum is developed.

CURRICULUM DESIGNS

The curriculum design reflects decisions that have been made about what actually must be planned for and delivered as a final result of the curriculum development activity. The design will reflect curriculum sources, major mediators, external influences, and developers' general orientations. In planning a curriculum design, curriculum developers must answer questions such as these:

What content is to be selected?
How is content to be selected?
How is content to be organized?
How is content to be sequenced?
How is content to be prioritized?
How is content to be transmitted?
How is content acquisition to be evaluated?
How are curriculum decisions to be reflected in written form?

Chapters 3, 4, 5, 6, 7, and 8 treat issues associated with these questions.

CURRICULUM IMPLEMENTATION

Once new programs have been developed, they must be implemented. There are a number of approaches that have been devised to facilitate implementation and to assure new programs are being used properly. Chapter 9 deals with this issue in some detail.

CURRICULUM EVALUATION

It is not enough for curriculum development activities to generate specific information about how learners are to be evaluated as they work with the transmitted content. There needs also to be planning for evaluation of the program as a whole. Program evaluation data allow curriculum developers to study the impact of the program as a whole, and additionally, when well designed, this kind of evaluation permits analyses of individual parts of a program. Such analyses provide a rationale for minor internal adjustments or for radical adjustments, if needed, to improve a program's effectiveness. A more detailed treatment of curriculum evaluation is provided in Chapter 10.

PHILOSOPHIES OF EDUCATION

Individual philosophies of education are clusters of ideas that have certain internal consistencies. Each philosophy reflects a unique view of what is good and what is important. These differences are significant because people who subscribe to alternative philosophies may interpret the worth of a given school subject or a given approach to learning in very different ways. It is possible for the work of an individual educator to be held up as a model of sound practice by someone subscribing to one educational philosophy and to be pointed to as an example of "what is wrong with education today" by someone subscribing to a different one.

BASIC PHILOSOPHICAL QUESTIONS

Philosophical perspectives in education stem from basic categories of philosophical inquiry. Among these major categories are *metaphysics, epistemology, axiology,* and *logic.*

Questions associated with *metaphysics* probe issues related to the nature of reality. Speculative questions such as "Is there an ultimate purpose to life?" "Do basic discoverable principles exist that can explain all things?" and "Is life more characterized by constancy or change?" are examples of metaphysical questions. Such questions may appear abstract, but answers do have relevance for school programs. For example, programs designed to teach citizenship presume that a body of knowledge about the characteristics of citizenship has been discovered.

Epistemology is concerned with questions about the nature of knowledge and about ways of knowing. "Are there some unchanging truths, or does truth vary with the situation?" is an example of an epistemological question. Epistemology also focuses heavily on what constitutes the appropriate approach to truth. For some, the answer is the scientific method. For others, it is revealed religion. For still others, it is folk wisdom passed orally from generation to generation. Educational decisions to teach for fact or to teach for process reflect implicit answers to epistemological questions.

Questions associated with *axiology* are concerned with ultimate values. These are examples of axiological questions: "Is life worth living?" "What constitutes 'right' conduct?" and "Should pleasure be immediate, or should pleasure be deferred?" Any examination of learners in schools immediately reveals behaviors reflecting many responses to axiological questions. Some individuals seek immediate gratification through drugs. Some study hard today in the firm conviction that they will be rewarded in the future. An understanding of axiological questions can provide curriculum developers with an important frame of reference as they consider program alternatives.

Logic is concerned with relationships among ideas. Logicians seek rules for separating "correct" thinking from "fallacious" thinking. Logic teaches us how to think clearly. Many instructional programs are organized using either deductive logic or inductive logic. Deductive instruction begins with a presentation of a broad explanatory principle or generalization. This is followed by introductions of examples that will broaden learners' understanding. On the other hand, inductive instruction begins by introducing learners first to the examples. By working with the examples, learners are encouraged to formulate their own broad explanatory principle or generalization. The selection of a deductive or an inductive approach has important implications for curriculum workers who must make content selection and content sequencing decisions.

Answers to questions related to metaphysics, epistemology, axiology, and logic have given rise to a number of influential philosophical systems. Among these are *idealism, realism, pragmatism,* and *existentialism.*

Proponents of *idealism* contend that ultimate truth cannot be known directly through the basic human senses. It can be found only in the intangible world of the mind. Development of insight is a primary objective of idealists. Such disciplines as philosophy, theology, literature, and other liberal arts are thought particularly suitable for developing the capacity of the mind to appreciate important truths and lasting values. Idealists believe these truths to be universally accessible to the mind sufficiently developed to appreciate them.

Realism shares with idealism a belief in the existence of unchanging principles or "truths." While idealists focus on the intangible truth of the mind, realists contend that truth can be verified in a very tangible way through the senses. Realists' tests for truth often involve careful human observation. Because they believe in rational organizational schemes, they often support science instruction, mathematics instruction, and other disciplined approaches characterized by systematic thinking.

Pragmatism challenges the conviction of idealism and realism that there exists a body of unchanging truth. Pragmatists emphasize the changing nature of the universe, contending that truth and values are relative to place, time, and situation. Pragmatists are interested in developing people's ability to think clearly and to solve problems. They favor school subjects that will develop problem-solving skills responsive to the changing conditions learners will face as they live out their lives in a world of change.

Existentialism has less historic standing than idealism, realism, and pragmatism. Its fundamental position is not so clearly defined. A general theme of existentialism is that human beings face one fundamental problem—coming to terms with the inevitability of their own death. This terrible reality is something with which each person must come to terms alone. For this reason, individual choice, freedom, and personal responsibility are strong values of the existentialist. Existentialists reject the imposition of one person's values on another. For curriculum workers, this suggests that electives and opportunities for free choice will be prized.

EDUCATIONAL APPLICATIONS
OF PHILOSOPHY

Over the years, a number of educational applications of philosophy have developed. Among them are *essentialism, perennialism, progressivism,* and *reconstructionism.*

Essentialism probably is more widely accepted among Americans than any of these other orientations. Essentialists believe that there is some specific, basic information that all learners should know. They believe that people need this "practical" knowledge to function as productive members of society.

Essentialists place heavy emphases on science and technical fields. They prize, as well, business and other subjects that have a clear connection to the world of work, and often are suspicious of offerings in the arts and humanities. They do not object to this content *per se* but find it less important. When budgets are tight, essentialists argue for reducing course offerings in these areas in favor of keeping "more practical" courses.

Essentialists hold that people are not naturally "good," and thus support strong adult leadership for younger learners. The ideas of hard work in the classroom and a disciplined classroom environment are integral to this perspective.

Perennialism assumes that a limited number of common themes have challenged humans through the ages. Perennialists believe that there are never any truly new problems; what we see as "new" are really variations on themes that have dominated human affairs for centuries. Since these historic problems have been studied for years, solutions offered by thinkers of the past continue to have validity even today.

For perennialists, the task of schools is to bring learners into contact with the great thinking of the past. This exposure will provide them with a set of insights that will serve them well as they grapple with the challenges of the modern era.

Perennialists favor having all learners encounter a common school program with contents drawn heavily from literature, humanities, and the classics. Classes must be rigorous, and teachers must work hard to assure that no learner leaves school without a solid grasp of those basic insights seen as a key to survival in a human community.

Perennialists are suspicious of vocational programs and of the whole idea of relevance, which may divert learners from the task of mastering "basic human truths." Perennialists argue that learners who leave school with these insights well in hand will have little difficulty in adapting to the demands of the world of work.

Progressivism has little in common with the perspective of the perennialists. Unlike the perennialist who argues that the basic nature of problems stays the same over time, the progressive sees problems varying dramatically in character over time. Hence, for progressives, yesterday's answers have little to offer people confronted with today's problems.

Progressives argue that learning experiences should be organized to provide many opportunities for people to develop individual problem-solving skills. They regard learners and human beings in general as basically "good," and thus assume that they will behave responsibly even when given a good deal of freedom of choice. They believe that learners should be allowed to make some personal learning choices as they go through a school program, and that learning to deal with that freedom is part of the process of growing to maturity in a democratic society.

Content from the social sciences is particularly prized by progressives, as it is thought to afford many opportunities for developing problem-solving skills. Furthermore, these disciplines expose learners to a wide range of dilemmas of types they may be expected to encounter throughout their lives.

Reconstructionism holds that modern technology and modern economies are out of control, and that human society is threatened because no limits have been placed on the evolution of dangerous technologies. Though modern economies have generated wealth at rates undreamed of in the past, poverty remains a particularly intractable problem. The only hope, suggest reconstructionists, is to rebuild societies along more humanistic lines.

This philosophy implies a need to raise learners' levels of social conscience. Programs drawing insights from such disciplines as sociology, with its emphasis on group and social behavior, are thus important to reconstructionists. Reconstructionists view learner activism positively, and would encourage learners to engage in political and other change processes assertively, with a view to bettering the human condition. Ideally, programs in schools would lead human society to reorganize itself.

These descriptions are very brief. They do, however, highlight distinctions among the cited positions. Curriculum developers need to be aware of these differences. They need to recognize, also, that, no matter how hard they work, programs they develop and install will not be supported by everyone. People with different philosophies apply different standards of excellence when they evaluate instructional programs. Figure 1-3 addresses the implications of various philosophical guidelines.

THEORIES OF LEARNING

Specialists vary in how they view the learning process. Specific theories have differing prescriptions for enhancing learners' likelihood of mastering new material. When individuals commit to a particular learning theory they simultaneously commit to a number of assumptions about how contents should be organized, sequenced, and delivered to learners.

There are a number of learning theories of possible interest to curriculum developers. Today, those associated with *behaviorism*, *perception*, and *developmentalism* dominate curriculum planning.

FIGURE 1-3   Implications for Curriculum Workers of Varying Guidelines

Educational policymakers have varying views about what priorities should be reflected in programs. Look below at the brief extracts from four separate policy statements. For each, respond to these questions:

1. What might be the most important subjects or courses in this setting?
2. What philosophical position(s) is (are) reflected?
3. How do you personally feel about each of these policy statements?

A. We believe learners, themselves, to be the best judges of what they should take away from their educational experiences. Programs should help them to make personal decisions about how they should live their own lives. Learners should develop into secure people who "know who they are."

B. After individuals leave our educational programs, they will be confronted by problems of all kinds throughout their lives. Therefore, our programs place very heavy emphases on development of the kinds of problem-solving skills they will need to engage life's challenges.

C. People who best serve our society possess basic skills and understandings. They have a solid grasp of the "practical." While our programs may properly expose learners to all domains of understanding, under no circumstances should we lose sight of the need to produce contributing citizens.

D. Today's answers fail to serve even today's needs. For tomorrow's, they are totally inadequate. We want to encourage learners to challenge present social realities. We want people who are uncomfortable with the world as it is and who will act to make it what it might become.

LEARNING AS BEHAVIOR

Learning theorists associated with behaviorism assume that the world as people take it in through their senses is "real." They believe that the totality of anything can be understood through a careful study of its parts, and that laws of behavior reveal consistent patterns. Learning is defined as a change in behavior.

Behaviorists begin program planning by identifying the nature of the final or *terminal* behavior. They carefully study this whole and identify its parts. They then organize programs that sequence the learning of these parts in an appropriate way, so that the pieces learned will lead gradually and purposefully to the intended outcome. Teachers and instructors study learners' observable behaviors at each step to check their progress.

A number of ideas and guidelines for curriculum specialists have come from the learning-as-behavior orientation. Wolfson (1985; p. 55) suggests the following insights from the behaviorists:

1. Reward, or immediate feedback, is necessary for learning to occur.
2. Learning proceeds by building from simple behaviors to more complex combinations of behavior.
3. Learning tasks should be presented in an ordered sequence.
4. Skills are hierarchical.
5. Desired performance should be specified in advance.
6. Repetition and practice are important to produce learning.*

LEARNING AS PERCEPTION

The basic position of those who view learning as perception is that reality consists not of what comes to us from the senses, but rather of what we make of what comes to us through the senses. Reality does not exist in any kind of absolute sense that can be divorced from human beings. It is, rather, what the world is *perceived* to be. Information is taken in through the senses, operated on by the thought processes, and transformed into information. Learning, then, is defined as a change in stored information or insight.

Adherents of learning-as-perception suggest that people do not tolerate ambiguity. There is a human drive to make sense out of the world by imposing explanations that may or may not be accurate. This tendency imposes an obligation on teachers and instructors to check frequently on the accuracy of learners' stored information.

Program planning begins with identification of broad "wholes," or problem areas. Learners are encouraged to bring their own thoughts to bear on selected topics and issues. Because of their drive to arrive at conclusions, they are provided concurrently with multiple pieces of information that form an information base adequate for responsible decision-making. Active learner thought and active learner manipulation of content are features of programs with a learning-as-perception orientation.

Wolfson (1985; p. 57) suggests a number of implications of the learning-as-perception point of view:

---

* Bernice J. Wolfson. "Psychological Theory and Curricular Thinking." *Current Thought on Curriculum*. Edited by Alex Molnor. 1985 ASCD Yearbook. Alexandria, VA: Association for Supervision and Curriculum Development, 1985, p. 55.

1. Each student's unique perspective is significant for learning.
2. Knowledge is personally constructed, but socially shared.
3. Any system of knowledge is a way of interpreting the world.
4. An individual makes decisions on the basis of his or her perceptions.
5. No matter how the curriculum is designed, learners create their own meanings.
6. Individuals develop self-concepts; that is, one's perception of self emerges in interaction with other people in a cultural context.
7. Students' self-concept is an important factor in their ability to learn.
8. Students and teachers pursue self-actualization in social contexts.*

LEARNING AS DEVELOPMENT

The learning-as-development point of view has more relevance for educators who work with children and young people than it has for the work of teachers and instructors as adults.

Learning-as-development proponents place great importance on physiological, emotional, and other changes young people experience as they grow to maturity. En route to adulthood, all people are thought to pass through identifiable periods or stages, and there are patterns of behaviors and emotional responses identified with each stage. These patterns suggest kinds of learning experiences that are appropriate and inappropriate for learners in different age groups.

Proponents of the learning-as-development perspective take care to tailor programs to the specific developmental stage of the intended audience. They believe that learners' prospects for success are enhanced when there is an appropriate "fit" between the program design and the developmental level of program users.

The following ideas are associated with the learning-as-development perspective:

1. Learners pass through a predictable series of stages as they grow to adulthood.
2. It is futile to challenge learners with work for which they are developmentally unprepared; this will lead only to failure and frustration.
3. The idea of "readiness" plays an important part in any curriculum planning.

---

* Bernice J. Wolfson. "Psychological Theory and Curricular Thinking." *Current Thought on Curriculum.* Edited by Alex Molnor. 1985 ASCD Yearbook. Alexandria, VA: Association for Supervision and Curriculum Development, 1985, p. 57.

4. Learners do best when educational experiences are well fitted to their developmental levels.
5. There are developmental levels with implications for cognitive learning as well as for emotional and moral development.
6. Diagnoses of learners' levels of development are an important precursor to program planning.

Many educational programs today draw insights from a number of learning theory orientations. Because of the importance of learning theory as a foundation for curriculum development, curriculum specialists have an obligation to be well grounded in this area.

SOCIAL AND CULTURAL INFLUENCES

Curriculum specialists operate within a social and cultural environment that imposes certain constraints. The constraints, or influences, are of two types. *Direct influences* are those that have the backing of constituted authority. They direct curriculum specialists to do certain things and to refrain from doing other things. *Indirect influences* are no less important, but their constraints are not the result of legal authority. They are of a *de facto* rather than a *de jure* nature. Indirect influences are certain realities of the social and cultural environment that push curriculum specialists to embrace some decisions and to disavow others.

DIRECT INFLUENCES

Direct influences result from policy decisions of governing bodies and may include actions of the federal, state, and local governments. For example, federal legislation mandates that public schools provide programs for learners with handicapping conditions. Curriculum specialists cannot ignore this requirement. When they develop programs, they are obligated to plan for *mainstreamed* youngsters (learners with handicapping conditions who spend part of the school day in regular classrooms).

Most state governments have provided directives regarding kinds of contents to be included in public school programs. These vary greatly from place to place. Some states prescribe only that certain courses be taught. Others, in recent years, have gone beyond this requirement to mandate specific topics that must be included within each authorized course. Almost universally, state laws say something about the age at which learners may leave school and about graduation requirements. This kind of state legislation provides curriculum specialists with a number of "givens" not open to debate by curriculum workers at the local level. Curriculum programs must meet the language of the law.

Sometimes local governments also pass laws that affect curriculum specialists' freedom of action. For example, there may be laws regarding use of public properties of various kinds during school hours (e.g., scheduling of time in parks, museums, and the like). These regulations place some restrictions on curriculum specialists.

The local authority more likely than a country, city, or town government to place restrictions on curriculum specialists, however, is the school board, which sets policies for the district. Within the range of authority allowed by the state, it can establish course and content requirements of its own. For example, in states requiring all students to take three years of English for high school graduation, a local school board has the option of requiring three and a half or four years for students in the district's own high schools. Other school board actions can place restrictions on what curriculum specialists can do.

In higher education, boards of regents and central administrators make policy decisions with implications for curriculum development. In business and industrial training operations, corporate policy often places certain limitations on kinds of decisions curriculum specialists can make. In virtually every setting where curriculum specialists work, they are faced with certain obligations that result from decisions of important policy-making bodies.

INDIRECT INFLUENCES

Indirect influences, though sometimes more difficult to see than direct ones, nevertheless definitely shape behaviors of curriculum specialists. Indirect influence takes many forms.

Pressure groups of all kinds are an example. Suppose a pressure group in a community favored modifying the secondary program to require all high school students to read at least two plays by Shakespeare in each English class from grades 9 through 12. Such a group might have a long-term objective of having the school board adopt such a policy. If they accomplished this, the requirement would become a mandated, direct influence on curriculum developers. However, even before this were to happen, if the group were large and respected, even the possibility of the board's ultimately being pressured to take such action could influence district curriculum specialists to alter the English program to include more study of Shakespeare's plays. It is not uncommon for new curricular programs to be designed to meet *some* of the desires of a powerful interest group in the hope of heading off a policy decision that would, in time, require that *all* of them be met.

Pressure groups beyond the local community also influence curriculum decisions. For virtually every academic subject, there exists a separate national professional organization dedicated to improvement of instruction in that subject. Among these are the International Reading Association, the National Council of Teachers of English, the National Council for the Social Studies, the National Council of Teachers of Mathematics, and the National Science Teachers Association. Other groups are dedicated to broader issues of program design and management. The Association for Supervision and Curriculum Development (ASCD) is concerned with such issues in public schools, and the American Society for Training and Development (ASTD), the professional group for curriculum specialists and training experts in business and industry, has similar concerns for quality program development in the private sector.

These groups represent only a small sample of the total number of professional organizations with some interest in issues related to curriculum development. Many of them publish guidelines from time to time regarding the characteristics of quality programs. Though these have no legal standing, still they do influence the decisions of curriculum developers. Often curriculum specialists use positions of these professional groups to build a rationale in support of their own decisions. Figure 1-4 cites some *extreme* results of actions by special interest groups.

The range of learning material available to support instruction represents another important indirect influence. Understandably, curriculum specialists are reluctant to develop programs for which no instructional material exists. If they did, teachers and instructors would be required to develop every bit of the print and nonprint materials used by their learners. While curriculum specialists do wish to encourage teachers to prepare materials tailored to specific needs of learners in their classes, it is not considered practical to expect teachers and instructors to deliver a program for which no external support materials are available.

Consider this example. Recently, curriculum specialists in one state were working to revise the entire grades K-to-12 social studies curriculum. At one point in their discussions, they decided to abandon the grade 8 United States history course and to replace it with a new grade 8 United States geography course. A number of logical arguments were made in behalf of the proposal, and initially it had broad support.

Before any final decision was made, a committee was charged with surveying commercial materials to determine the amount of instructional resources to support instruction in a grade 8 United States geography course. The committee failed to find a single available textbook specifically designed for United States geography at this level. Similarly, other support materials were scarce. As a result, the group voted to abandon the idea of requiring such a course.

A lack of available learning materials places no legal obligations on curriculum specialists. It does, however, impose a practical limitation that encourages the support of programs for which such materials presently exist.

FIGURE 1-4   Book and Film Censorship and Curriculum Development

Pressure groups of all kinds attempt to influence the nature of information to which school learners are exposed. Sometimes this takes the form of efforts to bar certain books and films from schools. Here are some recent examples:

- A school district banned William Faulkner's *As I Lay Dying* because of "filthy language."

- A pressure group succeeded in getting a school to remove a film version of *Romeo and Juliet* from a high school English program because of its "encouragement of drug use and suicide."

- Alice Walker's novel *The Color Purple* was challenged because of its "objectionable material."

- In one school district, a librarian responded to a personal objection to nudity by drawing pants on a figure of a naked child in Maurice Sendak's *In the Night Kitchen*.

- Mark Twain's *Huckleberry Finn* has been challenged as inappropriate for school-aged readers because "racist terms" are used to describe blacks.

1. How should a curriculum specialist respond to pressures such as those reflected in these examples?

2. How are conflicts in values between school programs and families of learners to be resolved?

3. In what ways can curriculum decisions reflect sentiments of a majority without trampling on rights of minorities?

4. Have you personally encountered other examples of attempts to restrict the use of certain materials in educational programs? If so, how was the issue finally resolved?

Standardized tests of all kinds influence decisions of curriculum specialists, especially in situations where test results assume great importance. In the state of New York, for example, college-bound secondary students must pass special regents' examinations. Thus, New York secondary school curriculum specialists feel pressure to develop programs that will prepare students for these examinations.

In other settings, where there is great emphasis on students doing well on examinations such as the Scholastic Aptitude Test, curriculum developers must consider the potential impact of projected program changes on students' scores. Though standardized tests again place no legal constraints on what curriculum developers do, they often place some very real practical limitations on the options they can consider.

ORIENTATIONS TO CURRICULUM

Curriculum specialists develop general orientations to curriculum development based on personal responses to information about content, reactions to philosophical alternatives, thoughts about learning theory, and considerations of direct and indirect constraints on their freedom to make decisions. One might think of these orientations as falling into four groups: the *academic orientation*, the *technological orientation*, the *personal orientation*, and the *social orientation*.

These orientations do not represent positions necessarily in conflict. Several of them share a number of common characteristics. The labels, however, reflect different priorities.

THE ACADEMIC ORIENTATION

Curriculum specialists with an *academic orientation* place heavy emphases on content drawn from traditional subjects or disciplines. Goals and objectives for curriculum development are drawn from the *structure* of the individual disciplines, or the basic ideas and questions that define their boundaries.

Curriculum planning is heavily concerned with organizing content from the academic subjects so that it can be mastered by learners. Transmission of information related to these subjects is a very high priority.

THE TECHNOLOGICAL ORIENTATION

Curriculum specialists with a *technological orientation* are extremely interested in how content to be transmitted to learners is broken down and organized. They are committed to a systems approach to instructional design and tend to subscribe to a behavioristic view of learning. They begin by carefully identifying the desired learning outcomes, continue by breaking these down into basic tasks to be mastered, and finally identify and sequence prerequisite skills to be acquired by learners. All elements of the instructional program are described in great detail.

The content of instructional programs may be drawn from many sources. The issue of whether content is drawn from the traditional academic subjects, of great concern to those with an academic orientation, is of less concern than the issue of whether it is systematically organized. The priority here is the nature of program design rather than the academic content to be transmitted.

THE PERSONAL ORIENTATION

Curriculum specialists with a *personal orientation* are very concerned about how learners will be exposed to programs and how they will develop as a result. Many of them are interested in issues related to human development. Often they sympathize with learning-as-development and learning-as-perception points of view.

The personal-orientation approach assigns high priorities to learning experiences oriented toward responding to learners' interests, needs, and capabilities. Content may be directed not only at development of thinking ability and motor skills, but also at clarification of personal values. The academic subjects themselves and the way in which content is organized are of lesser interest than issues related to how learners personally react to and profit from programs.

THE SOCIAL ORIENTATION

Curriculum specialists with a *social orientation* work to develop programs that will produce learners with abilities needed by society. They respond to changes in the society and are willing to modify programs to accommodate altering social needs.

Programs regarded as practical have a high priority. For example, if there is a national shortage of engineers, and leading political figures are lamenting the nature of secondary school mathematics instruction, developers with a social orientation are willing to modify existing school programs to remedy this deficiency. Programs of a vocational nature designed to train learners for productive social roles are important. In summary, the social utility of the school experience is more important than the tie of content to traditional subjects, a systems approach to design, or a concern for individual learner development.

In practice, few curriculum specialists are so narrow that their decisions reflect a commitment to a single orientation to the exclusion of others. As Gay (1980) points out: "curriculum practitioners frequently employ a combination of selective concepts and principles from different theoretical models, along with conventional wisdom and common sense, depending upon the particular planning activities being pursued at the moment and the sociopolitical context in which these activities take place" (pp. 136–137).

SUMMARY

How curriculum workers define curriculum influences what they do. Their roles vary enormously in scope. Some are engaged in macrocurriculum work involving central planning for large numbers of other professionals. Others work in microcurriculum, their roles requiring them to develop specific and detailed instructional plans for a single classroom setting.

Curriculum developers' work requires them to consider several important curriculum sources. They must be familiar with a number of philosophies of education and theories of learning. They must deal with mandates emanating from a number of authorities. They are compelled to respond to indirect pressures from organized interest groups, professional associations, developers of standardized tests, and producers of commercial learning materials.

As a consequence of their interactions with a large number of variables, there is a tendency for curriculum developers to make decisions based on one or more general orientations to curriculum. These are the academic orientation, the technological orientation, the personal orientation, and the social orientation.

EXTENDING AND APPLYING CHAPTER CONTENT

1. Interview someone responsible for curriculum development in a school district central administrative office or in a training-and-development department of a large business. You might wish to ask such questions as these: How do you begin to make decisions about which content to include? To what extent are you influenced by competing theories of learning? How do you deal with situations when people apply different standards of excellence in judging the worth of your work? What kinds of constraints place limitations on curricula you and your people develop?

2. An emerging area of interest to people concerned with learning-as-development is *brain-stage theory.* Researchers have found that the human brain does not grow at a constant rate as young people mature. Rather there are periods characterized by spurts of brain growth and periods when there is little or no growth occurring. Read some professional articles on brain-growth stages. Write a paper in which you cite some implications of this research for individuals developing curricula for young people in middle schools and junior high schools.

3. Prepare a paper in which you describe your own orientation to curriculum. Describe how this orientation is influenced by what you know about philosophies of education and theories of learning.

4. Arrange for a practicing curriculum specialist to visit the class. Ask this

person to indicate how he or she handles complaints from individuals who are philosophically opposed to some adopted curriculum decisions.

5. Consult with professional educational psychologists for some ideas about how similar content might be organized in different ways for different instructional purposes to maintain consistency, respectively, with positions of those who see (a) learning as behavior, (b) learning as perception, and (c) learning as development.

BIBLIOGRAPHY

Armstrong, David G., Kenneth T. Henson, and Tom V. Savage. 1989. *Education: An Introduction*, 3d ed. New York: Macmillan Co.

Bantock, G. H. 1980. *Dilemmas of the Curriculum*. New York: John Wiley and Sons.

Beane, James A., Conrad F. Toepfer, Jr., and Samuel J. Alessi, Jr. 1986. *Curriculum Planning and Development*. Boston: Allyn and Bacon.

Bigge, Morris L. 1981. *Learning Theories for Teachers*, 4th ed. New York: Harper & Row.

Brubaker, Dale L. 1982. *Curriculum Planning: The Dynamics of Theory and Practice*. Glenview, IL: Scott, Foresman and Company.

Connelly, F. Michael and Freema Elbaz. 1980. "Conceptual Bases for Curriculum Thought: A Teacher's Perspective." *Considered Action for Curriculum Improvement*. Edited by Arthur W. Foshay. 1980 ASCD Yearbook. Alexandria, VA: Association for Supervision and Curriculum Development, pp. 95–119.

Cremin, Lawrence A. 1961. *The Transformation of the School: Progressivism in American Education, 1876–1957*. New York: Alfred A. Knopf.

Curtis, S. J. and M. E. A. Boultwood. 1966. *A Short History of Educational Ideas*, 4th ed. London: University Tutorial Press.

Gay, Geneva. 1980. "Conceptual Models of the Curriculum Planning Process." *Considered Action for Curriculum Improvement*. Edited by Arthur W. Foshay. 1980 ASCD Yearbook. Alexandria, VA: Association for Supervision and Curriculum Development, pp. 120–143.

Oliva, Peter F. 1982. *Developing the Curriculum*. Boston: Little, Brown, and Co.

Phenix, Phillip H. 1962. "The Disciplines as Curriculum Content." *Curriculum Crossroads*. Edited by A. Harry Passow. New York: Teachers College Press, pp. 57–71.

Saylor, J. Galen, William M. Alexander, and Arthur J. Lewis. 1981. *Curriculum Planning*, 4th ed. New York: Holt, Rinehart and Winston.

Taba, Hilda. 1962. *Curriculum Development: Theory and Practice*. New York: Harcourt Brace and World.

Tanner, Daniel and Laurel N. Tanner. 1980. *Curriculum Development: Theory into Practice*, 2d ed. New York: Macmillan Co.

Tyler, Ralph W. 1949. *Basic Principles of Curriculum and Instruction*. Chicago: University of Chicago Press.

Wolfson, Bernice J. 1985. "Psychological Theory and Curricular Thinking." *Current Thought on Curriculum*. Edited by Alex Molnar. 1985 ASCD Yearbook. Alexandria, VA: Association for Supervision and Curriculum Development, pp. 52–72.

CHAPTER 2

Organizing for Curriculum Development

This chapter introduces information to help the reader

1. recognize settings where curriculum development can occur.
2. identify a number of basic curriculum-design tasks.
3. recognize the relationship between the complexity of a curriculum-development activity and the number of tasks that must be accomplished.
4. describe some patterns of administrative organization in school districts that may influence how curriculum leaders interact with principals.
5. point out some general patterns of decision-making in curriculum-development activities.

INTRODUCTION

Curriculum development embraces many different activities, some of them very broad in scope. In school districts where developers are planning and implementing programs for all grades in several subject areas, such projects may involve hundreds of people and go on for years.

Other curriculum activities are of a more modest dimension. For example, a relatively small curriculum-development activity might be organized exclusively for the purpose of planning and producing a limited number of instructional units in a given subject area. These units might include detailed information regarding content elements to be taught, objectives to be mastered, procedures for transmitting information to learners, sets of test items, and exhaustive lists of learning materials upon which both instructors and learners can draw.

Still another development project might be dedicated to producing an educational philosophy statement for a school district or for a training-and-development unit of a corporation.

Different curriculum-development tasks require different lengths of time to complete and involve varying configurations of people. Despite their differences, however, most curriculum-development projects share some common features. This chapter introduces some generic tasks that must be responded to by curriculum leaders as they plan and manage curriculum-development projects. The issue of personnel organization and management is also introduced.

CURRICULUM-DEVELOPMENT SETTINGS

Curriculum development goes on in at least five major settings: (1) the national setting, (2) the state or regional setting, (3) the local or divisional setting, (4) the individual institution setting, and (5) the individual classroom setting. There are important differences in curriculum-development activity at each level.

THE NATIONAL SETTING

National curriculum-development work can be directed toward a number of ends. Beginning in the mid-1950s and continuing throughout much of the 1960s, there was an effort to bring subject area professionals together for the purpose of developing comprehensive programs for the schools. These went beyond statements of goals and identification of content elements. A number of these programs developed classroom-ready materials and specific instructional guidelines for teachers. Among these projects were the Biological Science Curriculum Study, the Georgia Anthropology Project, the High School Geography Project, Developing Mathematical Processes, the School Mathematics Study Group, and Project English.

More recent work at the national level generally has been less comprehensive in scope. In particular, there has been less emphasis on developing complete programs that go so far as to provide specific suggestions for instructors. Developers have taken the view that general guidelines formulated nationally can be filled in with more specific information as they are adapted to state and local settings.

An example of curriculum development of this type is the work of such professional organizations as the National Council for the Social Studies to develop a basic program pattern listing contents that should be taught at each grade level. Decisions made by national groups such as this typically are supported by no legal authority.

National curriculum projects often engage the talents of experts in academic areas and experts in curriculum development. The involvement of these people tends to attract the attention of state and local authorities. Hence, guidelines developed at the national level do exert an important influence on state and local educational programming.

National curriculum development does not pertain only to programs designed for use in schools. Large corporations often centralize some of the planning for training and development programs that are delivered in widely scattered national locations. Top program-design specialists are involved in these efforts.

THE STATE OR REGIONAL SETTING

State boards of education and state departments of education set down many guidelines affecting school curricula. These agencies are charged with implementing broad policies outlined by legislators. They also monitor schools' compliance with state regulations. Often these authorities have the power to make policy in areas that have not been addressed directly by legislation.

In times past, state-level curriculum reform efforts were often directed toward winning legislators' support for certain programs or courses. Sometimes narrow interest groups lobbied for the inclusion of special topics into the existing curriculum. For example, in some states, drug education and free enterprise education were mandated by law.

Sometimes legislators were influenced to change basic components of the required program, such as adding a required course in state history or changing the number of years of English required for high school graduation.

Historically, curriculum work at the state level involved decisions going little beyond specification of particular courses or specialized units of study to be included in educational programs. In recent years, however, some states have begun to exert much more influence over specific elements of content treated within the authorized array of school courses. Texas is one such state.

Texas has a list of *essential elements* for every subject taught in grades K to 12. These specify content elements that, by law, must be treated in each school subject. See Figure 2-1 for an illustration of the essential elements for one course.

FIGURE 2-1   Content That, by Law, Must Be Included in Each United States Government Course Taught in the Schools of Texas

(e)   United States government (½ unit). United States government shall include the following essential elements:

(1)   Foundations of the United States political system. The student shall be provided opportunities to:

(A)   explain reasons governments are established;

(B)   analyze the differences between direct and representative democracy;

(C)   compare United States political institutions, processes, and values with other governmental systems;

(D)   trace political ideas from the Ancient World, Western Europe, and the 13 colonies that formed the foundation of the United States system of government;

(E)   trace the growth of the two-political party system in the United States; and

(F)   analyze major historical documents relating to the political development of the United States.

(2)   Development of the United States governmental system. The student shall be provided opportunities to:

(A)   analyze the purposes and political and economic philosophies of the United States Constitution, Bill of Rights, and Declaration of Independence;

(B)   recognize significant individuals who played important roles in establishing the government of the United States;

(C)   analyze the impact of Supreme Court decisions on the American governmental system; and

(D)   explain due process of law.

(3)   Structures and functions of the United States governmental systems. The student shall be provided opportunities to:

(A)   describe the structures and functions of governments at federal, state, and local levels;

(B)   identify executive, legislative, and judicial authority roles on national, state, and local levels;

(C)   understand the taxing and spending functions of national, state, and local levels of government and the impact of these functions; and

(D)   analyze techniques for maintaining a division of power among branches of government and between national and state levels.

(4)   Participation and decision making in civic affairs. The student shall be provided opportunities to:

(A)   examine factors that influence an individual's political beliefs and behavior;

(B)   understand the functions of political parties in the United States political process;

(C)   analyze the functions of minor political parties and interest groups in the American political process; and

(D)   interpret the concept that the United States has a "government of law, not men."

1. How might state regulations such as these affect the work of curriculum specialists in local school districts?
2. What is your personal reaction to guidelines of this type? Why do you feel this way?

Source: *State Board of Education Roles for Curriculum: Principles, Standards, and Procedures for Accreditation of School Districts.* Austin, TX: Texas Education Agency, 1984. pp. 147–148.

Though this pattern is by no means universal, there is a tendency for curriculum activity at the state level to result in program decisions that, formerly, were left to state departments of education, local school districts, and teachers. Though curriculum specialists may play some role at the state level, in many cases decisions are heavily influenced by the opinions of legislators. Since legislators react to what they hear from their voting constituents, the judgments of informed curriculum leaders and educators may carry less weight here than at the local and institutional levels.

Not all curriculum development at the state level involves political decision-making by legislators. State organizations of educators, for example, state English and mathematics groups, sometimes establish guidelines for instruction in their respective subjects. Often, these guidelines suggest general patterns and leave more specific implementation decisions to curriculum specialists and educators at the local, institutional, and classroom levels.

Private sector curriculum development that is analogous to school curriculum development at the state level often occurs at the regional level as well. Large corporations often divide the country into a few large regions for administrative purposes. For example, a Western Region might encompass the thirteen western states. Because of specialized problems, corporate curriculum leaders in regional offices sometimes develop programs designed for exclusive use within the region's training and development units.

THE LOCAL OR DIVISIONAL SETTING

Much curriculum development continues to occur locally, where curriculum leaders play very important roles. It is here that master plans guiding instructional programs are developed, and here that steps are initiated that will result in more specific building-level and individual-classroom-level plans.

Curriculum leaders at the local level oversee curriculum development at the school-system level, the building level, and the individual-classroom level. These specialists have important managerial responsibilities, including overseeing the development of programs that are internally consistent. For example, they aim for programs that encourage instructional practices in individual classrooms consistent with goals adopted at the school-district level.

The work of the individual curriculum leader varies with the size of the local setting. In a large school district, a curriculum director may supervise a staff of curriculum specialists. In smaller operations, one curriculum specialist may be responsible for all curriculum-development work.

In the private sector, some large corporations subdivide their major regions into small units that may be called divisions. These might span parts of several states, include all of one state, or include only a portion of a large state. For example, there might be a Northern California Division and a Southern California Division. Where employee training needs in one division of a corporation differ from those throughout the region or throughout the corporation as a whole, division-level curriculum leaders develop programs tailored specifically for use within their own divisions.

THE INDIVIDUAL INSTITUTION SETTING

In a school district, the individual institution is a single public school. Curriculum development at this level involves planning, developing, and implementing instructional programs for use in the individual building. Typically, district-level curriculum leaders work closely with building administrators and with teacher representatives in curriculum-development projects. Special attention is given to providing for the instructional needs of both building administrators and classroom teachers.

In corporate settings, the individual institution is a single factory or business location. Programs planned are those to be implemented at that site. Directors of training and other top training-and-development officers play an important role in managing the curriculum-development effort.

Curriculum development at the level of the individual institution tends to tie planning to more general guidelines developed at the local school district level (in the case of school programs) or the division level (in the case of private-sector programs). School or corporate administrators play a role along with some teachers and instructors in an effort to produce guidelines that can be refined and made more specific by classroom teachers and instructors.

THE INDIVIDUAL CLASSROOM SETTING

Curriculum development at this level requires direct participation of large numbers of teachers and instructors. It focuses on careful planning of instructional units that are "classroom ready." Curriculum development in this setting has a heavy nuts-and-bolts orientation directed at providing teachers and instructors with highly specific information regarding what is to be taught, practical suggestions for introducing content, testing ideas, sources of needed learning materials, and other issues of importance to teachers and instructors. Figure 2-2 addresses some problems that can arise when local teachers write their own instructional units in isolation.

FIGURE 2-2   Development of Instructional Units by Local Teachers

Two school district curriculum directors recently discussed some problems they were facing. One of them made these comments:

> "I am very much committed to the *idea* that teachers should help develop the new teaching units in the social studies revision, but I have had some real problems. There is just so much difference in what these people know. Their writing skills are all over the place. Some can follow a format, but others can't.

> "My staff and I are having to rewrite practically everything that comes in. I'm about at the point of giving up on our own people. I think we might be better off to find some professional curriculum writers. I would want people with teaching experience, of course. I'm convinced they would produce better materials than our own teachers. In the long run, I think we might get a better program."

1. How do you react to the speaker's position?
2. How would you respond to this argument?
3. What kinds of things might a curriculum specialist do to respond to the varying levels of expertise local teachers bring to a curriculum-development task?

Curriculum leaders and administrators play an important information-dissemination role at the individual classroom level. They provide information regarding general guidelines that may have been developed at the local or divisional level and the individual institutional level. They may suggest general models for teachers and instructors to follow as they prepare instructional units. Curriculum specialists' roles here are, in large measure, directed to overseeing the development of instructional units that will be consistent with more general institution-level and local- or division-level guidelines.

A CURRICULUM-DEVELOPMENT MODEL

Curriculum-development tasks are those steps that must be accomplished en route to completing a curriculum-development project. Numbers of tasks will vary with the intended result of a given activity. For example, a relatively small number will be required to prepare a new school district philosophy statement. On the other hand, a project aimed at installing a new English program in every elementary school classroom will involve identification and completion of a much larger number of tasks.

Over the years, experts in curriculum have developed a number of curriculum-development models (Tyler, 1949; Gagne and Briggs, 1979; Hunkins, 1980; Miller and Seller, 1985). These include curriculum tasks that must be performed by individuals involved in the development of a wide variety of curriculum-development projects.

There is no master list of essential curriculum tasks, because different authorities conceptualize needed tasks in different ways. The following list, however, includes tasks that are representative of those found in many curriculum-development models:

1. Identify needs and purposes.
2. Select and organize participants.
3. Develop a master program management scheme.
4. Develop components needed for each setting.
5. Pilot test/assess/reorganize.
6. Disseminate and implement.
7. Evaluate and revise.

Curriculum development today is frequently viewed as a continuous or circular activity rather than a linear activity with a fixed beginning and end (Miller and Seller, 1985). There are times during a curriculum project when certain tasks are being performed and others are largely ignored. However, over a longer period of time, tasks that for a time appear to be finished will need to be done again. Curriculum activity is dynamic rather than static. Figure 2-3 depicts a curriculum-development model featuring the seven tasks introduced above.

IDENTIFY NEEDS AND PURPOSES

The first task curriculum developers face is to identify needs and purposes. Curriculum development does not go forward in the absence of some kind of a need. Analyses may begin with a consideration of "what ought to be" in light of "what is." Discrepancies are identified, and these needs help establish purposes for the curriculum-development activity.

Purposes may be very broad or very narrow. For example, there may be an expectation that a detailed revision of a high school mathematics program will require the development of new instructional units for all high-school level mathematics courses. On the other hand, there might be an interest only in revising a single unit of work within a given course.

A clear conception of purpose is essential if rational decisions are to be made about other critical curriculum-development tasks. Lacking such

FIGURE 2-3   A Curriculum-development Model

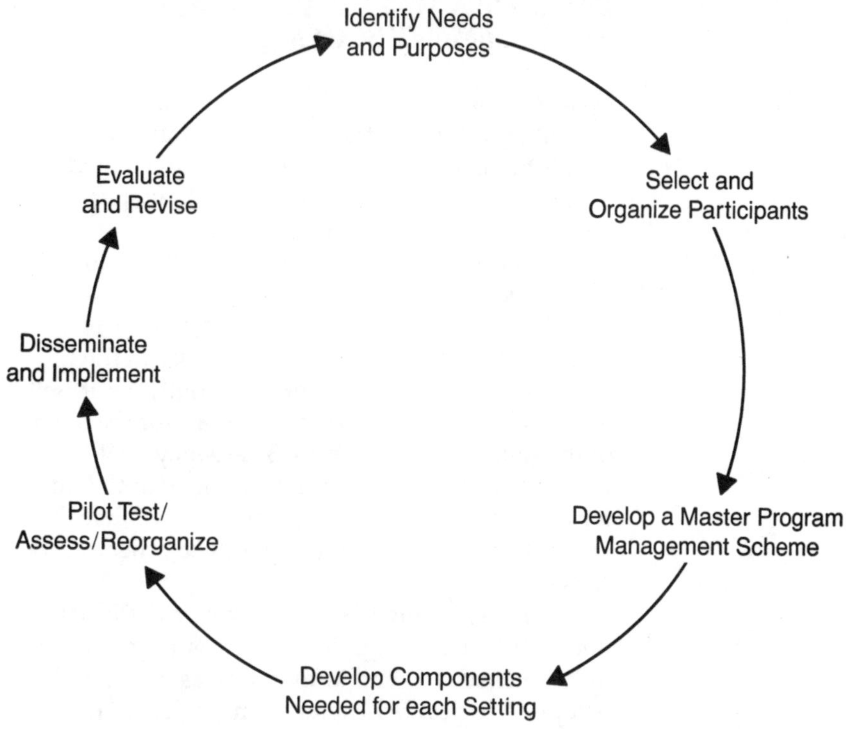

a focus, a curriculum-development activity may wander off in unproductive directions.

SELECT AND ORGANIZE PARTICIPANTS

The identification of project needs and purposes guides the selection of people who will participate. In part, these purposes should help to identify the kinds of people who will be users of any materials and programs that are developed. If these users are to be instructors, it makes sense for some instructors to be directly involved in the development activity. If the purpose is to improve a philosophy statement that will be disseminated to members of the community, then, perhaps, lay citizens have some role to play in its development.

People involved in curriculum development divide into two broad categories: professionals and nonprofessionals (Doll, 1986). Part of the task of the curriculum leader with responsibilities for a curriculum-development activity is to identify and organize people from both of these categories who will participate. Attention to organizing people and laying out fair but firm rules for making decisions smooths the curriculum-development process.

DEVELOP A MASTER PROGRAM MANAGEMENT SCHEME

This step looks beyond the organization of the curriculum-development project and the selection and organization of people to the need to provide for a management scheme for the finished project. In a curriculum-development project with a very limited purpose—for example, the revision of the philosophy statement—there would not need to be a master program management scheme. There would be no complex program developed that would require it.

On the other hand, a large-scale project devoted to making major changes in something as broad in scope as the English program in a high school calls for careful thinking about how it will be managed. For example, changes will have implications for the overall scope and sequence of the total district program. There may well have to be modifications of the master scope and sequence document. Additionally, course guides for English in individual high schools will have to be modified. For individual English teachers, there will be a need to prepare sets of new instructional units.

Decisions must be made that will allow for a consistency among documents used to guide programs in each setting, local school district, individual school, and individual classroom. Subsequent chapters of the text provide detailed explanations of functions and formats of some useful program management documents.

DEVELOP COMPONENTS NEEDED
FOR EACH SETTING

Once the master program management scheme has been identified, there is a need to develop information for each relevant setting. This task is simpler and can be completed more quickly when the curriculum-development activity involves preparation of only a single product for use in a single setting. If the curriculum-development purpose is limited to producing a philosophy statement, then this task is done once a format for the document is established, general categories of information to be included are identified, and the document is written.

More complex curriculum-development projects require much more time. A project to design an English program for a high school will involve many people, result in the publication of numerous documents, and require several years of work. At any given time in a large-scale project, individual components of the project may be at different stages of completion. For example, some instructional units may be finished and available for pilot testing in the schools before work has begun on other instructional units

PILOT TEST, ASSESS, REORGANIZE

This task requires the use of preliminary versions of components of new programs. Pilot testing involves identification of a small sample of *final users* who react to elements of what has been developed. In the case of instructional units, pilot testing may involve small numbers of teachers who will teach from these materials, note their reactions and those of their students, and report findings back to leaders of the curriculum-development project. Similarly, a draft of a proposed philosophy statement may be provided to selected community leaders, school officials, parents, and teachers for comment. Their reactions are channeled back to the leaders of the group charged with developing the material.

Results of pilot testing are used by the curriculum-development group as they analyze what has been prepared and review and reorganize materials. This review process allows curriculum developers to produce programs and materials ready to be adopted and implemented.

DISSEMINATE AND IMPLEMENT

This task focuses on the distribution of the new program and supporting materials and their actual implementation in each relevant setting. Curriculum leaders need to develop plans both to get program information distributed and to oversee its initial and continuing use. Monitoring use is particularly critical. The new program and material at this stage may be in the hands of many people who know relatively little about it, and the way a new program is used has much to do with its effectiveness. Important skills associated with dissemination and program monitoring that curriculum leaders should have are discussed in some detail in Chapter 9.

EVALUATE AND REVISE

Once a new program has been implemented, curriculum leaders must monitor its effectiveness. To do this, they need to be familiar with some program assessment procedures. Several of these are introduced in Chapter 10.

Evaluation results may well suggest a need to revise certain program components. Evaluation data are analyzed with a view to identifying certain weak spots. These are targeted for special attention. Ideally, adjustments are made that eliminate problem areas and contribute to improving overall program quality. Furthermore, evaluation results are kept for the purpose of providing a more substantial data base should a decision be made in the future to undertake a massive program revision. This information can be used to analyze needs and to reconceptualize purposes before the new curriculum activity begins.

ORGANIZATION OF PERSONNEL

The organization of personnel for curriculum work has two important dimensions. First, there is the formal, ongoing structure of the school district or corporate entity that employs curriculum specialists. Their status within this structure implies what they can and cannot do. The relative clout of curriculum leaders within their respective organizations varies from setting to setting.

Beyond this formal, ongoing structure, curriculum-development tasks generate personnel needs that are project-specific. Some large and complex curriculum-development schemes require the services of large numbers of people from diverse backgrounds. Others require smaller numbers. Curriculum leaders must analyze specific project personnel needs and develop plans that bring in the talents necessary to complete a job properly and on time.

CURRICULUM LEADERS IN SCHOOL ORGANIZATIONS

To understand how curriculum leaders function within the administrative structure of a school district, some understanding of the terms *line relationship* and *staff relationship* is necessary. A line relationship refers to a relationship in which someone has a clear authority to impose a decision on his or her subordinates. For example, a superintendent exercises line authority over his or her assistant superintendents. The school board exercises line authority over the superintendent.

A staff relationship is of a different character. It is a relationship that is advisory in nature. Someone in a staff relationship to another may suggest that he or she do something, but has no power to force the adoption of the suggestion. A supervisor of social studies education may work hard to convince a principal to assign a certain teacher to a given course. However, the supervisor, in most districts, cannot force the principal to do this. His or her relationship to the principal is staff, not line.

Within a large school district, people tend to have staff relationships with some people and line relationships with others. For example, a curriculum director usually has line authority over subject-area curriculum specialists but a staff relationship with the superintendent.

The exact nature of these staff and line relationships influences the behavior of curriculum personnel. An organizational model found in many school districts features an assistant superintendent for curriculum and instruction who is a direct subordinate of the superintendent. This person has line authority over the director of curriculum and other subordinate curriculum specialists. On the other hand, the assistant superintendent for curriculum and instruction has a staff relationship with building principals. The principals report directly to the superintendent. A diagram of this kind of administrative structure is illustrated in Figure 2-4.

This arrangement makes it necessary for the assistant superintendent for curriculum and instruction and for all subordinate central-office curriculum personnel to become very adept at public relations. Principals hold key roles in their schools, often having the final say (unless contradicted by the superintendent) on implementing changes in their schools' instructional programs. Curriculum leaders must work closely with each other to win principals' support for any curricular change.

In this arrangement, the relationship between the assistant superintendent for curriculum and instruction and the superintendent is also very important. The superintendent, if convinced, may be willing to support a curriculum decision some principals are resisting. The assistant superintendent for curriculum and instruction may well find himself or herself aligned against the position of another assistant superintendent who is also trying to get a decision from the superintendent. The assistant superintendent for curriculum and instruction must be a good thinker and an able negotiator.

Not all school districts configure their central administrative office in this way. In some places, where curriculum has been assigned a very high priority, principals report not directly to the superintendent but rather to the assistant superintendent for curriculum and instruction. A diagram illustrating this kind of an arrangement is depicted in Figure 2-5.

FIGURE 2-4   A School District Organization Reflecting a Staff Relationship Between the Assistant Superintendent for Curriculum and Instruction and Principals

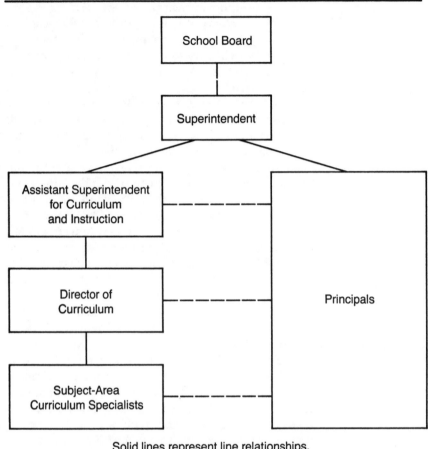

Solid lines represent line relationships.
Dotted lines represent staff relationships.

Note how in this arrangement the assistant superintendent for curriculum and instruction exercises a line authority over principals. Theoretically, principals should be very willing to respond to their responsibilities in the areas of curriculum and instruction, but this arrangement puts real power over school programming in the hands of the assistant superintendent for curriculum and instruction. It tends, too, to enhance the status within the district of all curriculum specialists. The public relations function of curriculum leaders is still very important. However, this administrative setup tends to make principals attentive to the assistant superintendent for curriculum and instruction and his or her professional staff.

These two administrative schemes exemplify many that are found in

FIGURE 2-5   A School District Organization Reflecting a Line Relationship Between the Assistant Superintendent for Curriculum and Instruction and Principals

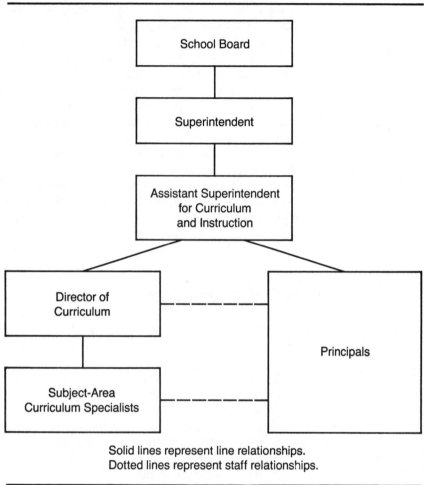

Solid lines represent line relationships.
Dotted lines represent staff relationships.

school districts. It is fair to say that curriculum leaders most frequently have staff relationships with school principals. This suggests a need for individuals who are articulate, personable, and able to make their case with educators who must respond to pressures from many other sources.

MANAGING THE CURRICULUM-DEVELOPMENT FUNCTION

School districts have developed a number of schemes for managing curriculum development. Small districts may have no formal organizational arrangement. The superintendent or, in slightly larger districts, an assistant superintendent may organize *ad hoc* groups to work on specific curriculum tasks. Larger districts have permanent administrative arrangements for dealing with issues related to curriculum development. An example of a permanent scheme is illustrated in Figure 2-6.

The arrangement depicted in Figure 2-6 reflects a decision to vest overall curriculum policy decisions in a small central district curriculum council, which includes a selection of administrators, teachers, learners, and community members. Typically, in an organizational plan of this type, supervision of hands-on curriculum-development work (preparation of new courses, new instructional units, and so forth) is managed by program area curriculum councils.

Participants in specific curriculum-development activities often will include people in individual buildings who may be organized into ad hoc curriculum groups as part of their participation in individual projects. In some buildings, such groups exist more or less continuously. They transmit ideas to and react to ideas from program area curriculum councils and from the central curriculum council.

TASK-SPECIFIC PERSONNEL SELECTION

People from seven categories often play roles in a curriculum-development activity:

1. curriculum specialists
2. teachers/instructors
3. learners
4. principals/corporate unit supervisors
5. central office administrators/corporate administrators
6. special experts
7. lay public representatives

The nature of the involvement of people from each group will be determined by the nature of the individual curriculum-development activity. Hunkins pointed out that "in addition to the question of whom to involve are questions directed at determining the special backgrounds, skills, and abilities individuals require for particular curriculum involvement. What talents do participants require? Where are such talents to be used?" (1980; p. 113).

Hunkins raises some excellent points. Selecting personnel for the cosmetic reason of getting someone from a given category is shortsighted. These individuals will be called upon to commit a good deal of time and will be expected to contribute ideas. In short, when the hard work begins, people are needed who are capable of doing the job.

FIGURE 2-6 An Organization Plan for Managing Curriculum Development in a Large School District

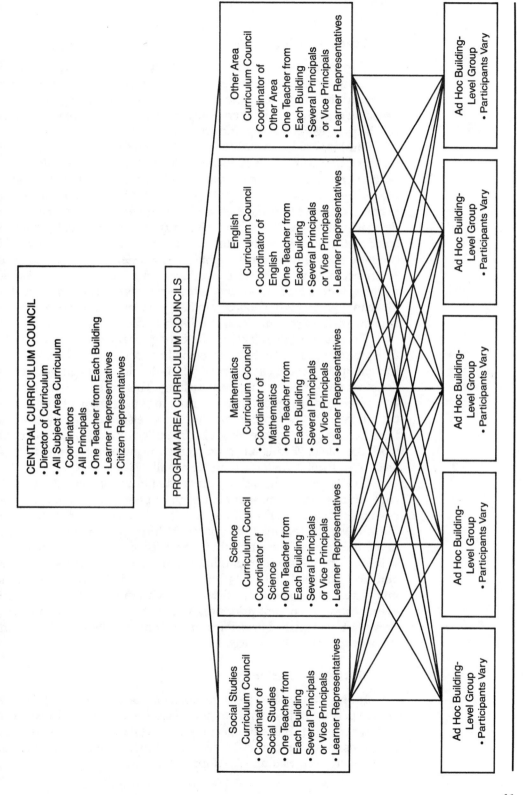

41

Curriculum Specialists

Curriculum specialists will generally take a leadership role in a curriculum-development project. Sometimes someone else will be titular head, but the expertise of the curriculum specialist is required to established an organizational scheme, suggest tasks for participants, and oversee the progress of the ongoing activity.

The curriculum specialist often will decide upon the composition of the group involved in a particular activity. If this is a small-scale effort, directed perhaps at developing some new instructional units for a specific secondary school course, the total effort might involve only three or four people. A project to revise the programming for gifted and talented students in grades K to 12 might involve forty or more people. Such a project could well take several years to complete and the organization would be complex. For example, there might be a small steering committee of six or seven people plus a variety of working committees. (Some possibilities might include: a grades K–3 committee, a middle grades committee, a middle school/junior high school committee, a senior high school committee, a student advisory committee, and a citizens advisory committee.)

Curriculum specialists work to help members of a curriculum-development team take their responsibilities seriously. When this kind of leadership is lacking, some curriculum-development groups resort to "scissors-and-paste" curriculum making. This occurs when, through a lack of leadership, members of a curriculum-development project spend their time reviewing programs developed elsewhere. They snip parts from here and there, assemble a hodgepodge of ideas, and declare their work complete. This is a certain recipe for mediocrity, and curriculum leaders who know their business do not allow it to happen.

To ensure that the task is approached in a professional manner, the curriculum specialist has an obligation to provide necessary training in essentials of curriculum building to individuals who may lack it. Suppose the task were to develop a new course, including a complete set of instructional unit plans. The curriculum specialist must ensure that those involved have a basic understanding of how course development proceeds and how instructional units might be framed. Beyond these general guidelines, some specifics related to such issues as content selection, identification of content priorities, and content sequencing must be addressed. Some general principles curriculum specialists draw on to make these decisions are introduced in Chapters 3 and 4.

Teachers/Instructors

Individuals who will be responsible for implementing programs should play a part in designing them. This is a fundamental axiom of curriculum building. Since much curriculum work is directed at producing programs for classroom use, teachers and instructors are often included as members of curriculum-development teams.

As individuals who are in regular contact with learners, teachers and instructors are in a position to comment upon the practicality of suggested alternatives. Their involvement in program development adds an important dimension of credibility to whatever is developed, particularly in the minds of other teachers and instructors.

Teachers and instructors who participate in curriculum-development activities must be selected with care. First they must be individuals who are well regarded by their teaching colleagues. If they are not, their involvement will hardly be a selling point to other teachers and instructors. Additionally, these teachers and instructors should be people who have reasonably good working relationships with principals and other administrators, as these administrators will play an important role in managing new programs. When there is a bond between those teachers and instructors and those administrators involved in a curriculum-development activity, chances for successful implementation of new programs are enhanced.

Many teachers who are invited to participate in curriculum-development activities do not bring with them a substantial background in curriculum. They tend to be well versed in instruction, but program design is not an area that receives extensive attention in some preservice teacher preparation programs. As may be the case with others involved, teachers and instructors often need guidance in curriculum matters from the curriculum-development specialist.

Learners

Learners are the ultimate consumers of programs and materials resulting from curriculum-development activities. Consequently, they may provide useful perspectives as programs and materials are being developed. Figure 2-7 raises some concerns related to learner participation.

Curriculum leaders face difficulties in identifying learners who can work as members of a curriculum-development team. One problem has to do with time commitment. Some curriculum-development activities occur during the school or working day. It may be difficult for learners to attend meetings. Curriculum work that occurs in the evening, on weekends, or during vacation periods also may pose attendance problems for learners.

Another difficulty has to do with age and maturity levels. It may not be practical to make extremely young and immature learners formal members of a curriculum-development team. Suppose a curriculum project were dedicated to producing instructional units for use in kindergarten. Youngsters at this age are not sufficiently mature to make substantive contributions to program and material planning. Their reactions, as learners, to learning materials and activities being considered can be probed (for example, during pilot tests), but this kind of involvement is somewhat different from that of people who are actually part of the curriculum-development team.

FIGURE 2-7   Learner Participation in Curriculum Development

Using learners in curriculum development activities has sometimes spawned controversy. A parent recently requested a meeting and made these comments to a school board member:

> "My son is a good kid . . . a hard worker, but no great shakes academically. He gets C's, a few B's, and every once in a while impresses everybody with an A. He plays football, belongs to a bunch of clubs, and generally gets along pretty well. In fact, I think he's a pretty typical high school junior.

> "I read in the school newsletter that the Jameson boy . . . that's Eric Jameson . . . has been assigned to work with the district on the revision of the English curriculum. It said that he was chosen because the committee wanted somebody who 'could speak from the perspective of the student.'

> "Now, look. I've got nothing but praise for Eric Jameson. He comes from a fine family. But Eric Jameson as somebody to speak for the student? Come on! He's a kid who's never received anything but an A. He plays first chair violin in the community orchestra. He's already had a short story published. I mean, Eric's a really competent kid, but what business does he have suggesting to anybody what a more typical high school student like my son thinks about changes to your English program. You couldn't have picked a more atypical student."

1. How do you react to this parent's concern?
2. If the school board member called you regarding the decision to select Eric Jameson, how would you respond?
3. What criteria would you use in selecting students to participate on curriculum development teams?

There are other difficulties when the proposed program is to be directed at older (even adult) learners. One of these has to do with how representative the learners are who are selected to participate. Sometimes, there is a tendency to select bright, highly motivated learners. These people may have the sophistication to master basic curriculum-building principles and to make important contributions to discussions. Their perspectives, however, may not generalize well to the total group of learners to be served. What they see as interesting or motivating or exciting may not appear that way to the more typical learner.

Learners invited to participate in curriculum-development activities rarely bring any initial expertise in curriculum-building with them. The curriculum specialist must work carefully to provide them with this information and to integrate them into the overall activity in a meaningful way.

Principals/Corporate Unit Supervisors

In a school setting, the principal is a key individual whose attitude toward program modification has enormous impact on the success or failure of implementation. In the corporate setting, the administrator responsible for the overall operation of the training and development unit exercises a similar influence.

Principals and corporate unit supervisors have responsibilities ranging well beyond instructional programming. For this reason, sometimes it is difficult to involve them directly in curriculum-development activities. They have many demands on their time. However, many of these individuals take very seriously their roles as instructional leaders and can make important contributions to a curriculum-development activity.

Principals and corporate unit supervisors are in a position to see how a suggested modification might have implications for other programs and for other elements of the school or corporate unit operation. Often their comments will help a group shape decisions that will ease the task of program introduction. Their insights relating to management of new programs are particularly useful.

Given the many roles principals must play, their professional preparation programs must include training in a large number of areas. Though principals may have had a brief introduction to curriculum development, curriculum leaders still need to help them sharpen their skills.

Central Office Administrators/Central Corporate Administrators

In school districts, central administrators might include the superintendent and the assistant superintendents. In corporations, they might include top corporate administrators at the site housing the training and development unit.

Generally, administrators at this level will not be active participants in curriculum-development activities. Although they may make appearances from time to time as general representatives of higher administration, they have a broad range of responsibilities, and simply are not able to commit the time required to do much of the nuts-and-bolts work of curriculum development.

Occasionally, however, there are curriculum-development tasks that bear rather directly on the interests of upper-level administrators. For example, top officials in a school district must consider public reactions to school programming. A district's philosophy statement is a public document that communicates the general intents of the district's programming. Negative reactions to such a document can pose problems for administrators. Consequently, some top administrators, perhaps an assistant superintendent or two, may play an active role in the development of a new district philosophy statement.

Special Experts

The degree to which special experts are involved in a curriculum-development activity depends on its purpose. Nearly all projects require expertise beyond what individuals involved are personally capable of providing. However, in many cases this expertise can be obtained from articles, position papers, books, and other information sources.

Sometimes, though, it makes good sense to involve special experts as part of the group. If a school district is planning a revision of a biology program, science education experts and biology experts might well be included. In some corporate training settings, it is common for a curriculum specialist to work directly with a content expert who possesses a technical skill but who knows nothing about curriculum development. For example, in a project designed to produce instructional materials for training airline pilots, a curriculum specialist and a professional pilot might be teamed.

Citizen Representatives

In public school curriculum development, representatives of the local community are sometimes included as members of curriculum-development teams. This is particularly likely when new programs and materials might be regarded as controversial by some school constituents. Lay members can serve as a bridge to the community. Their presence can give the community some sense of "ownership" of programs and materials that are developed.

A major problem facing curriculum leaders is the selection of citizen representatives. Sometimes school board members are included. In addition to representing the community, they typically are individuals known by large numbers of school patrons. On the other hand, school board members often have personal, business, and professional responsibilities that place heavy demands on their time. Duties associated with their membership on the school board may not allow them to commit to membership on a curriculum-development team. Often when school board members are involved they attend occasional meetings of the group but do not do much hands-on curriculum-development work.

When school board members are not involved, other community representatives may be selected to represent constituencies with a particular interest in the project. For example, if there is an organization for parents of gifted and talented learners, then someone from this group might be invited to join a curriculum-development project focusing on revising a district's gifted and talented program.

One difficulty in selecting lay representatives concerns the "representativeness" of the individuals selected. The general public speaks with many voices and diverse perspectives. There is always a danger that people will be invited who are members of highly vocal pressure groups but who do not represent general community opinion.

There is no configuration of people good for all curriculum-development activities. The nature of the task is the primary consideration in determining who should be involved. Figure 2-8 illustrates some groupings of individuals and suggests levels of their involvement for several different tasks.

DECISION-MAKING IN
CURRICULUM-DEVELOPMENT ACTIVITIES

Curriculum specialists may exercise leadership in different ways. Some favor a highly centralized approach. This means that basic goals and objectives, frameworks for accomplishing such tasks as developing courses and instructional units, and perhaps even much of the content of these courses and units are established by the curriculum specialist and his or her staff. This information is then provided to others involved in the project. While there may be some room for discussion, these participants are generally expected to produce programs and materials consistent with the provided guidelines. Some programs in the military services are examples of those developed using this approach.

An argument often made in opposition to highly centralized curriculum-development leadership is that it removes decision-making from the hands of individuals who, ultimately, will have to use the new programs and materials. Specifically, there is a concern that teachers will not find the products of curriculum development useful and, hence, may have difficulties implementing what has been developed.

Taba (1962) was particularly concerned about this issue. She proposed what has sometimes been called an *inverted approach* to curriculum-development leadership. She suggested that curriculum revision begin by asking teachers and instructors to develop and pilot test new instructional units. Presumably, they would develop materials to which they were personally committed and that would work in the classroom. Only after such units had been developed would curriculum specialists enter the picture to identify certain common themes and organizers, which would then be used as bases for developing individual courses and overall programs of study.

The inverted approach has been criticized on the grounds that individual teachers vary tremendously in their ability to develop instructional units. Without provision of a framework, these materials might prove

**FIGURE 2-8   Levels of Involvement Varying with the Nature of the
Curriculum-Development Activity**

The chart illustrates some possible differences in levels of involvement of
different groups that often play a part in curriculum development.

Purpose of the Activity

Development of Training Materials for New Pilots
    heavy involvement: instructors
                           curriculum specialists
                           special experts

    moderate involvement: corporate unit supervisors
                              students

    low/no involvement: corporate administrators
                           lay public

Revision of a K–12 School Social Studies Program
    heavy involvement: teachers
                           curriculum specialists
                           principals

    moderate involvement: students
                              central office administrators
                              special experts
                              lay public

Development of a Philosophy Statement for a School District
    heavy involvement: curriculum specialists
                           principals
                           central office administrators
                           lay public

    moderate involvement: teachers
                                special experts

    low/no involvement: students

Revision of a Master Scope and Sequence Document for a School District
    heavy involvement: curriculum specialists
                           principals
                           central office administrators

    moderate involvement: teachers
                                special experts

    low/no involvement: students
                           lay public

Development of a New Science Program for Elementary Gifted and Talented Students

heavy involvement: curriculum specialists
teachers
special experts

moderate involvement: students
principals
central office administrators
lay public

---

very difficult to organize in any systematic way. Curriculum specialists may have difficulties finding common themes and organizers.

In reality, decision-making in most curriculum-development activities reflects a blend of centralized and inverted leadership. Curriculum leaders tend to suggest general directions and to provide suggested writing frameworks as alternatives to which teachers and others react. The group then collectively determines procedures to be followed. This collaborative procedure builds a sense of ownership in the activity that will be very important when participants are asked to help "sell" what has been developed to people not involved in the curriculum-development activity.

SUMMARY

Curriculum-development activity occurs in many settings: (1) the national setting, (2) the state or regional setting, (3) the local or divisional setting, (4) the individual institution setting, and (5) the individual classroom setting. The specific character of a given curriculum-development activity is influenced by the setting in which it takes place.

In any curriculum-development project, a number of tasks must be completed. The range of these tasks and their complexity will vary with the sophistication of the project. A number of curriculum-development models have been developed that are particularly useful in identifying tasks to be accomplished in large and complex projects.

Among curriculum leaders' most important responsibilities are organizing and working with other people. These people may include teachers and instructors, learners, principals or corporate unit supervisors, central office or corporate administrators, special experts, and lay public representatives.

The kinds and numbers of individuals involved in a given curriculum-development activity will vary with the demands of the activity and its complexity. Once a project has begun, the curriculum specialist often develops a management style characterized by a willingness to provide general guidelines while, at the same time, standing ready to consider seriously suggestions and comments from other members of the group.

EXTENDING AND APPLYING CHAPTER CONTENT

1. Prepare a clipping file from magazines, newspapers, and other print sources illustrating kinds of curriculum development occurring at various settings. Find at least one article for each of these five settings: (1) the national setting, (2) the state or regional setting, (3) the local or divisional setting, (4) the individual institution setting, and (5) the individual classroom setting. Share files with others in the class, and discuss your findings.

2. Ask a local curriculum director to visit the class. Interview him or her about the kinds of pressures he or she feels from curriculum activities going on in settings beyond the local level. Are these influences direct or indirect? In what ways do they influence local groups involved in curriculum-development activities?

3. A large number of curriculum-development models have been proposed. Look for them in other curriculum texts and in professional articles directed at curriculum leaders. You might look for such articles under the heading "curriculum" in the *Education Index*. Bring at least one such model to class. Your instructor may wish to duplicate several of these to use as bases for a discussion. What similarities and differences are there among models? What assumptions seem to undergird each? To what kinds of curriculum-development activities is each applicable? Conclude by developing and defending a curriculum-development model of your own.

4. Organize a panel of curriculum directors trom several school districts. Ask members to discuss the nature of their relationships with others in their school districts. Specifically, ask about their relationships with superintendents, assistant superintendents, and school principals. Ask them how they influence people over whom they have no direct line authority.

5. Interview a number of teachers or instructors who have been involved in curriculum-development projects. Focus on their perceptions of the leadership provided by curriculum specialists. You might ask questions such as these: Did the curriculum specialist provide you with a clear set of instructions? Did you have input into the nature of what was to be done? Did you sense that the project was well organized and that time was put to effective use? Overall, how would you rate the quality of project leadership? If you had been able to make some changes in how the project was organized and managed, what would you have done?

BIBLIOGRAPHY

Beane, James A., Conrad F. Toepfer, and Samuel J. Alessi. 1986. *Curriculum Planning and Development*. Boston: Allyn and Bacon.

Doll, Ronald C. 1986. *Curriculum Improvement: Decision-Making and Process*, 6th ed. Boston: Allyn and Bacon.

Gagne, Robert M. and Leslie Briggs. 1979. *Principles of Instructional Design*, 2d ed. New York: Holt, Rinehart and Winston.

Hunkins, Francis P. 1980. *Curriculum Development: Program Improvement*. Columbus, OH: Charles E. Merrill.

Miller, John P. and Wayne Seller. 1985. *Curriculum: Perspectives and Practice*. New York: Longman.

Neagley, Ross L. and N. Dean Evans. 1967. *Handbook for Effective Curriculum Development*. Englewood Cliffs, NJ: Prentice-Hall.

Taba, Hilda. 1962. *Curriculum Development: Theory and Practice*. New York: Harcourt Brace and World.

Tanner, Daniel and Laurel N. Tanner. 1980. *Curriculum Development: Theory into Practice*, 2d ed. New York: Macmillan Co.

Tyler, Ralph W. 1949. *Basic Principles of Curriculum and Instruction*. Chicago: University of Chicago Press.

Wulf, Kathleen M. and Barbara Schave. 1984. *Curriculum Design: A Handbook for Educators*. Glenview, IL: Scott, Foresman and Company.

The Anthony Wayne Library
The Defiance College

CHAPTER 3

Curriculum Designs

This chapter introduces information to help the reader

1. describe examples of such basic curriculum design concepts as *scope, sequence, articulation, continuity,* and *balance*.
2. differentiate among a number of general curriculum designs including *academic-subject designs, fusion designs, broad-fields designs, special-topic designs,* and *learner-centered designs*.
3. identify features of *structure-of-the-discipline designs* and *correlation designs* and point out how each differs from more common academic-subject designs.
4. point out features of two specialized learner-centered designs, the *core curriculum* and the *activity curriculum*.
5. distinguish among such content selection criteria as *legal constraints, content significance, content authenticity, motivational appeal, content complexity,* and *instructors' backgrounds/support-material availability*.

INTRODUCTION

Anybody *can* select and organize content. A review of content alternatives, a hasty choice of specific topics, and an arbitrary decision about sequencing will complete the task. Although such an arrangement may respond to somebody's idea of form, it may also be woefully deficient in substance. Sometimes people do learn from instructional programs fashioned in this way, but such learning often results as much from personal perseverance as from adequacy of program design.

Specific elements of good design are not always recognized by individuals exposed to instructional programs. For example, they may not think about the mesh between the end of a previous learning sequence and the one they are about to begin. They may reflect little on relationships among lesson objectives, techniques used by the instructor, and supporting learning resources such as textbooks, films, and other media. A person who has had a satisfying learning experience tends to recall its overall excellence rather than the design features that contributed to its quality.

This chapter introduces basic curriculum design concepts associated with selection and organization of content. These concepts are part of the professional language of curriculum professionals.

BASIC DESIGN CONCEPTS

Many specialized terms are associated with curriculum design. Regrettably, these terms are not always used in the same way by all people in the field. This section introduces a selection of major design concepts and attempts to define them in ways that many curriculum specialists would support.

SCOPE

The term *scope* refers to the extent and depth of content coverage. Scope has relevance at many levels of curriculum development. For example, scope decisions may relate to an entire K-to-12 program, and regard which content elements should be included at each grade level and how much time should be devoted to each.

Sometimes scope decisions are dictated by state legislation or by policy decisions of state boards of education. Such decisions may require that certain percentages of instructional time or certain numbers of minutes per week be devoted to particular kinds of content or to particular types of learning activities. Texas has a law requiring that 40 percent of the time spent in secondary-school science classes be spent in laboratories. This regulation establishes a priority for kinds of content that can be demonstrated in a laboratory setting and clearly affects the scope of the secondary science programs in this state.

In a local school district that is hierarchically oriented, scope decisions may be made and passed on to building level administrators and teachers by officials higher up the administrative ladder. In more participatory systems, classroom teachers, community representatives, learner representatives, and others may play important roles in making K-to-12 scope decisions.

Regardless of how district-level scope decisions are made, individual teachers almost always have some control over the scope of content they will cover. They make many decisions about how much material to cover related to a given topic and how much to expect of learners as a result of instruction related to this topic. At the individual classroom level, teachers may implement their scope priorities by preparing larger numbers of objectives related to those issues, topics, and other areas of content selected for particular emphasis. A larger number of objectives will guide planning that can assure more breadth and depth of coverage of these priority areas.

Decisions of scope are particularly important because they have implications for instructional time. Time is a fixed-sum commodity. When a decision is made to expand coverage in one area, time must be taken away from instruction in another. Scope decisions involve important value choices relating to the relative worth of alternative learning experiences. As there are broad differences among educators regarding the relative importance of individual subjects and topics, decisions relating to scope are extremely difficult. Curriculum workers often find it difficult to achieve consensus (or, sometimes, even a simple majority) when making decisions that will result in varying allocations of instructional time for different subjects and topics. Figure 3-1 addresses some specific issues related to scope.

SEQUENCE

Sequence refers to decisions about the order in which learners encounter content. As is the case with scope, sequence decisions are made at many levels. In a public school system, curriculum committees, comprising curriculum specialists, teachers, administrators, and others, will often be charged with making decisions about which courses and learning experiences must precede others. At the classroom level, individual teachers will decide which lessons should come first, second, third, and so forth.

Some sequencing decisions almost "make themselves" because tradition and the logic of the content suggest an ordering that few will challenge. For example, in foreign language classes, there is virtually unanimous agreement that instruction related to the past tense of verbs should follow instruction related to the present tense and not the other way around. Similarly, no algebra teacher would attempt to teach the binomial theorem on the first day of class. The logic of this subject matter requires its instruction to come after much other critical content has been introduced.

At other times, the sequence decision is not so obvious. Some instructional experiences are more or less freestanding and do not depend

FIGURE 3-1   Issues Related to Scope in Textbooks

Decisions related to scope are shaped by a number of influences. Among these are legal constraints, tradition, national values, community values, and personal values. Individual textbooks treating the same content may not treat exactly the same topics. Furthermore, the extent of treatment of those topics that are included may differ.

For example, American history textbooks designed for use in senior high schools may vary in their relative emphases on such topics as (a) the California Gold Rush, (b) the Spanish American War, (c) the Muckrakers, (d) Building the Panama Canal, (e) the Great Depression, and (f) Famous Twentieth Century Writers and Painters. Numbers of pages devoted to each topic may be quite different from book to book.

As an exercise, locate two or more textbooks dealing with an area in which you are interested. Identify five topics often taught in courses where this textbook is used. Then, respond to these questions.

1. Is there a single one of these five topics that receives more pages of coverage in each text than do any others?
2. What general patterns of difference in extent of coverage of these topics do you find from book to book? How do you explain these differences in scope?
3. What would you decide as a proper scope of treatment for each of your topics? On what would your decision be based? How acceptable do you think it would be to others?

---

on a mastery of critical prerequisite content. For example, though many history courses are organized using a chronological approach, this is by no means the only alternative available. Similarly, courses in language arts and the fine arts can be organized in a variety of ways. Decisions about sequencing in such cases often come only after exhaustive discussions of alternatives.

ARTICULATION

Articulation is one of those terms that has not always been defined in the same way by curriculum professionals. The approach to the term taken here follows an explanation developed by a leading professor of curriculum, Albert Oliver. Oliver suggests that articulation refers to a relationship between two or more elements of curriculum that is simultaneous rather than sequential (Oliver, 1977). Often the term articulation is used to refer to attempts to correlate experiences a learner has in one subject area with those he or she has in another.

Suppose a high school student were enrolled at the same time in a U.S. history course and an American literature course. Often, learning experiences in each are quite independent of one another. However, planning could result in an articulated or correlated series of learning experiences. One possibility would be to arrange both courses chronologically. Were this done, students might study the political and social history of the Civil War period at the same time they studied the literature of the period.

One driving force behind the idea of articulation is the view that grade levels and subject areas are artificial human inventions. "Reality" is not divided in this way. Therefore curriculum specialists should make an effort to assure that learners do not take away from their school experience the idea that knowledge or truth exists only as it is typically organized and presented within subjects or grade levels.

Because of its emphasis on the importance of interconnections among different kinds of content, sometimes the term *correlation* is used instead of articulation. And, since the focus is on concurrent learning experiences, sometimes *horizontal articulation* is used as the term has been defined here. Both of these alternate terms emphasize that articulation reaches out laterally to cross subject-area boundaries in an effort to maximize potential relationships among many kinds of content.

CONTINUITY

Continuity focuses on the relationship between a subsequent learning experience and its predecessor. Another term sometimes used for continuity is *vertical articulation*. Continuity suggests a need for instruction to be organized so that the ending points of a given learning experience mesh well with the beginning points of the next one. Continuity operates at many levels. Within their classrooms, teachers must plan for smooth transitions even within individual lessons. At quite another level, curriculum planning should assure some relationship between learning experiences provided at the end of a course or grade and those introduced at the beginning of the next course or grade level. Continuity is also important in transitions from one level of schooling to another. For example, the elementary program should be organized in such a way that it flows logically into the secondary program.

Continuity seeks to avoid interference with learners' progress. A French language program that required learners to begin their study of highly complex subjunctive verb forms directly after their first exposure to the present tense of -er verbs would fail the test of continuity. Because the program did not provide learners with prerequisites needed to succeed at the new task, many, probably most, individuals would find their progress blocked.

BALANCE

There are many important components in an instructional program. *Balance* refers to the need to assure that no one of them is emphasized to the diminishment of others. Considerations related to balance are relevant at many levels of curriculum planning.

In planning lessons and units teachers seek to assure that there is an equitable coverage of all important content. At the district level, curriculum planners consider balance when revising the contents of existing courses and grade-level programs. State high school graduation requirements also reflect decisions made about what a balanced high school program of study should be.

Issues related to balance sometimes generate heated arguments. This is, in part, true because these decisions often affect how money is to be spent. Suppose an organized group of parents succeeds in having a higher percentage of a district's budget directed to programs for the gifted and talented. This decision will require diversion of funds from other programs, and thus will influence the balance of the entire district program. Whether this new alignment of priorities reflects a good balance is a topic that will almost certainly be debated.

GENERAL CURRICULUM DESIGNS

Curriculum designs in public schools (and in other settings) are not uniform from place to place. In virtually every setting curricula are tailored to meet special conditions and interests, but despite these differences, there are a number of general design patterns. This section introduces a selection of these.

Curriculum planning occurs at many levels, among them lesson plan, unit plan, grade-level plan for each subject, and course design. To illustrate the differences among selected general curriculum designs, this discussion will be limited to the implications of each for course design.

ACADEMIC-SUBJECT DESIGNS

Academic-subject designs are responsible for the traditional school courses in such familiar areas as history, mathematics, and English. These courses have had a long history as staples of the public school curriculum.

In these familiar designs, academic subjects lend their titles to school courses and classes. In elementary schools, the subjects reading, mathematics, and so forth, and in secondary schools, courses such as biology, chemistry, economics, English, and trigonometry clearly are tied to recognized academic disciplines.

This design orientation persists for many reasons. First, the various subjects keep content current by drawing on the organized scholarship of the individual academic disciplines. Since colleges and universities in most cases are organized along disciplinary lines, academic scholars find their work judged by peers working within their individual subject areas. The whole process of creating and validating new knowledge, then, is heavily influenced by the separate academic disciplines.

Second, most teachers have graduated from colleges and universities organized into departments of professors who specialize in separate academic subjects. As a result, many find this familiar organizational pattern to be quite natural.

Third, organization of knowledge into various subject areas at the college and university level makes it relatively convenient for primary and secondary schools to divide knowledge in the same way. For example, a teacher of a course entitled "United States History" may find it much more convenient to locate information than would a teacher of a course entitled "The Special Identity of Americans." This latter course might well require the teacher to draw upon information from a variety of academic subjects.

This is not to suggest such a course might not be a good one, but it may place extra and unfamiliar work on the teacher. This is one reason why large numbers of courses in schools today continue to reflect a traditional subject-matter orientation.

Most commonly, courses reflecting an academic-subject design take findings from a single subject and organize them in ways appropriate for transmission to elementary and secondary school learners. This procedure produces the familiar array of classes in such subjects as English, algebra, chemistry, and so forth. There are also organizational variations that represent subsets of the general academic-subject design. Among these are *structure-of-the-discipline designs* and *correlation designs*.

Structure-of-the-Discipline Designs

Traditionally, academic-subject designs have introduced elementary and secondary school learners to findings of professionals in such traditional academic disciplines as history and mathematics. The shock waves sent through the American educational establishment, however, after the Soviets launched the first earth-orbiting satellite in 1957 led to a critical reexamination of school curricula.

One group of reformers suggested that the nation's intellectual power could be better developed were learners exposed to the structure of individual disciplines rather than to findings of professional specialists. Such figures as Joseph Schwab (1962) argued that mastery of the structure would enhance learners' intellectual powers and better prepare them for the academic challenges they would face as college and university students.

Supporters of structure-of-the-discipline designs wanted school programs that would teach learners how professional scholars go about the business of weighing evidence and establishing "truth." In essence, elementary and secondary programs were to be revised to produce learners who would master professional investigative techniques and who, to the extent practical, would be directly involved in the production of new knowledge.

In the late 1950s, throughout the 1960s, and into the 1970s, a number of programs were developed that reflected this orientation. Among these were the Biological Science Curriculum Study (BSCS), the Physical Science Study Committee (PSSC), The Earth Science Curriculum Project (ESCP), and the Intermediate Science Curriculum Study (ISCS).

Elements of many structure-of-the-discipline programs are still found in some schools. However, the approach is not nearly so popular today as it once was. Some critics argued that the programs were too heavily oriented toward the interests of the college-bound learner. Others found it difficult to find consensus among professionals in some disciplines about what the structure of their discipline was. Still others felt that the approach placed too much emphasis on academic disciplines and that other topics and subjects deserved more attention in school programs. Figure 3-2 offers a challenge to the traditional structure-of-the-discipline approach.

Correlation Designs

Correlation designs are concerned with the articulation of learning experiences in two or more areas. These designs attempt to build on relationships between and among subject areas, but continue to emphasize the individual subjects' identities.

Suppose two teachers, an English teacher and a social studies teacher, were working with some college-bound seniors. They might decide to develop part of the English program and the social studies program in a correlated manner. For example, the two teachers might focus on the role of India in World War II and events leading to India's independence. The English teacher might have the students read the four novel's in Paul Scott's *Raj Quartet*. The social studies teacher could assign students to read historians' accounts of India's role in World War II and its eventual independence. The intent would be to broaden learners' understanding by providing them with concurrent treatment of a common topic from the perspectives of two subjects.

FUSION DESIGNS

Fusion designs, similar to correlation designs, attempt to build on relationships between and among two or more separate subject areas. However,

FIGURE 3-2   Response to the Organization of All Academic Programs in Schools According to a Structure-of-the-discipline Approach

Suppose you overheard someone making these comments:

> "We're falling behind. The Japanese, the Germans, people in a dozen other countries are leading the world to a new and exciting technological future. Relative to other countries, our national store of brainpower is on the decline. Schools must react to this dangerous situation.
>
> "Our programs, especially at the high school level, need to be made more intellectually demanding. We need to have leading research scientists and engineers take charge of an effort to replan courses. Courses should train students early to use skills that will be useful to them when they pursue more advanced college and university study. We want them to enter college knowing much more than they do today. It is not too much to expect them to begin work that will lead to modest creation of knowledge and even of scholarly publication while they are still in high school."

Think about these comments. Then, respond to these questions.

1. What strengths do you find in the arguments presented? What weaknesses?
2. What might be some reactions of the general public were there attempts to implement these ideas?
3. How do you personally feel about them?

---

whereas correlation designs preserve the identities of the individual subjects, in fusion designs, these identities disappear. Rather, related content from several subjects is joined together under a brand new subject label.

Fusion can result in the creation of new courses either within a given academic discipline or between two or more academic disciplines. The high school world history course really represents a fusion of more specific history courses (European history, Asian history, and so forth). This is an example of fusion within the given academic discipline history.

Fusion also occurs across disciplines. For example, today many colleges and universities offer a course in biophysics. This course represents a fusion of content from the disciplines of biology and physics. At the elementary school level, the Elementary School Mathematics and Science Project represented an effort to create a new program from disciplinary "parents" in mathematics and the sciences (Tanner and Tanner, 1980).

Fusion designs are not so common as academic-subject designs. A major barrier to their development has been the difficulty of achieving agreement on theoretical rationales to justify the blending of contents from independent disciplines into something new (Tanner and Tanner 1980).

BROAD-FIELDS DESIGNS

Whereas fusion designs attempt to blend content from several subjects into a single new subject, *broad-fields designs* seek to create a unity that cuts across an entire domain or branch of knowledge. The intent is somewhat the same as in fusion designs: to create a new unity from constituent subjects that lose their individual identities once the process is complete. The major difference between fusion and broad-fields designs is that the scope of broad-fields design is grander.

Some examples of broad fields approaches include industrial arts, humanities programs, and courses labeled "social studies." As Tanner and Tanner (1980) point out, there is no broad-fields program when a department of social studies continues to offer separate courses in history, economics, and so forth. To be a broad-fields program, these subject labels must disappear and content must be integrated from many different sources.

One rationale for the broad-fields approach is that it provides a basis for avoiding program fragmentation. Instead of seven or ten separate courses, a school can offer single programs called "humanities" or "industrial arts." Planners are free to draw content from a variety of sources. Often broad-fields programs are organized around a theme. For example, a humanities program might use a title like "Human Accomplishments Through Time," and an industrial arts program might identify a focus such as "Preparing for the World of Work in an Era of Technological Change."

One problem people have had in developing broad-fields designs is identifying which elements of content should be drawn together and blended. A result is that there may be important differences in contents treated within broad-fields programs having the same name. For example, learners enrolled in a humanities program in one high school may have an experience that is little related to that of learners in a similarly titled program at another school.

SPECIAL-TOPIC DESIGNS

The term *special-topic design* is a generic one applied when learning experiences are organized around a specific focus topic. Some special-topic designs appear to be quite similar to correlation designs. Unlike correlation designs, however, those focusing on special topics tend to be much less particular about drawing content from recognized academic subjects, such as history and English, that continue to maintain their own individual identities.

Some special-topics designs do draw content only from recognized academic disciplines, but others incorporate information from a wider array of sources such that the academic "parentage" of the course may be difficult to identify. Figure 3-3 gives an example of a special-topic design.

Special-topic designs are very flexible. They can embrace serious content centering on profound social problems or they can focus on much more mundane issues. Some examples include courses on such diverse topics as real estate licensing, developing self-awareness, threats to the environment, revolutions and their causes, and beginning aerobics.

A strength of special-topics designs is their ability to organize courses that respond to changing social conditions and changing learner interests. A weakness of the approach is that some special-topics courses have been accused of being too easy. Nothing inherent in the design sug-

---

FIGURE 3-3   Example of a Special-topic Design

Special-topic designs can draw content from a variety of sources. As is the case with the design illusrated here, sometimes information is derived from recognized academic disciplines as well as from less formal sources. For example, newspaper accounts might provide information useful for a study of this topic. Such accounts include information not tied to a single academic discipline.

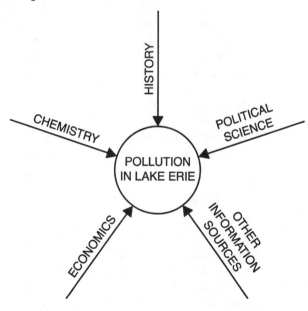

gests that courses planned in this way will not be rigorous and challenging. There is not, however, the kind of history behind highly individual special-topics courses that there is, for example, behind a standard high school algebra course. For this reason, standards of academic excellence in such courses are harder to establish.

In practice, there are good and bad examples of both courses reflecting a special-topics' design and courses reflecting an academic-subjects' design. The critical variable is how the design is executed rather than the nature of the design itself.

LEARNER-CENTERED DESIGNS

The term *learner-centered design* may be confusing at first. To some extent, all curriculum designs are learner centered. Regardless of the design selected, planning goes forward with some attention to the characteristics and needs of learners to be served. What is special about learner-centered designs is that the needs and desires of learners are the *major* focus of program planning.

At the secondary-school level, students are sometimes asked to suggest ideas for mini-courses, and if a sufficient number of learners want something, a mini-course is developed. Community education programs also tend to have many learner-centered courses. Courses come and go in response to the learners' changing interests.

Though there are learner-centered courses in the schools, their numbers are somewhat limited. Accreditation requirements and graduation requirements pose certain obstacles. As mentioned earlier, most teachers are products of college and university training that featured academic-subject designs, and many are not comfortable with the idea of placing the focus for a course so heavily into the control of learners. Some critics also wonder whether issues of short-term interest to learners serve their long-term interests well.

Despite these difficulties, two learner-centered designs that have appeared in elementary and secondary schools are worth noting, the *core curriculum* and the *activity curriculum* designs.

Core Curriculum

This term has not always been defined in a consistent way. As Beane, Toepfer, and Alessi (1986) have commented, in recent years some people have used it simply as a label for the courses learners are required to take in school. Historically, however, the term encompassed the idea that learners have certain common needs that should be addressed in the curriculum. It is in this historical sense that the term is used here.

This view of the core curriculum implies that a school program should be primarily directed at making schooling relevant to the lives of learners. It places a heavy emphasis on the study of social and personal problems. Tanner and Tanner (1980) identified two basic types of core curriculum, the *preplanned core* and the *open core*.

In the preplanned core, teachers and others involved in the curriculum development process work to identify important social and personal issues that can be organized into a structure for learners at each grade level. In the open core, no preplanning occurs. Learners and their teachers cooperatively decide what is to be studied. What learners want and perceive as relevant is given the highest priority.

Activity Curriculum

The traditional core curriculum is based on the idea that learners have certain social and personal needs, and that, given free choice, they will choose to learn things that will be responsive to these needs. The activity curriculum likewise places a heavy emphasis on the learners' right to choose. But this view stresses that active involvement or *activity* is the key to productive learning.

The activity curriculum promotes learners' development by giving them opportunities to become active participants in the learning process. Curriculum planning involves creating environments that will maximize learner opportunities for active engagement with the content. Teachers are admonished to stay out of the learners' way to allow them to pursue their own interests creatively.

The curriculum designs described here are samples of those most often used to plan learning experiences. The public schools, as large comprehensive institutions, include courses and programs from these as well as other designs. The diversity of designs reflects the broad range of views in this country regarding what constitutes responsible school programming.

EXAMPLES OF CONTENT-SELECTION CRITERIA

People involved in curriculum development apply certain criteria as they select specific elements of content to be included in instructional programs at many levels. Classroom teachers must make decisions about what to include in specific lessons and units. Individual school districts make decisions about courses to be offered in their elementary and secondary schools. A state may impose graduation requirements that specify the kinds of content that must be part of certain required courses.

Part of the difficulty associated with content selection is the tremendous volume of information that could be included. This volume always exceeds what *can* be included given the time limitations associated with

individual lessons, units, and courses. These limitations often force curriculum developers to make hard choices. Some examples of content selection criteria that assist with these choices include the following:

1. legal contraints
2. content significance
3. content authenticity
4. motivational appeal
5. content complexity
6. instructors' backgrounds/support-material availability

LEGAL CONSTRAINTS

Some content selection decisions lie beyond the control of curriculum developers. Almost every state mandates some content to be included at certain grade levels or in certain courses. There may also be requirements
that certain amounts of instructional time be devoted to certain subjects or
topics. (By mandating that certain numbers of minutes or hours be devoted to treatment of topic X, the treatment of alternative topics Y and Z
consequently becomes limited. In this sense, such legislation does affect
content selection.)

Several examples illustrate specific legal constraints states impose
on content selection. Alabama requires that the grade 4 social studies program treat Alabama history, while California's Hughes-Hart Educational
Reform Act requires high school students to take three years of social science. Texas requires that at least sixty minutes of each instructional day in
grades 1 through 3 be spent on mathematics instruction.

As a matter of practice, when curricula are being developed legally
mandated contents are incorporated early. Once these have been established, then decisions can be made about discretionary elements of content for which room still remains.

CONTENT SIGNIFICANCE

Some content is obviously more important than other content. Content
such as that associated with basic skills represents prerequisite knowledge necessary for further educational development. Basic number facts,
patterns of letter and sound recognition, and recognition of key positions
on a typewriter or computer keyboard by touch are some examples of significant basic skills content. Without mastery of this important content,
learners will experience difficulty in mathematics, reading, and typing
courses.

Another kind of significant content is that which helps learners to
understand broad ranges of information and to transfer what they have

learned to settings beyond the classroom. This kind of content is not easy to identify. Often, curriculum specialists will call on the services of subject-matter specialists, educational psychologists, and other professionals to assist them in making these judgments. Even experts often have very different views about what is important. These differences and those of individual curriculum specialists, administrators, teachers, learners, parents, and interested school patrons result in curricula that reflect varying priorities from one community to another.

CONTENT AUTHENTICITY

Specific information related to the general categories of content selected should be as accurate as possible. Accuracy is not especially difficult to judge when matters of fact are at issue. The area of *authenticity* presents more challenges to curriculum specialists when issues of judgment are involved.

The curriculum developer shies away from the view that one person's opinion is always just as good as another person's opinion. Authenticity is more than a matter of simply counting the votes of people who happen to be involved in a curriculum development effort. It requires the curriculum specialist to obtain opinions supported by verifiable expertise in the area or areas in question. It also requires a willingness to check research evidence. The search for authenticity requires the curriculum specialist to validate content selection decisions by seeking the concurrence of the best-informed professional opinions.

Authenticity may play a role in how content is received by learners. In certain areas, for example, some learners may know as much or more about a certain issue as their teachers. If content is not authentic, the teachers' and the program's credibility will suffer.

Consider the push for drug awareness education that has become very popular in recent years. Few will deny the seriousness of the problem and many endorse the idea that schools should help do something about it. The tremendous interest in the issue has spawned development of a huge volume of instructional materials, some of which may have been put together by groups so adamantly opposed to drug use that they overstate their case. Students, consequently, may reject such an approach as "just so much emotional propaganda." Whereupon the sound intentions of the drug-awareness-education program would have been undermined by the failure to attend to the authenticity issue.

MOTIVATIONAL APPEAL

Curriculum developers are concerned with the potential interest learners will have in their programs. Even with a recognition that learners are very

FIGURE 3-4   Inquiring About Learners' Interests in Content Alternatives

Curriculum developers are urged to give some consideration to learners' relative interest in individual content alternatives when programs are being developed. Suppose you were working on a curriculum development team. After legal constraints and all other considerations that play a part in content selection had been reviewed, several acceptable content alternatives remained. It was decided to solicit some opinions from learners who would be the ultimate consumers of the new program. How would you respond to issues raised in the following questions as you prepare to seek learners' opinions?

(In responding to these questions, you might wish to make some assumptions about what is being planned. Is it a new course? A new instructional unit? A new lesson? You might also want to make some assumptions about age-level and/or grade-level of learners to be served.)

1. How many learners would you question?
2. How would you explain content alternatives to the learners?
3. Specifically, what would you ask?
4. How would you assure that learners questioned were reasonably representative of the total population of learners who would be exposed to the new program?
5. How would you organize responses for purposes of making a report back to the curriculum-development group?

diverse, it is folly to pretend that any program will be equally appealing to all. Instead, developers must attempt to put something together that will enable teachers to spark interest in as large a number of learners as possible.

Information about the relative appeal of alternatives is gathered in many ways: by consulting learning theory specialists, by interviewing a selection of learners, or by pilot testing initial versions of programs and monitoring learners' reactions. Review of this information can lead to adjustments that, it is hoped, will make learners more receptive to what is taught. A discussion of methods for gathering learner opinion is presented in Figure 3-4.

CONTENT COMPLEXITY

Selected content needs to be appropriate to the population of learners for whom it is intended. One would never think of introducing kindergarteners to the Pythagorean theorem. Similarly, a lesson titled "Our Friends the Firefighters" in a civics course for high school seniors would be laughably inappropriate. In general, the sophistication of content should become greater as learners mature and progress through the school program.

Exceptions do exist. For example, curricula planned for even quite young gifted and talented learners can deal with content that would be far too complex for more typical learners. Similarly, young people with certain learning disabilities may not be able to profit from exposure to content that many others of their age and grade level can handle with ease.

Selecting content at an appropriate level of complexity rarely involves just a single decision, as there are wide ranges of ability levels in most classrooms. Curriculum developers try to select content that can be introduced at different levels of compexity to respond to variations among learners.

The complexity issue prompts curriculum developers to look carefully at the instructional materials that will be used as learning resources. Developers examine these to assure that they provide reasonably good "fits" with the population of learners to be served. Textbooks, especially, are given careful scrutiny.

At one time, some high school textbooks were basically reworked college and university books, perhaps with the typeface enlarged and photographs added. However, little attention was given to readability levels and other pedagogical features such as levels of within-text skills development exercises and within-chapter and end-of-chapter questions. Today much attention is paid to the suitability of secondary textbooks as resources for secondary-school learners.

INSTRUCTORS' BACKGROUNDS/ SUPPORT-MATERIAL AVAILABILITY

When new programs are developed, one important consideration is the background of the teacher or teachers who will be presenting them in the classroom. This issue varies greatly in its importance according to the nature of the curriculum-development task. An individual teacher developing a new lesson or a new unit typically will select material with which he or she is familiar. Additionally, he or she will take advantage of existing materials or seek new ones that will be needed to support instruction.

The situation becomes more complex when a school curriculum-development group at the district level plans a new course. Those individuals who are involved may develop a sense of "ownership" in the new program. During their work, they may have come into direct contact with various specialists and feel themselves well steeped in the new content. They may also have become quite familiar with a variety of instructional resources.

Other teachers in the district who will be potential users of the program will not be nearly so familiar with a proposed new course as those who developed it. This situation calls for staff development to familiarize these teachers with the new course. (For a treatment of the staff-development issue, see Chapter 9.)

Curriculum developers involved with a new course or instructional program must wrestle with the question, "How divergent can the new content be from what teachers now know and do?" If large numbers of teachers are expected to make profound changes in a course yet lack knowledge about a high percentage of the content to be included, staff-development work will be lengthy and expensive. Sometimes the decision has to be made to make more modest changes with a view to encouraging easier adoption of a program by teachers not involved in its initial development.

Support-material availability can also be a limiting factor when a curriculum-development group is considering a change. Textbooks, films, software, and other commercial materials are desirable aids to teachers. Although teachers certainly can and do develop materials of their own, curriculum specialists must consider what resources (financial, released time, and so forth) can be made available to assist teachers in preparing their own materials and whether the teachers have the levels of expertise required to produce quality materials.

SUMMARY

Many curriculum professionals regularly use a number of terms that relate to curriculum design, among them the concepts of *scope, sequence, articulation, continuity,* and *balance.* These terms, comprising part of the professional language of the curriculum field, describe specific considerations to be weighed when curriculum designs are being selected.

Curriculum designs, themselves, take many forms. Often different designs exist within a given school. Each establishes a somewhat different set of priorities and provides for a program being developed to respond to a particular set of needs considered worthy by important learner, parental, and community constituencies. Some examples of curriculum designs include *academic-subject designs, fusion designs, broad-fields designs, special-topic designs,* and *learner-centered designs.*

Curriculum developers must make choices from among available content alternatives. Constraints, including available instructional time, will not allow more than a limited sample of possible content to be included within any instructional program. Among criteria considered when deciding whether or not to include a given element of content are *legal constraints, content significance, content authenticity, motivational appeal, content complexity,* and the instructors' backgrounds and support-material availability.

EXTENDING AND APPLYING CHAPTER CONTENT

1. A number of basic terms related to curriculum design comprise part of the professional language of curriculum professionals. Among the terms introduced in this chapter are scope, sequence, articulation, continuity, and balance. Not everyone in the curriculum profession defines these terms in exactly the same way. Examine a cross-section of curriculum texts and articles to determine how these terms are used. As you read, take note of additional key terms that others have suggested are important curriculum-design concepts. Present your list to your instructor. As a class, you may wish to prepare a master array of key design concepts and to begin work at framing some operational definitions of each.

2. Find a listing of courses and their descriptions from a local secondary school, community education program, community college, or large-scale training-and-development operation in industry. Alone or in cooperation with several students analyze this material to identify the kinds of instructional designs that most probably were used to develop each listed course. As a class, it might be interesting to analyze differences (if any) among different types of educational institutions in terms of prevalence of individual curriculum designs. For example, are learner-centered designs more frequently reflected in community-education courses than in secondary-school courses?

3. Beginning in the late 1950s and continuing throughout the 1960s, enormous sums of money were invested in projects that brought in leading academic scholars and involved them directly in the development of school curricula. Many such projects had a heavy structure-of-the-discipline emphasis, and many had much less impact on school practices than had been hoped. As a class activity, assign several members of the class to do background reading on individual projects such as The High School Geography Project, Project English, The Biological Sciences Curriculum Study Project, Project Physics, Sociological Resources for the Social Studies, and others suggested by the instructor. Have each group share a report with the class that provides the following information:

   a. What was the project designed to do?

   b. How different was it from existing curricula in its area of focus?

   c. What success did it have in changing school programs?

   d. What continuing influences does this project have on curricula in its area of focus?

   e. What factors contributed to successes and failures of the project?

4. Interview curriculum leaders familiar with the total K-to-12 programs in their districts. Ask them about features of the programs that are consistent with the ideas of those who initially conceived the core curriculum and the activity curriculum. To prepare for your interview, you will need to do some additional background reading to broaden your base of understanding of the core curriculum and the activity curriculum. Your instruc-

tor may be able to suggest some source materials. One book you may wish to consult is Daniel Tanner and Laurel Tanner's *Curriculum Development: Theory into Practice*, 2d ed (New York: Macmillan Co., 1980).

5. Review requirements in your state that govern what must be taught in public schools. What specific courses are mentioned? What kinds of topics referred to must be included within other courses? What requirements are there relating to how much time (expressed as years, semesters, days, or even hours or minutes) must be spent on specific subjects or topics? Do the same requirements apply to every learner? Or, are there some requirements that apply only to certain categories of learners, for example, to learners in special advanced programs?

   If you can secure a copy of a similar set of requirements from another state, do so. Compare and contrast the requirements of the two states. Then as a class discuss the constraints both place on curriculum developers and consider whether these are desirable or undesirable.

BIBLIOGRAPHY

Beane, James A., Conrad F. Toepfer, Jr., and Samuel J. Alessi, Jr. 1986. *Curriculum Planning and Development*. Boston: Allyn and Bacon.

Bruner, Jerome. 1960. *The Process of Education*. Cambridge, MA: Harvard University Press.

Bybee, Rodger W. and Robert B. Sund. 1982. *Piaget for Educators*. 2d ed. Columbus, OH: Charles E. Merrill.

Good, Carter V., ed. 1973. *Dictionary of Education*. 3d ed. New York: McGraw-Hill Book Company.

Hunkins, Francis P. 1980. *Curriculum Development: Program Improvement*. Columbus, OH: Charles E. Merrill.

Miller, John P. and Wayne Seller. 1985. *Curriculum: Perspectives and Practice*. New York: Longman.

Oliver Albert I. 1977. *Curriculum Improvement: A Guide to Problems, Principles, and Process*, 2d ed. New York: Harper & Row.

Saylor, J. Galen, William M. Alexander, and Arthur J. Lewis. 1981. *Curriculum Planning for Better Teaching and Learning*, 4th ed. New York: Holt, Rinehart and Winston.

Schwab, Joseph J. 1962. "The Concept of the Structure of a Discipline." *The Educational Record* (July 1962): 197–205.

Tanner, Daniel and Laurel Tanner. 1980. *Curriculum Development: Theory into Practice*, 2d ed. New York: Macmillan Co.

Walker, Decker F. and Jonas F. Soltis. 1986. *Curriculum and Aims*. New York: Teachers College Press.

CHAPTER 4

Organizing Course Content

This chapter introduces information to help the reader

1. **identify content-organization issues.**
2. **describe bases for organizing and sequencing course content.**
3. **point out general criteria to be used in establishing priorities among content elements in courses.**
4. **indicate the curriculum-development implications of assigning different priorities to different content elements.**
5. **suggest how tables of specifications can be used to denote relative emphases on different content elements.**

INTRODUCTION

Use of general curriculum designs to organize learning experiences into overall programs is a macrocurriculum activity. It involves broad, strategic planning and reflects decisions made at the national, state, and local levels. The result of this work usually is a set of guidelines including information related to courses that may be offered, courses that are required, course sequences, and the time to be devoted to each course. (The word "course" is used in this chapter to denote grade-level programs in individual subjects at the elementary level and separate subjects as they are taught at the secondary and university levels, in the military, and in government and private sector training-and-development settings.)

Often these guidelines do not provide information regarding specific content to be covered in individual courses, but this is not always the case. In some parts of the country, state legislatures have mandated that certain elements of content be taught within individual courses. Sometimes these mandates involve directives to include a particular topic. For example, there might be a regulation that a unit on drug abuse awareness be included in secondary school health courses. A few states even specify required content to be covered in each K-to-12 grade level and subject area. Texas, for example, has such regulations (Texas Education Agency, 1984).

The task of organizing content within an individual course is a microcurriculum activity and can occur at a number of levels. Textbooks reflect an organizational plan resulting from decisions made by the author and a team of editors. Courses designed by the military services often are centrally planned and distributed to instructors throughout the world. Training and development specialists at a corporation's national headquarters sometimes prepare courses used by the company's corporate trainers throughout the nation. Professional groups of educators in such subject areas as English, mathematics, the sciences, and the social studies occasionally produce prototype courses that include quite specific information about content and content sequencing.

Much work associated with course content organization occurs in local school districts. This work often is done by curriculum development groups led by a district-level curriculum specialist. These groups may include, among others, teachers with interests in the course(s) involved, subject-matter specialists, administrators, and community members.

SOME COURSE-ORGANIZATION ISSUES

No course or subject divides automatically into a natural array of major topics or unit titles. Existing breakdowns reflect decisions made after a consideration of alternatives, several of which may be equally good. Adopted schemes always reflect the priorities of individuals who have played a role in organizing course content. Since different people have different priorities, an arrangement that one person views as working wonderfully well may be seen by another as a disaster.

Though people differ in what they want in a course, certain general approaches to the task of course organization are applied by people having a variety of personal preferences. For example, in identifying specific topics or unit titles to include, it makes sense to select those deemed "powerful," or relatively broad in scope. Powerful topics are capable of organizing a large amount of subordinate information, thereby eliminating the need for an excessively high number of topics.

How many topics or unit titles are needed? This is a subjective question that requires the weighing of a number of variables. First, the perspectives of teachers who have worked with learners who will take the course must be considered, along with the factors of learner age-level and sophistication. In general, there need to be more subdivisions in content directed at younger and less-sophisticated learners than in that designed for older and more-sophisticated learners. Second, if standardized tests are given regularly to learners who take the course, consideration may have to be given to selecting topics or unit titles that are reasonably consistent with the content assumed by the tests.

In addition to the number of topics, the nature of the topics themselves will vary from situation to situation. For example, a first-grade reading program may have a heavy skills orientation. If this is the case, content should be organized so that learners are exposed to each needed skill and provided opportunities to practice it under the watchful eye of the teacher. On the other hand, a course intended to help develop learners' abilities to apply, analyze, synthesize, and evaluate information should plan an organizational scheme that facilitates the development of lessons directed at promoting these higher level thinking skills. Some arrangements are better suited for this purpose than others.

A great variety of organizational schemes can be applied to similar content. Consider the three possible arrangements on the following pages for a course titled "United States History."

Arrangement One

Our Country's Beginnings
  Our People
  Our Land
  The First Americans
  Exploring the Americas
Developing the English Colonies
  The Southern Colonies
  The New England Colonies
  The Middle Colonies
The New Nation Is Born
  The Road to Revolution
  Governing the New Nation
  The New Nation Begins to Grow
Expanding the Nation's Frontiers
  Americans Move West
  On to the Pacific
  A Changing Nation
The North and South in Conflict
  A House Divided
  The Civil War
  Reconstruction
The Nation in a New Industrial Age
  The Twilight of the Old West

Growth of Industry
Immigrants Help Cities Grow
The United States: A New World Power
Becoming a World Power
Challenges in the New World and in the Old
Prosperity and Depression
World War II and the Atomic Age
Our Country Today and Tomorrow

What are some characteristics of Arrangement One, and what do they tell us about the priorities of the course developers? For one thing, the large number of topics and subtopics tends to indicate a design prepared for use with a group of younger, less-sophisticated learners.

Furthermore, some periods seem to be targeted for more intensive study than others. For example, topics dealing with early American history are more numerous than those focusing on more recent American history. Note that only two of the seven major topics deal with events occurring after Reconstruction. What might account for this arrangement?

Arrangement One is a typical layout of content for a grade 5 United States history course. Though the course, by title, suggests an overview of all of United States history, traditionally treatment at this grade level has placed a heavy emphasis on the earlier periods. This has tended to be counterbalanced by subsequent United States history courses at the junior and senior high school levels that have placed more emphases on later periods.

Arrangement Two

Settlement in the Colonial Period
    The East-to-West Pattern
        From the Atlantic Coast to the Fall Line
        West of the Mountains
    The South-to-North Pattern
        The Southwest
        Florida
Settling the United States
    East-to-West Settlement
        1800–1850
        1850–1910
        1910–Present
    South-to-North Settlement
        1800–1850
        1850–1910
        1910–Present

Developers of Arrangement Two assigned heavy priority to patterns of settlement in the United States. This does not necessarily suggest that no other content elements will be treated in this course, but it does indicate that they will be taught in the context of major topics and subtopics related to settlement patterns. Furthermore, there is a general chronological overlay applied to the topics. Note that each subtopic is further divided into sections related to blocks of time.

An interesting feature of this framework is its attempt to break away from a more familiar treatment of United States' historical development as an unbroken east-to-west sequence. The framers of this course have recognized that this perspective fails to account for a substantial flow of people and ideas into the area of today's United States from south-to-north. Their design reflects a desire to provide learners with a perspective that development proceeded both from east-to-west and from south-to-north.

Arrangement Three

Earning a Living
  Age of Discovery to 1776
  1776 to 1820
  1820 to 1870
  1870 to Present
Inventions and Innovations
  Age of Discovery to 1776
  1776 to 1820
  1820 to 1870
  1870 to Present
Social Life and Recreational Practices
  Age of Discovery to 1776
  1776 to 1820
  1820 to 1870
  1870 to Present
Making Political Decisions
  Age of Discovery to 1776
  1776 to 1820
  1820 to 1870
  1870 to Present
Involvement in World Affairs
  Age of Discovery to 1776
  1776 to 1820
  1820 to 1870
  1870 to Present
Contributions to the Fine Arts
  Age of Discovery to 1776
  1776 to 1820
  1820 to 1870
  1870 to Present

This arrangement focuses learners' attention on a number of key themes. Developers have taken the position that these major topics or unit titles are important enough to serve as organizers for the United States history course. This design lends itself to the development of lessons that will require learners to analyze and to use other higher-level thinking skills both within and across major themes.

For example, within the major theme Inventions and Innovations, learners can be asked to compare and contrast numbers and kinds of innovations appearing during the several time periods treated under this topic or unit title.

Similarly, after learners have been exposed to several of the major themes, cross-theme comparisons can be made. For example, members of a class might be asked to capsulize what generally was happening with regard to each major theme during a given period of time. Relationships between and among developments related to selected themes at a given time can also be explored. (For example, students might be asked to find connections between the role of the American colonies in world affairs and the way political decisions were made in the period from the Age of Discovery to 1776.)

These three alternatives are among dozens of possible frameworks that might be used to organize a United States history course. Each reflects a set of decisions made by the individuals responsible for developing the course. Others might have arrived at quite a different set of arrangements. The next section introduces some basic approaches to making organizational decisions.

ORGANIZATIONAL APPROACHES

A number of general approaches to content organization have been devised. Four frequently used are (1) the chronological approach, (2) the thematic approach, (3) the part-to-whole approach, and (4) the whole-to-part approach.

THE CHRONOLOGICAL APPROACH

In a chronological approach, content elements are sequenced in terms of calendar time. The sequence may be from past to present or from present to past. This approach makes sense only when the subject matter to be treated has some logical connection to chronological time. Often a chronological approach is used to sequence content in history courses. It is by no means, however, the only approach that can be used. Chronological approaches sometimes are used in English courses, as well, particularly if course planners hope to familiarize learners with the development of a certain literary genre over time.

THE THEMATIC APPROACH

In this approach, content elements first are organized under any one of several major themes. Decisions about which themes are to be taught first, second, third, and so forth may be left entirely to the discretion of the instructor. Freedom to vary topic or unit order is particularly likely to be a feature of courses where individual topics or units are relatively independent of one another, meaning they do not require learners to master information presented in one topic or unit before they can begin their study of another. For example, an elementary school language arts program may feature such thematic topics as short stories, creative writing, plays, and poetry. None of these topics necessarily builds on any of the others.

Sometimes, however, developers of thematically organized courses suggest that certain topics or units should precede others. For example, in high school English programs, learners may be introduced to a unit on short stories before they are asked to read a novel. There are some similarities in the skills needed for success in each topic, but many instructors believe that when learners succeed at reading short stories they will have less difficulty in dealing with longer reading assignments in a subsequent unit on novels.

THE PART-TO-WHOLE APPROACH

In the part-to-whole approach, topics or units are sequenced so that basic elements of content precede more complex elements. This arrangement is reflected in the design of many mathematics and foreign language courses. Mathematics courses regularly expose learners to problems involving manipulation of one variable before asking them to solve multivariable problems. The present tense in foreign language classes is likewise taught before the imperfect tense.

The part-to-whole approach by no means is restricted to mathematics and foreign language courses, however. It is used in many other courses where complex content can be conveniently broken down into clearly identifiable constituent parts, including some science and social studies courses.

THE WHOLE-TO-PART APPROACH

The whole-to-part approach reverses the sequencing order used in part-to-whole course planning. In a whole-to-part design, general information is typically introduced first, providing class members with a broad overview of what they are to learn. Only after they have a good grasp of this overview is more specific information introduced that allows them to study smaller parts of this "whole." A geography course reflecting this basic design might introduce learners initially to all of the continents, then move on to coverage of large regions, and finally focus on individual countries and regions and cities within countries.

Often the planning of an individual course draws upon a combination of approaches. As noted in the previous section, a history course can be organized and sequenced using a combination of thematic and chronological approaches. Major themes can be selected as titles for course topics or units, then within each theme, content can be subdivided further using periods of time. This procedure can also be reversed. Periods of time can become the topic or unit titles, with individual themes treated under each.

ESTABLISHING PRIORITIES AMONG TOPICS OR UNITS

In some instances, curriculum work directed at course planning stops once content has been organized into major topic or unit titles and related subtopics. Often, however, curriculum developers wish to provide additional information to potential course instructors about the relative value of the included topics.

The issue of priorities is an important one, as instructors work within very restricted time limits. If every topic or unit and related subtopic in a given course were of equivalent importance, then the time issue could be resolved easily with instructors devoting the same amount of class time to each. This, however, is almost never the case. As a result, some effort needs to be made to identify more important topics or units and related subtopics to encourage teachers to allocate more instructional time to the high-priority parts of the course.

The identification of important content in some ways is similar to the effort made early in course development to decide which topics or unit titles to include and which to exclude. As they seek to establish the relative importance of course topics and subtopics, curriculum developers often consider the opinions of subject specialists and other authorities. These individuals may be part of the curriculum-development group itself, or they may be brought in as temporary special consultants. On still other occasions, the views of experts are solicited by telephone or letter.

A review of professional literature in education (identified from such sources as the *Education Index*) may reveal how highly regarded authorities view content priorities within a given course. Sometimes professional groups such as the National Council for the Social Studies or the National

Council of Teachers of Mathematics also publish materials calling for increased emphases on certain areas of content.

The views of experts are useful, but many curriculum groups have found experts to have varying opinions regarding the importance of individual topics. At some point, the curriculum-development group must weigh the relative merits of experts' views, consider the positions of those who are directly involved in the curriculum development effort (as well as those of some potential users), and make a decision. In general, there is merit in assigning high priorities to content elements characterized by high explanatory power, a focus on critical issues, and potential for providing knowledge with a broad transfer value.

Some curriculum groups find it useful to suggest amounts of instructional time needed for each major course topic or unit. Figure 4-1 illustrates the results of such work by one curriculum-development group.

Teachers and instructors should be encouraged to allocate more instructional time to high-priority content than to low-priority content. Assigning additional time, however, means more than simply spending more clock hours on a topic or unit. It also suggests that, as a result of this extended period of instruction, learners will be able to think about high-

FIGURE 4-1   Instructional Time Recommendations Reflecting Topic Priorities for a Course in United States History

The curriculum-development group that made these suggestions was planning a course for which 16 instructional weeks were available. They decided to identify topics as "high priority," "intermediate priority," or "low priority." High-priority topics were allotted 3 instructional weeks. Intermediate-priority topics were allotted 2 instructional weeks. Low-priority topics were allotted 1 instructional week each. The following matrix reflects their decisions.

Course Topics	Recommended Instructional Time
Age of Discovery	1 week
The Colonial Era	2 weeks
The Revolutionary War, Independence and the Constitution	3 weeks
Foreign and Domestic Affairs to 1820	2 weeks
Foreign Affairs, 1820–1850	2 weeks
The Rise of Sectionalism	2 weeks
The Civil War	3 weeks
Reconstruction	1 week

priority content in more sophisticated ways than they are able to think about low-priority content.

This expectation has led some curriculum groups to provide information that goes beyond the identification of topic or unit titles and related subtopics. Such additional information helps teachers and instructors to plan learning experiences that will lead to levels of learning consistent with the quantities of instructional time allocated to each topic or unit. In providing this information, course planners must consider three major categories of learning: (1) cognitive learning, (2) psychomotor learning, and (3) affective learning.

COGNITIVE LEARNING

Cognitive learning involves rational or intellectual thinking. Learning of traditional academic content associated with history, chemistry, English, and other basic school subjects is cognitive learning.

A scale, often referred to as the *cognitive taxonomy*, has been developed to indicate the relative sophistication of different kinds of cognitive learning. The name comes from the title of the book that introduced this scaling system, *Taxonomy of Educational Objectives: Handbook I: Cognitive Domain* (Bloom, 1956). There are six levels on the cognitive scale, ranging from least complex to most complex: (1) *knowledge*, (2) *comprehension*, (3) *application*, (4) *analysis*, (5) *synthesis*, and (6) *evaluation*.

Knowledge

Learning at the *knowledge* level requires only recall of isolated elements of information. No interpretation is required. There is also no expectation that the learner will be able to apply the new information to a different setting. ("What are the elements of the halogen family?" "Who was the leading character in the story?"—These are examples of knowledge-level questions.)

Comprehension

At the level of *comprehension*, learners must focus on several elements of information and must do more than simply identify them or repeat their names from memory. In addition they must grasp important relationships among these elements. They may also be required to change the form of information they have learned in a minor way. ("What voting patterns do you see on this chart that tell us how young voters, middle-aged voters, and older voters voted in the election?" "What would you expect to happen next in the story?"—These are examples of comprehension-level questions.)

Application

At the *application* level, learners are able to take information learned in one setting and apply it in another. The idea is for them to *do something* they were not able to do before. ("Use your map symbols to locate and identify cities in China having over one million people." "Write a ten-line poem in which at least four lines feature some use of alliteration."—These instructions are designed to encourage learners to operate at the level of application.)

Analysis

At the level of *analysis*, learners are required to understand a large phenomenon of some kind by examining its constituent parts and making inferences. Analysis involves the study of "pieces" of a larger "whole" with a view to better understanding that whole. ("Identify this unknown chemical by conducting analyses necessary to identify the elements." "Describe the 'character' of the central figure in the story after considering how he acts in various situations that develop as the plot unfolds."— These tasks require learners to operate at the level of analysis.)

Synthesis

At the level of *synthesis*, learners must put together individual elements of content to create a new "whole," or at least one that is new to them. ("Prepare a logical plan for the defense of Western Europe." "Write an original short story." "Suggest what might happen to weather in the Midwest if a huge range of mountains were to appear along the Gulf Coast of the United States."—These tasks involve synthesis-level thinking.)

Evaluation

At the level of *evaluation*, learners must make judgments in the light of criteria. They must make their criteria explicit, and they must cite evidence to support their conclusions. ("Critique the argument in terms of accepted standards of logical fallacy." "Evaluate two pieces of seventeenth-century French drama in terms of their relative consistency with the 'rules' of classical drama."—These tasks require evaluation-level thinking.)

The cognitive levels at which it is hoped learners will perform at the end of their exposure to given content elements have implications for instructional time and program planning. Some curriculum specialists have found it convenient to use a scheme that allows for a display of course topics or units in terms of the cognitive levels expected of learners. This is the *table of specifications* (Bloom, Hastings, and Madaus, 1981). A table of specifications lists major topics or unit titles down one axis and the intended highest levels of cognitive outcome across the other.

To understand how a table of specifications might be used, look again at the recommendations for a United States history course described in Figure 4-1. For purposes of comparison, tables of specifications have been prepared for two of the course topics or units, The Age of Discovery, a low-priority unit for which one week of instructional time has been recommended, and The Civil War, a high-priority unit for which three weeks of instructional time has been suggested. Look at the tables of specifications for these two units in Figure 4-2.

Note how the tables of specifications visually portray differences in expectations for learners in the low-priority unit and the high-priority unit. The X's indicate the cognitive levels expected of learners. An X has also been included in each cell to the left of the highest level. This is because the cognitive taxonomy assumes that someone capable of thinking at a given cognitive level has the ability to think at every lower cognitive level as well.

Figure 4-1 indicates that three times as much instructional time is planned for the Civil War unit as for the Age-of-Discovery unit. Notice that the table of specifications for the Civil War unit indicates that learners should be able to think about this content in considerably more sophisticated ways than they will be expected to think about the Age-of-Discovery unit. Since instructors are expected to devote only one week to the Age-of-Discovery material, there will not be sufficient time to develop large numbers of sophisticated thinking skills related to this content.

The table of specifications provides an excellent beginning point from which individual instructors can plan their units in detail. The X's suggest the cognitive levels of instructional objectives that need to be developed. Instructional objectives are statements that specify what learners should be expected to do after having been exposed to instruction related to a given topic, the conditions under which they should be expected to do it, and their proficiency. A given instructional objective will reference a particular topic and the expected cognitive level of learner thinking. (For more information about formatting objectives and the relationship of objectives to instructional units, see Chapter 8.)

Teachers designing complete instructional units for the Age-of-Discovery material might look at the table of specifications in Figure 4-2 and conclude that they would need one or more knowledge-level objectives for the subtopics Important Explorers and Lands Explored. They would need comprehension-level objectives for the subtopics European Motives and Technology and Exploration. And for the subtopic Legacies of Exploration they would prepare one or more analysis-level objectives.

PSYCHOMOTOR LEARNING

Psychomotor learning refers to outcomes that require learners to use the body's muscular system. The degree of coordination required varies from

FIGURE 4-2   Tables of Specifications for (A) a Low-priority Unit and (B) a High-priority Unit in a United States History Course

A: Unit Title: "Age of Discovery" (Low-Priority Unit)

Subtopics	Knowledge	Comprehension	Application	Analysis	Synthesis	Evaluation
Important Explorers	X					
European Motives	X	X				
Technology and Exploration	X	X				
Legacies of Exploration	X	X	X	X		
Lands Explored	X					

B: Unit Title: "The Civil War" (High-Priority Unit)

Subtopics	Knowledge	Comprehension	Application	Analysis	Synthesis	Evaluation
Resources of North and South	X	X	X	X		
Characteristics of Major Battles	X	X				
Economic Conditions of North and South	X	X	X	X		
Social Characteristics of North and South	X	X	X	X		
Legacies of the Civil War	X	X	X	X	X	X
Civil War Era Political Leaders	X					
Reading Battlefield Maps	X	X	X			

activities involving the use of very large muscles to those demanding the skilled use of fine-muscle systems. All learning involves some elements of psychomotor learning. For example, even as cognitively oriented a learning activity as reading requires use of the large and small muscle systems. Pages must be turned. The eyes must be capable of moving to scan lines. (Indeed, all learning involves elements of all three major learning types: cognitive, psychomotor, and affective.)

A number of attempts have been made to describe taxonomies of psychomotor behavior (Simpson, 1966; Harrow, 1972; Jewett and Mullan, 1977). Each of these frameworks has certain strengths and weaknesses. Savage and Armstrong (1987) suggested a simplified framework for psychomotor learning that drew upon several ideas introduced in the work of Simpson (1966) and of Jewett and Mullan (1977). Their framework includes four levels of psychomotor learning: (1) *awareness*, (2) *individual components*, (3) *integration*, and (4) *free practice*.

Awareness

At the *awareness* level, the learner must describe correctly how the psychomotor task should properly be performed. This level is quite similar to the cognitive level of knowledge. ("Describe where the feet should be positioned when the bowling ball is released." "Tell me how the clay should be placed on the potter's wheel before you begin to turn."—These are examples of awareness-level tasks.)

Individual Components

Many complex psychomotor activities are composed of several parts and learners may become frustrated if asked to perform all of a new complex activity at one time. This possibility is recognized in the second level of psychomotor activity, *individual components*. At this level, the learner is asked to demonstrate individual parts of a complex activity one at a time in an effort to work through the entire sequence with no errors. ("Show me where the club should be at the beginning of the swing. Good. Now show me how your feet should be positioned. Now where should the club be at the end of the swing. Excellent."—Instructions such as these are typical of those provided at the individual-components level.)

Integration

People who are capable of performing a psychomotor skill proficiently move smoothly through the entire activity. They do not pause at the conclusion of each part. Instead boundaries separating parts tend to disappear as the activity is performed in a smooth, continuous flow. These individuals have unified the total performance into an integrated whole.

The learner, at the level of *integration* is asked to perform the entire sequence under the guidance of the teacher or instructor. ("Throw the discus as far as you can. Pay careful attention to feet position at each phase of your throw. I'll be watching."—Instructions similar to these are typical of the integration level.)

Free Practice

The learner at the *free-practice* level is asked to perform the activity on several occasions with no direct teacher supervision. He or she is assumed to have internalized the process and to require little or no direct instruction. Furthermore, at this level, mastery is so complete that the learner may adapt and modify the skill in accordance to his or her personal preferences. ("Using the guidelines we have learned, prepare at least six different dry flies of recognized standard patterns." "Make four drawers fitted together with joints consistent with or derived from dovetail patterns."—These instructions are characteristic of those provided at the free-practice level.)

As is true in the cognitive area, the higher the level of expected psychomotor performance, the more instructional time generally required. A table of specifications focusing on psychomotor outcomes may be helpful to curriculum specialists.

Suppose a curriculum-development group had been charged with making recommendations regarding major topics or units to be covered in a crafts class. After consulting experts, reviewing available local resources, considering the nature of learners to be served, and thinking about the relative "power" of alternative content elements, the group decided upon the following contents and priorities:

Priority 1: Turning Pots on the Wheel
Priority 2: Leatherwork
Priority 3: Enamelware
Priority 4: Lost-Wax Casting
Priority 5: Wood Carving
Priority 6: Candle Making

A table of specifications looking something like that featured in Figure 4-3 could be prepared.

The table of specifications clearly indicates an intent to devote more time to turning pots and to leatherwork than to other units. This is reflected in the higher expected level of final performance indicated for these areas as compared to the others. Because of time limitations, the topics of wood carving and candle making will barely be touched. Learners will not be expected to go away with much more than a basic understanding of fundamental processes associated with each.

FIGURE 4-3   Table of Specifications for Psychomotor Learning

Course: Beginning Crafts

	Awareness	Individual Components	Integration	Free Practice
Turning Pots	X	X	X	X
Leatherwork	X	X	X	X
Enamelware	X	X	X	
Lost-Wax Casting	X	X	X	
Wood Carving	X			
Candle Making	X			

AFFECTIVE LEARNING

Affective learning focuses on issues relating to attitudes and values. It embraces a broad array of topics that are of interest to curriculum developers, including moral development, values clarification, and learners' attitudes toward subject-matter content.

Lawrence Kohlberg has suggested that there exists a moral-development taxonomy (Kohlberg, 1975; 1980). As people mature and grow in their sensitivities to the world, they are capable of moving from lower to higher levels of moral development. Individual moral development stages are characterized by the kinds of logic or reasoning people use to make decisions.

People at higher levels make decisions based on concerns that are more universal and less self-centered than those at lower levels. For this reason, proponents of Kohlberg's ideas contend that schools have an interest in helping learners progress to higher levels. Kohlberg and others subscribing to his views have described approaches for assisting learners in moving to higher levels of moral development. Of particular interest on this subject is Lawrence Kohlberg's "Education for a Just Society: An Updated and Revised Statement," in Brenda Munsey's *Moral Development, Moral Education, and Kohlberg* (1980).

Values clarification refers to teaching approaches directed toward helping learners identify and understand values that underlie their personal behaviors. Too frequently these values remain at an unconscious level. Values clarification techniques seek to help learners grasp clearly what their own values are and how these values affect what they do. Two useful texts in this area are *Values and Teaching* (Raths, Harmin, and Simon, 1978) and *Values Clarification: A Handbook of Practical Strategies for Teachers and Students* (Simon, Howe, and Kirschenbaum, 1972; 1985).

Individuals concerned about affective learning are also interested in how learners feel about academic content. They recognize that long-term commitment to content learning will result only if individuals have positive reactions to academic experiences. A given program may produce splendid short-term results in terms of enhanced learner performance on tests. However, if, as a consequence of exposure to this program, learners develop a distaste for the subject matter, their long-term interests probably are not being well served.

The idea of imposing values has a negative connotation for most Americans, yet there is a reluctance to abandon all consideration of values and attitudes when educational programs are planned. Carried to its logical conclusion, a failure to address values might lead to the acceptance of the actions of a mass murderer on the grounds that he was simply following his own conscience.

The trick for the curriculum developer is to find an appropriate balance between the one extreme of imposing narrow, restrictive attitudes and the other of doing nothing and, by implication, endorsing socially destructive behavior. Generally, curriculum workers have resisted attempts to embed within programs hard-line positions on values' issues that are very much open to debate. For example, a curriculum document that appeared to mandate a "correct" position on such issues as mercy killing, abortion, or capital punishment would be certain to draw fire from opponents of whatever position was taken.

The kinds of attitude and value statements found in curriculum documents tend to be those related to the learning process. Often they focus on the importance of generating learners' interest in content to be taught and on developing their commitment to rational thinking processes. Since such attitudes and values are broadly accepted, few people will challenge attempts to nurture their development among learners.

Rarely are entire topics devoted specifically to teaching attitudes and values. More frequently, affective learning is viewed as an overlay on topics that more directly seek to promote certain cognitive or psychomotor outcomes. In a history course, there may be an affective interest in developing youngsters' enthusiasm for history and appreciation for methods historians use to make decisions. A physical education instructor, in addition to teaching the rudiments of bowling, may hope learners develop an enthusiasm for lifelong recreational pursuits.

There have been several approaches to scaling attitudes and personal values. Armstrong and Savage (1983) developed a framework for scaling affective-domain learning experiences that draws together and simplifies some of the categories included in previous work by Krathwohl, Bloom, and Masia (1964) and Raths, Harmin, and Simon (1978). Their scheme features four levels: (1) *receiving*, (2) *approaching*, (3) *deciding*, and (4) *sharing*.

Receiving

Receiving is a level of behavior characterized by a learner's willingness to be exposed to new content with an open mind. The intent is to remove any blockages caused by misconceptions or general hostility to the content. ("Learners are willing to take in new material without any preconceived feelings that it is somehow lacking in worth, importance, or merit."—This is an example of behavior one would expect at the level of receiving.)

Approaching

While receiving is concerned with a willingness to take in new content, *approaching* goes a step further. It refers to a learner's predisposition to look at individual aspects of content, one at a time, with no preset views that might lead to a rejection of information before it has been adequately considered. The level of approaching is characterized by a learners' willingness to suspend judgment and to weigh individual issues on their own merits. ("Learners will consider individual issues on their merits and will not let preconceived ideas stand in the way of their ability to make judgments based on the best available evidence."—This is an example of expected behavior at the level of approaching.)

Deciding

At the *deciding* level, learners are expected to arrive at personal decisions that have been made after a suspension of judgment and a consideration of issues on their merits. ("Learners will make choices based on their own best judgments after prejudice-free consideration of alternatives."—This is an example of the kind of behavior one would expect at the level of deciding.)

Sharing

At the level of *sharing*, learners evidence a willingness to share personal decisions with others. ("Learners will take action to interest others in reading science fiction."—This example of sharing-level behavior might characterize a person who, having decided that science fiction stories are good, undertakes to share this interest with others.)

Sometimes curriculum workers develop tables of specifications for the affective domain. In those relatively unusual situations when specific

FIGURE 4-4   A Table of Specifications for Affective Learning

Course: Biology

	Receiving	Approaching	Deciding	Sharing
Watching Biology-Oriented Segments of "Nova"	X	X		
Reading Assigned Biology Text Materials	X	X	X	
Reading Nonassigned Material about Biology	X	X		
Starting a Personal Insect Collection	X	X	X	X

The decision here was made to assign highest priority to starting a personal insect collection. Clearly others might have a different view as to the relative importance of each listed activity.

topics might be almost exclusively devoted to teaching for affective outcomes, a stand-alone table of specifications such as that depicted in Figure 4-4 might prove useful.

More typically, an affective component is added to a composite table of specifications such as that introduced in the next subsection.

BUILDING A COMPOSITE TABLE OF SPECIFICATIONS

Individual tables of specifications for courses or parts of subject areas are useful, but they do have some limitations. Many individual courses have parts that are chiefly cognitive, other parts that are chiefly psychomotor, and perhaps still others that are chiefly affective. When this is true, working with several tables of specifications can be cumbersome. To solve this problem, some curriculum developers use a *composite* table of specifications.

The composite table of specifications lists major topic titles down one axis and major elements of the cognitive, psychomotor, and affective scales on the other. To complete the table, the curriculum specialist places

FIGURE 4-5   Prototype for a Composite Table of Specifications

	Cognitive						Psychomotor				Affective			
	Knowledge	Comprehension	Application	Analysis	Synthesis	Evaluation	Awareness	Individual Components	Integration	Free Practice	Receiving	Approaching	Deciding	Sharing
Topic A														
Topic B														
Topic C														
Topic D														
Topic E														
Topic F														
Topic G														
Topic H														

X's in each relevant cell. When finished, the table indicates the relative emphasis to be given each topic in terms of cognitive, psychomotor, and affective outcomes (Figure 4-5).

The composite table of specifications typically will not have marks in each of the domains (cognitive, psychomotor, affective) for every listed topic, as some topics will focus on learning related to only one or two learning types.

SUMMARY

A number of general approaches to organizing and sequencing selected content are available. The chronological approach sequences content in terms of calendar time. The thematic approach organizes content under a number of major themes. When individual themes are unrelated, the sequencing of topics or units may be left to the discretion of the instructor. In cases where some thematic topics include content prerequisite to that taught in other topics, however, the topics including the prerequisite information must be taught first.

In the part-to-whole approach content is organized such that simple, less complex parts of a more complicated whole are taught first. This kind of course design is reflected in large numbers of mathematics and foreign language courses. Whole-to-part approaches reverse this process. They begin by orienting learners to a broad, general body of information, then deal subsequently with more specific elements of this whole. Some geography courses, among others, are organized in this way.

In most courses, some units and topics are thought to be more important than others. Sometimes curriculum developers provide guidelines of suggested topic and unit priorities to instructors. These carry with them an expectation that learners will emerge with deeper, more sophisticated understanding of high-priority topics than of low-priority topics. To achieve this expectation, more instructional time needs to be allocated to high-priority areas and objectives need to be developed that reflect the expectations of more sophisticated learning outcomes.

To communicate differences among topic or unit priorities and in intended outcomes, tables of specifications are sometimes used. These list course topics or unit titles down one axis and expected levels of cognitive, psychomotor, or affective outcomes across the other. A visual examination of a table of specifications will reveal the suggested importance of each unit or topic and the nature of objectives that need to be developed for each.

EXTENDING AND APPLYING CHAPTER CONTENT

1. A number of national professional organizations from time to time have published guidelines related to topics or units that should be covered in certain courses. Identify a professional group of which you are a member or one in which you are interested. Write to the national headquarters of this group or check in your library for information about guidelines for a specific course's contents that it may have published. Compare and contrast these guidelines with one or more of the following: (a) the topic breakdown in a textbook used in the course; (b) the topic breakdown reflected in a local curriculum document focusing on the course; (c) comments from a teacher of the course regarding the topics covered. Share your findings with your curriculum course instructor and the class. In general, do you feel the national guidelines to be fairly compatible with what is reflected elsewhere? Do you find them to be setting a standard to be aspired to, but far ahead of present practices? Or do you draw still other conclusions?

2. Examine several textbooks designed for use in a course in which you are interested. Prepare a short paper in which you discuss the priorities reflected in the scheme of topics in each. How do you account for these

differences? What does the topic organization in each text reveal about the authors' views regarding which content is high priority and which is low priority? Which arrangement do you prefer, and why?

3. Think about a course you are interested in teaching. Develop a scheme for breaking down contents of this course into topic titles or unit titles. Explain your rationale for this arrangement in terms of the following: (1) the nature of the learners for whom the course is intended, (2) the kinds of expected learning outcomes, (3) expert opinion regarding the importance of topics, (4) potential acceptability to other instructors, and (5) compatibility with available learning resources.

4. Identify a course you are interested in teaching. Find a textbook, a curriculum document that includes topic or unit titles, or any other source of information that will reveal a pattern of organizing and sequencing content. First, identify the general sequencing approach as being either (1) chronological, (2) thematic, (3) part-to-whole, (4) whole-to-part, (5) some combination of chronological, thematic, part-to-whole, or whole-to-part, or (6) something else entirely. Then, try to devise a content arrangement consistent either with a part-to-whole or whole-to-part approach. Bring results of your work to class. With others, discuss the strengths and weaknesses of alternative arrangements.

5. For a course you are interested in teaching, identify major topics or unit titles. Label each as a high-priority, intermediate-priority, or low-priority topic. Provide a rationale for your ranking. Develop a table of specifications for this course including your topics or unit titles and, as appropriate, expected levels of cognitive, psychomotor, or affective outcomes. Prepare a short paper explaining how this table of specifications might be useful to instructors in planning their courses.

BIBLIOGRAPHY

Armstrong, David G. and Tom V. Savage. 1983. *Secondary Education: An Introduction*. New York: Macmillan Co.

Berelson, Bernard and Gary Steiner. 1967. *Human Behavior: Shorter Edition*. New York: Harcourt, Brace, Jovanovich.

Bloom, Benjamin S., ed. 1956. *Taxonomy of Educational Objectives: Handbook I: The Cognitive Domain*. New York: David McKay Co.

Bloom, Benjamin S., J. Thomas Hastings, and George F. Madaus. 1981. *Evaluation to Improve Learning*. New York: McGraw-Hill Book Company.

Brandt, Ronald S., ed. 1988. *Content of the Curriculum*. 1988 ASCD Yearbook. Alexandria, VA: Association for Supervision and Curriculum Development.

Bruner, Jerome. 1960. *The Process of Education*. Cambridge, MA: Harvard University Press.

Harrow, Anita J. 1972. *A Taxonomy of the Psychomotor Domain*. New York: David McKay Company.

Jewett, Ann E. and Marie R. Mullan. 1977. *Curriculum Design: Purposes and Processes in Physical Education Teaching—Learning*. Washington, D.C.: American Alliance for Health, Physical Education, and Recreation.

Kohlberg, Lawrence. 1975. "The Cognitive-Developmental Approach to Moral Education." *Phi Delta Kappan* (June 1975): 670–675.

Kohlberg, Lawrence. 1980. "Education for a Just Society: An Updated and Revised Statement." *Moral Development, Moral Education, and Kohlberg*. Edited by Brenda Munsey. Birmingham, AL: Religious Education Press, pp. 455–470.

Krathwohl, David R., Benjamin S. Bloom, and Bertram B. Masia. 1964. *Taxonomy of Educational Objectives: Handbook II: Affective Domain*. New York: David McKay Company.

Miller, John P. and Wayne Seller. 1985. *Curriculum Perspectives and Practice*. New York: Longman.

Raths, Louis, Merrill Harmin, and Sidney B. Simon. 1978. *Values and Teaching*, 2d ed. Columbus, OH: Charles E. Merrill.

Rest, James. 1983. "Morality." *Handbook of Child Psychology*, Vol. 4. Edited by P. Hussen. New York: John Wiley and Sons.

Rokeach, Milton. 1979. *Understanding Values: Human and Societal*. New York: Free Press.

Savage, Tom V. and David G. Armstrong. 1987. *Effective Teaching in Elementary Social Studies*. New York: Macmillan Co.

Simon, Sidney B., Leland W. Howe, and Howard Kirschenbaum. 1985. *Values Clarification: A Handbook of Practical Strategies for Teachers and Students*. New York: Hart Publishing Company, 1972; Dodd, Mead and Company, 1985.

Simpson, E.J. 1966. "The Classification of Educational Objectives, Psychomotor Domain." *Illinois Teacher of Home Economics* (Winter): 110–144.

Stahl, Robert H. 1981. "Achieving Values and Content Objectives Simultaneously within Subject-Matter-Oriented Social Studies Classrooms." *Social Education* (November/December): 580–585.

Taba, Hilda. 1962. *Curriculum Development: Theory and Practice*. New York: Harcourt, Brace, and World.

Texas Education Agency. 1984. *State Board of Education Rules for Curriculum: Principles, Standards, and Procedures for Accreditation of School Districts*. Austin, Texas: Texas Education Agency.

CHAPTER 5

Introduction to the Written Curriculum

This chapter introduces information to help the reader

1. **identify characteristics and major purposes of selected curriculum documents.**
2. **describe major components of curriculum documents.**
3. **point out document types that might be included in a complete set of interrelated curriculum documents.**
4. **explain how a notation system can tie together common elements in different curriculum documents.**
5. **identify audiences for selected curriculum documents.**

INTRODUCTION

Curriculum documents are the physical carriers of the curriculum. They embrace all written forms a curriculum might take, including, but not limited to, such documents as philosophy statements, scope and sequence documents, curriculum guides, course plans, grade-level plans, instructional unit plans, and courses of study.

Each document type has a specific purpose and is intended for primary use by a specific audience. In the following section, a number of curriculum documents are introduced and described in terms of their basic characteristics and of the audience to which they are directed.

A SELECTION OF BASIC DOCUMENT TYPES

Documents introduced here represent a sampling of those in use in school settings and in other environments. Those included are among the most common types.

PHILOSOPHY STATEMENTS

Major Characteristics

Philosophy statements are collections of ideas about the overall intentions of a program. They tend to be nonspecific in nature and to reference a number of major goals. The lack of specificity in philosophy statements suggests an important political purpose of documents of this type. In part, the wording of philosophy statements attempts to bridge profound philosophical differences regarding the characteristics of "good" educational practices. The language in the sample philosophy statement in Figure 5-1 is a good example.

The statement in Figure 5-1 mentions many different kinds of major program goals. There is something here for constituents who, respectively, believe the school program should (1) develop intellectual competencies, (2) produce learners ready for the world of work, (3) promote learners' self-understanding, (4) develop problem-solving skills, and (5) produce individuals committed to reform. Because the philosophy statement seeks to comfort people representing many philosophical constituencies, language that attempts to weave a number of broad and sometimes conflicting goals into a single fabric is typical.

Philosophy statements, by design, attempt to bring together many perspectives regarding purposes of instructional programs. To assure that many views are incorporated in the document, there is often an effort to include in the document-preparation process individuals who hold varying opinions. When a philosophy statement is being prepared for a school district, the development effort often is led by a very senior central-office curriculum specialist. Others involved may include representatives of administrators, teachers, parents, learners, and interested citizens.

Primary Users

Philosophy statement documents are directed primarily at the general community. Rarely is language sufficiently specific to provide clear guidelines for the kind of program development that might interest curriculum developers, program administrators, or teachers. Philosophy statements inform the community at large about general intentions of the school program.

FIGURE 5-1   An Example of a Philosophy Statement

Purposes of Education: Smith City Public Schools

The Smith City Public Schools seek to develop each child's potential to its maximum. This goal will be accomplished through the provision of learning experiences that respond to legitimate learner interests, promote clarity of understanding of the larger world, foster development of citizenship and economic-survival skills, and develop learners' feelings of self-understanding and personal worth.

Smith City Public Schools commit strongly to the concept of educational balance. Sound academic skills are critical for survival in today's competitive world. Certainly, too, young people must have solid control over those basic skills they will need in the workplace. As future citizens, they will be helped to develop a commitment to participate in democratic efforts to improve the quality of local, state, national, and international life. All of these skills should be developed both within the academic program and in extracurricular and cocurricular experiences.

Tomorrow's world will confront people with challenges barely dreamed of today. All programs, therefore, should develop learners' problem-solving and thinking skills. Intellectual toughness will be critical in a world where change is becoming one of life's few "constants."

Programs to meet all of these goals must be developed by people representing the whole community. Parents, leading citizens, and learners themselves are among those who must join with professional educators to plan the best array of learning experiences for Smith City's future—its children.

Because philosophy statements sketch the broad outlines of an instructional program, they may serve as references for individuals who are involved in developing other curriculum documents. Developers of these other documents seek to maintain some consistency with the philosophy statement that gives general direction to the overall instructional program.

GENERAL SCOPE AND
SEQUENCE DOCUMENTS

Major Characteristics

General scope and sequence documents include information about major features of offerings in all subject areas included in the total program. In some school districts, these documents are split into two sections: one to reference all elementary programs (typically grades K to 6) and the other to reference all secondary programs (typically grades 7 to 12). Other school districts prefer to have a single comprehensive document covering the entire K-to-12 program.

Scope and sequence documents ordinarily are prepared by groups led by top-level curriculum specialists. Since the purpose of these documents is to identify key components in the total instructional program, central management of their design is essential. Some decisions regarding content elements to be included may be mandated by state law. Others may be determined locally. In addition to central office curriculum leaders, teams of individuals charged with developing general scope and sequence documents often include administrators and teachers, and sometimes learner, parent, and community representatives.

The general scope and sequence document is a basic tool of overall program management. It may serve as one basic component of a core set of interrelated documents, which also includes curriculum guides, grade-level plans or course plans, and instructional unit plans. For additional information about scope and sequence documents, see the material later in this chapter under the heading "A Basic Curriculum Document System" and in Chapter 6, which provides specific guidelines for preparation of general scope and sequence documents.

Primary Users

The primary user of a general scope and sequence document is the person charged with overall program management. In a school, this might be the assistant superintendent or the curriculum director. In a corporate setting, this person might be the chief training-and-development administrator.

The general scope and sequence document contains information about parts of programs in all subject areas and at all levels (grade levels in school settings). This information is most needed by people who must verify that a program meets legal requirements, implements administrative policies about instruction, and addresses components mandated by other authorities. It also is of primary interest to people whose responsibilities span the entire instructional program. Others—subject area specialists, building principals, and teachers—from time to time may have a need to look at a general scope and sequence document, but for the most part, other documents serve their needs better.

CURRICULUM GUIDES

Major Characteristics

A general scope and sequence document deals with all subject areas and grade levels. Curriculum guides have a narrower focus. A given guide generally includes either information relating to what is done with a particular subject at all grade levels or what is done at one grade level with all subjects.

For example, a science curriculum guide might contain information about the total grades K-to-12 science program or, in districts with separate general scope and sequence documents for elementary and secondary program, about the K-to-6 science program and the 7-to-12 science program. Information about all other subjects is absent. A grade 3 curriculum guide, however, would contain general information about all subjects covered at the third grade level.

If a general scope and sequence document has been previously prepared, a curriculum guide can be created by extracting the portion of the document referring to a single area, for example science or mathematics. When there is no general scope and sequence document, curriculum guides typically are developed by groups led by central-office curriculum specialists. Since these guides frequently deal with a specific subject area, individuals involved may include subject specialists as well as administrators, teachers, learners, and community members.

Primary Users

Curriculum guides are of primary interest to two groups of people. Single-subject curriculum guides are of special interest to those charged with the management of specific subject areas within the overall program. In school districts, such people may include the curriculum director and subject-area supervisors (for example mathematics supervisors, coordinators, directors, or consultants). Similarly, curriculum guides for individual grade levels will be of great interest to people with responsibility for programs at specific grade levels (for example, primary grades coordinators, intermediate grades coordinators, grade 5 specialists, and so forth).

Building-level administrators and individual teachers may have some interest in curriculum guides, although generally these documents do not provide as much specific information to these people as do other documents. Administrators and teachers find other kinds of documents more useful.

GRADE-LEVEL PLANS AND COURSE PLANS

Major Characteristics

Grade-level plans contain information about what is included within a given content or subject area at a particular grade level. For example, a grade-level plan might specify what is to be done in the area of social studies at grade 4. In schools with complete curriculum document systems, each grade has a separate grade-level plan for each content or subject area.

Course plans perform a function similar to grade-level plans, the major difference being that they are designed for secondary rather than elementary programs, or for nonpublic-school instructional settings. In the secondary schools, because programs typically are divided into individual courses such as American history, ideally, there should be a course plan for every course.

Grade-level plans and course plans often are developed by teams led by central-office curriculum leaders. In districts large enough to have curriculum specialists charged with supervising specific subject areas or grade levels, these individuals may well play leadership roles. In smaller places, curriculum specialists with broader responsibilities may be in charge.

Although some administrators may be involved in the preparation of grade-level plans and course plans, teachers responsible for individual grades and courses tend to be well represented on teams charged with preparing these documents. The teams may also include a few subject-area specialists, psychology-of-learning specialists, and instructional-design specialists.

Grade-level plans and course plans include information about the purposes of instruction. Furthermore, they suggest general approaches for delivering and evaluating instruction. More specific information about these documents is provided later in this chapter under the heading "A Basic Curriculum Document System" and in Chapter 7.

Primary Users

These documents are of great interest to people wanting specific information about the contents of each content or subject area at the elementary school level, and of each secondary-level course. Primary users include such people as building principals, subject-area specialists, and teachers responsible for coordinating instruction (perhaps a grade-level coordinator in an elementary school or a department head in a secondary school).

Other users may include central-office curriculum people with responsibilities for managing the total instructional program. These documents focus most heavily on the basic contents of instructional programs. They do not deal with the nuts-and-bolts of day-to-day instruction, nor do they include highly specific instructions regarding how learners and programs are to be evaluated.

Grade-level plans and course plans are of great interest to teachers as beginning points for planning daily instruction. However, by themselves, they generally lack the kind of detailed information that many teachers like to have. In terms of their usefulness as guides to daily instructional practice, grade-level plans and course plans are not of as much interest to individual teachers as are the more detailed instructional unit plans.

INSTRUCTIONAL UNIT PLANS

Major Characteristics

These documents provide very specific guidelines regarding how the individual parts of an instructional program, or the units, are to be organized and delivered. Instructional unit plans include complete lists of performance objectives, information regarding diagnosis of learners' individual characteristics, step-by-step directions for introducing content, tests for assessing progress, and other relevant material needed to support instruction.

Central-office curriculum specialists may provide some general leadership in an effort to develop instructional unit plans. However, teachers and instructors often do most of the actual document preparation. The detailed information in these materials is designed to provide very explicit suggestions regarding how elements of content might be introduced and evaluated. It is very difficult for individuals who have not had practical experience working with learners in given subjects and at given grade levels to develop instructional units that other teachers will regard as credible. While certainly many teams do attempt to involve university specialists with expertise in subject matter, learning theory, and instructional design, individual classroom teachers typically constitute a majority in groups charged with preparing instructional unit documents.

Instructional unit plans may comprise part of a basic set of interrelated documents. For more information about such an interrelated-document set, see the section of this chapter titled "A Basic Curriculum Document System." Other information regarding instructional units is found in Chapter 8.

Primary Users

Teachers and instructors working with learners are the primary audience for instructional unit plans. These documents include exceptionally detailed information about actual delivery of classroom instruction. This attention to the specifics of content delivery makes them especially useful to individuals teaching a given grade-level or subject for the first time.

Others who may have some interest in instructional unit plans are content specialists, building administrators, and district-level curriculum managers. However, the level of detail included in instructional unit plans goes beyond the information needs of most people other than teachers. In most cases, the needs of these others are better served by the documents previously discussed.

COURSES OF STUDY

Major Characteristics

Courses of study describe the required courses and options available for learners. In school districts, courses of study are more frequently developed for secondary rather than for elementary programs, because there are more electives open to students at the secondary than at the elementary level.

Many secondary-school courses of study suggest alternative courses and sequences of courses for students planning to go to college, students planning to enter the work force after graduating, and still others who have not made definite plans. This information is useful to students and their parents as they decide which elective courses are most appropriate.

These documents may be prepared by groups organized by central-office curriculum specialists, or sometimes by groups working within individual schools. In addition to curriculum specialists, administrators, teachers, counselors, and parents may be involved. Counselors have an obligation to make course alternatives known to learners and their parents, and when counselors participate in the preparation of courses of study, they are often able to provide better rationales to support their recommendations.

Administrators may be called on to determine the consistency of any proposed changes with state and school district regulations. In any case, since courses of study tend to be read by audiences that go beyond professional educators, central office administrators closely monitor their development.

Primary Users

The primary users of courses of study are learners and, in the case of elementary and secondary school learners, their parents. These documents are also frequently used by teachers and counselors who assist learners in selecting electives and in developing schedules of courses. Building-level and central office administrators may well also use these documents as they respond to questions about courses and course sequences.

A number of sources are available to individuals wishing to see examples of the document types discussed in this section, as well as others. Many college and university libraries include some curriculum documents in their curriculum collections. Sometimes professional organizations, such as the Association for Supervision and Curriculum Development (ASCD), display curriculum documents at regional and national meetings. A particularly useful place to find examples of documents is the Kraus Curriculum Development Library.

The Kraus Curriculum Development Library (KCDL) includes thousands of curriculum documents on microfiche, and new documents are added each year. The collection contains examples of documents developed for use in many different settings. General information about the KCDL may be obtained by writing to: Kraus International Publications, Route 100, Millwood, NY 10546.

CURRICULUM-DOCUMENT QUALITY: SOME ISSUES

Curriculum development is demanding and time-consuming. The results of such hard work deserve to be packaged in high-quality documents that signal to users the professionalism of the curriculum-development effort. This section describes a number of issues associated with document quality that are derived from those identified by Armstrong and Shutes (1981).

This discussion focuses on documents that are designed to be used by someone other than the person or persons who designed them. For example, sometimes teachers will work together informally to develop instructional units that are created exclusively for use in their own classrooms. The issues regarding document quality raised in this section are only marginally related to this kind of a situation. They apply much more directly to those curriculum documents designed for fairly wide use by individuals who, in many cases, have played little if any role in their preparation.

LEGITIMACY OF THE DOCUMENT

The issue of legitimacy has to do with the willingness of potential users to believe the prescribed program has some authority behind it. This does not mean that, in a public school setting, members of a school board need to read and approve every instructional unit plan. It does suggest, however, a need to reference somewhere in each document that it was developed under the authority of the school district. This tells users that there probably was a quality check before the document was printed and distributed.

Because knowledge about subjects and about how people learn changes over time, users will also be interested in the age of a curriculum document. This information can easily be provided by printing the date of publication on the title page.

CREDIBILITY OF THE DEVELOPERS

Credibility has to do with whether document users believe developers have the expertise to prepare documents that are conceptually sound and functional. For example, some individuals find suspect any instructional unit plan developed by someone other than a classroom teacher working in a context similar to the one in which the unit is to be taught.

What constitutes credibility is very much open to debate. Developers of curriculum documents must appreciate that concerns about a document's credibility are very real, and a failure to identify individuals involved in developing it may raise needless concerns among potential users of a described program. Document writers can alleviate some fears by identifying developers by name and making some reference to their qualifications for this work.

SPECIFICATION OF INTENDED LEARNERS

Educators deal with many different kinds of learners, varying in age, abilities, and interests. Such variety poses an important question for document preparers, who must decide whether contents are applicable to all or nearly all learners within a given category (for example, all fourth graders) or to only a few (only gifted and talented). Specific information provided at the beginning of a document should prevent a sixth grade teacher from reading about a program designed for use in more advanced grades or for more advanced learners.

SPECIFICATION OF MAJOR DOCUMENT USERS

At varying times, any curriculum document might interest different categories of people. However, curriculum documents usually are developed to be of primary interest to certain groups. Though a school superintendent might have an occasional interest in looking at an instructional unit plan, this document type usually is developed by and for classroom teachers.

Individuals and groups of individuals involved in document development need to consider who will have an interest in the document's contents. Often, curriculum development leaders require writers to identify within the document those individuals to whom the document is directed. This information can help users who encounter a document for the first time to make judgments about the relevance of its content to their own administrative or instructional roles.

SPECIFICATION OF DOCUMENT SCOPE

As they plan for document preparation, curriculum developers must consider the scope of content coverage. Some documents, for example general scope and sequence documents, have a wide range of content coverage, but include few specific details regarding individual elements. Instructional unit plans, on the other hand, may be restricted in scope, but richly detailed in terms of ideas for implementing a limited body of content. Inclusion of information about scope alerts users quickly to a given document's relevance to their needs.

CLARITY OF FORMAT AND ORGANIZATION

Document writers must be concerned with communicating clearly with document users. Attention to layout can facilitate ease of document use. A document's organization should make the relationships among its various components clear, and this scheme should be laid out concisely in the front matter. A comprehensive table of contents allows readers to locate individual parts and pages quickly.

Many documents use a notation system to label certain elements of content so that document users can identify common elements easily regardless of where they appear. Well-formatted and clearly organized documents are more likely to be used than those deficient in these areas.

INTERNAL AND EXTERNAL CONSISTENCY

Often many people are involved in preparing a single document, and when several documents are being developed, the number of individuals playing active roles grows even larger. With this kind of participation, maintaining consistency within a single document or within a group of related documents is difficult. It is the curriculum leaders' job to ensure that documents are of a fairly uniform quality throughout.

Each document needs to be *completely worked out*. This means that the level of detail provided in one section should be about the same as that provided in another. A common problem is that initial sections tend to be much more detailed and complete than sections toward the end, a pattern which may result from writers' fatigue or from pressures to meet deadlines.

Another issue arises in cases where a number of related curriculum documents already exist: language must be consistent when describing common elements. If a standard notation system has been used, it needs to be applied consistently throughout all the documents.

EVIDENCE OF PROFESSIONAL EDITING AND REPRODUCTION

High-quality editing and reproduction leads to a curriculum document that looks professional. Though people who have worked hard to produce a document might hope that potential users are prompted to use it solely because of its excellent content, appearance does exercise some influence.

Not all people agree that it is a good idea to make curriculum documents appear too polished. They argue that documents that are "too professional looking" may come to be regarded as unchangeable. Such documents could possibly have a stultifying influence on attempts to modify and improve described programs.

A counterargument claims that many existing documents appear to have been produced with little attention to their final appearance. Often curriculum developers work months on a given program. If the document that describes it is produced on an old spirit-master machine so that copies look like faded classroom handouts, many who participated may wonder why their work has been so little appreciated. Furthermore, users may infer that poorly edited and cheaply reproduced documents signal a lack of central-office commitment to described programs. Though the issue is debatable, the evidence seems to tilt slightly in favor of the production of well-edited, neatly printed documents.

There are no well-established standards for assessing the quality of individual documents. This section, however, introduced some issues that document writers might consider as they produce new curriculum documents and review those prepared by others. A scheme for looking at documents in light of this criteria is displayed in Figure 5-2.

A BASIC CURRICULUM-DOCUMENT SYSTEM

One approach to managing a large and complex instructional program is to develop a set of interrelated curriculum documents. There are many variations in the kinds of documents included in basic curriculum-document systems. One such system, for example, features a three-tiered arrangement of documents, including (1) a general scope and sequence

FIGURE 5-2   Issues to Consider in Improving a Curriculum Document

1. Legitimacy of the Document
   strengths:
   weaknesses:
   specific suggestions for improvement:
2. Credibility of the Developers
   strengths:
   weaknesses:
   specific suggestions for improvement:
3. Specification of Intended Learners
   strengths:
   weaknesses:
   specific suggestions for improvement:
4. Specification of Major Document Users
   strengths:
   weaknesses:
   specific suggestions for improvement:
5. Specification of Document Scope
   strengths:
   weaknesses:
   specific suggestions for improvement:
6. Clarity of Format and Organization
   strengths:
   weaknesses:
   specific suggestions for improvement:
7. Internal and External Consistency
   strengths:
   weaknesses:
   specific suggestions for improvement:
8. Evidence of Professional Editing and Reproduction
   strengths:
   weaknesses:
   specific suggestions for improvement:

document, (2) grade-level plans and course plans, and (3) instructional unit plans. Some elements will be common to all three documents; others will be unique to a document type.

Each document in the set has specific and somewhat limited purposes. For example, the general scope and sequence document describes many facets of the overall program. In contrast, each instructional unit provides information about a narrow range of issues, including suggested instructional approaches and evaluation procedures.

Differences among curriculum documents are there by design, because of the varying needs of their users. Though these differences are important, there needs to be some consistency among different document types. This consistency assures that the program described in general terms in the scope and sequence document is logically connected to what is described in more specific language in grade-level plans, course plans, and instructional units. Consistency is provided by including certain common elements in all documents in the set, which then provide a basis for accountability throughout the program.

A basic curriculum-document system facilitates program management by enabling administrators and central-office curriculum specialists to audit a program easily in terms of its consistency with state and local policies. Additionally, such a system provides useful guidelines for others who wish to develop documents consistent with the format used in those in the basic set.

For example, writers of instructional unit plans for a typical basic set generally take care to assure teachers that their ideas for introducing content and evaluating learners are provided only as suggestions. Individual teachers are invited to adapt these ideas to their own needs. As they do so, they may find the format of the instructional units used in the basic document set to be a helpful organizational tool. This format suggests a layout scheme and suggests ways for cross-referencing content to other documents such as the general scope and sequence document and the course plans.

The documents in a basic document set by no means represent all curriculum documents that might be developed and used. Personnel in school districts may well prepare other documents, including philosophy statements and courses of study, that are outside of the basic set. Documents purchased from commercial sources would also lie outside of the basic, interrelated document system.

SUMMARIZING CONTENT
IN BASIC DOCUMENTS

Before the designs of the documents can be determined, some scheme must be developed for summarizing content. Space considerations make it necessary to delimit information. At the same time, care must be taken to assure that summaries are not so general that they fail to communicate the plans for instruction in given courses and at given grade levels.

One approach to summarizing content is based upon the "structure of knowledge," derived from the work of Bruner (1960) and Taba (1962). The structure of knowledge has three major levels: (1) generalizations, (2) concepts, and (3) facts. Relationships among these levels are illustrated in Figure 5-3.

The most important of these components for the curriculum-development process is the *generalization*. Generalizations are idea-dense

FIGURE 5-3 The Structure of Knowledge

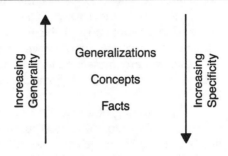

statements of "truth," or at least of what the best evidence suggests "truth" to be. Generalizations draw together tremendous quantities of content in the form of succinct statements, along with identifying the relationship between and among key concepts.

Here are two examples of generalizations:

1. Opinions that originate in an early period persist to be influential in a later period, both within a single lifetime and over generations (Berelson and Steiner, 1967).
2. As a society becomes more educated and industrialized, its birth rate declines.

The use of generalizations in curriculum documents allows for information about a good deal of content to be conveyed in a space-efficient way. Generalizations are often used to summarize content in general scope and sequence documents, curriculum guides, grade-level and course plans, and instructional unit plans.

In selecting generalizations to provide a focus for instructional programs, curriculum developers try to choose more "powerful" ones. Although there is no purely objective technique for assessing a generalization's power, Fraenkel (1980, p. 77) suggested that general criteria can be applied to evaluate the worth of a generalization. The following criteria are derived from those introduced by Fraenkel: range, research support, importance, and power of the concepts.

Range refers to the scope of phenomena for which the relationship implied by the generalization might have relevance. When two generalizations are being considered, curriculum developers often select the one with the broader reach.

Research support focuses on the strength of the research base that supports the generalization; those generalizations with a strong base are to be preferred over those less well grounded.

A generalization's *importance* is tied to its potential to develop insights applicable to a wide variety of phenomena. Important generalizations describe relationships that help to explain persistent problems.

The *power of the concepts* in a generalization, or the number of complex and important concepts it contains, should influence whether or not it is selected over another otherwise similar generalization.

Concepts are the second level in the structure of knowledge. As organizers, they tie together a great deal of specific information under one label.

The meaning of a concept derives not from a consideration of evidence, as with a generalization, but from its definition. A concept's meaning is stipulated or "given." Because the "truth" of a generalization results from a continuous process of testing against the best available evidence, a generalization may change as new evidence is found. A concept, however, has been defined in a certain way, and, therefore, usually does not change.

To understand a generalization, a learner must first be familiar with the concepts embedded within it. For example, the second generalization provided earlier references the concepts *society, educated society, industrialized society*, and *birth rate*. A learner ignorant of any of these concepts would never grasp the meaning of the generalization.

There are three important types of concepts: *conjunctive concepts, disjunctive concepts*, and *relational concepts* (Bruner, Goodnow, and Austin, 1962). These categories are important for curriculum developers because some concept types are generally more difficult for learners to grasp than are others.

The specific defining features of a concept are referred to as its *attributes. All* of the defining attributes of a *conjunctive concept* must be present in order for a thing to be considered a proper example of the concept. For example, the conjunctive concept "triangle" has these attributes: (a) a closed plane figure with (b) three sides, and (c) three interior angles. If any one of these attributes is missing, the thing under consideration is not a triangle.

Disjunctive concepts have several defining attributes. However, not all must be present for something to be considered a proper example of the concept. Fraenkel (1980; pp. 58–59) cites the extra point in football as an example of a disjunctive concept. There are several alternate ways of scoring an extra point: The ball can be run into the end zone; it can be passed to a receiver in the end zone; or it can be kicked through the uprights. The presence of any one of these conditions will suffice. Learners generally find disjunctive concepts more difficult to master than conjunctive concepts (Martorella, 1972).

Relational concepts feature a relationship between or among the defining attributes. For example, in the concept *miles per hour*, there is a relationship between an attribute having to do with distance traveled (miles) and with time (hours). Mastery of relational concepts requires learners not only to understand the defining attributes but also to understand the nature of the relationships among these attributes. Hence, relational concepts are also sometimes more difficult to teach than conjunctive concepts.

Complex concepts with numerous attributes, such as *democracy, socialization*, and *industrialization* are much more difficult for learners to grasp than simpler concepts having only a limited number of attributes. Generalizations which contain large numbers of highly complex concepts, therefore, will require more instructional time than those in which the concepts are less complex.

The third level of the structure of knowledge, *facts*, deals with much more specific and limited information than the levels of either generalizations or concepts. A fact references a specific situation. Often a fact is bound by time or place. "All the facts" can never be included in a given course or topic: There are simply too many of them.

Facts, though, have an important role to play in helping learners to master concepts and generalizations. The selection of facts is an important responsibility of curriculum developers. The problem they face is deciding which facts to include.

Generalizations and concepts can serve as screens to assess the merit of including or excluding specific facts. Identifying important generalizations and concepts in advance simplifies the matter of selection. Facts that will help learners to understand these concepts and generalizations can be selected, while facts that have no power to explain these matters can be excluded.

In summary, the structure of knowledge provides a convenient framework for summarizing large amounts of content. This efficient summary then provides a beginning point for the detailed preparation of curricula, or, initially, the development of a basic set of curriculum documents.

A SCHEME FOR INTERRELATING DOCUMENTS

Curriculum developers interested in establishing consistency within programs should ask themselves two questions: Do selected generalizations logically tie together the units? Can the relationship of individual units to individual courses be verified? Answers to these questions can emerge from the examination of well-formatted, interrelated curriculum-document sets.

One way to establish these relationships is to use a system that references key areas from the general scope and sequence document whenever they appear in a grade-level plan, course plan, and instructional unit plan.

For example, suppose a scope and sequence document contained information related to these four key areas:

1. The curriculum area
   A listing of such major parts of the overall program as social studies, mathematics, English, science, and so forth.
2. Grade-level or course titles
   The grade-levels or secondary-school courses where certain content would appear.
3. Unit or topic titles
   The names of each unit or topic covered in each grade level or each course in each major curriculum area.
4. Generalizations
   The insights provided by content introduced in each grade level, unit or topic, and major curriculum area.

To assure consistency in all documents, these key elements are referenced again in all documents subordinate to the general scope and sequence document in which they initially appear. In some cases, the information related to these elements is written out in full, exactly as it appears in the scope and sequence document. In others, a notation scheme is used as a kind of shorthand. The notation scheme indicates the relationship between these key areas of the scope and sequence document and the components provided in subordinate documents such as grade-level plans, course plans, and instructional unit plans.

A Basic Notation System

A notation scheme designed to tie together documents in a basic document system must be capable of referencing key areas in the scope and sequence document. If four key areas had been developed, as in the example just cited, then the notation system would have to be capable of identifying each of them. Such a system might look something like the example introduced in Figure 5-4.

The general pattern used in the notation system depicted in Figure 5-4 is as follows:

.01.01.01.01

Curriculum Area_____| | |____Generalization
Grade-Level or |____Unit or Topic Title
Course Title_____|

This notation scheme allows curriculum developers at their discretion to print either the notational reference *and* a complete description of the key area to which it refers *or* to print only the notation scheme. For

FIGURE 5-4   A Sample Notation Scheme

Curriculum Area

.01 English (includes reading, language arts)
.02 Mathematics
.03 Science
.04 Social Studies
.05 Music
.06 Art
.07 Physical Education
.08 Health
.09 Industrial Arts
    (same scheme follows for other areas)

Grade-Level or Course Title

.01 English
    .00 reading—kindergarten
    .01 reading—grade 1
    .02 reading—grade 2
    .
    .
    .
    .12 world literature, grade 12
.02 Mathematics
    .00 number readiness—kindergarten
    .
    .
    etc.
.03 Science
(same pattern for all other curriculum areas)

Unit or Topic Titles

.01 English
  .01 reading—grade 1
    .01 Word Attack Skills
    .02 Vocabulary Development
    .03 Comprehension Skills etc.
(same scheme for other curriculum areas and grade-levels or course titles)

Generalizations

.01 English
  .01 reading—grade 1
    .01 Word Attack Skills
      .01 Reading expertise is facilitated when learners first master simple, one-syllable words and then move on to more complex words of two or more syllables, etc.

(same pattern for other curriculum areas, grade-level or course titles, and units or topics)

---

example, under some conditions, it might be desirable to make this kind of comprehensive entry in a document:

    .01 English
      .01 Reading, Grade 1
        .01 Word Attack Skills
          .01 Reading expertise is facilitated when learners first master simple, one-syllable words and then move on to more complex words of two or more syllables.

At other times, this kind of complete listing might not be desirable. Such a display takes up a good deal of space. If space is a consideration, a decision might be made to display only the notation referencing this information. Were this done, the following notation would result:

.01.01.01.01

Notation is always written from left to right. In the display above, the first two digits refer to curriculum areas. The second two indicate the grade level or the course title. The third two identify the unit or topic title. The fourth two denote the generalization.

The exact meaning of a line of notation is determined by referring back to an initial explanation of each digit. A display such as the one introduced in Figure 5-4 typically is developed when the scope and sequence document is first produced. This display can be conveniently included in all other documents in the basic set (grade-level plans, course plans, and instructional unit plans). Ordinarily, the display is presented in the opening pages of each document, thereby alerting users to the significance of the notations they will see in subsequent sections of the document.

Illustrations of Notation System Application

Notation-system layout in individual documents may vary according to developers' preferences and space limitations, among other influences. The examples introduced here are not intended to represent the only correct applications of notation systems. They should, however, illustrate acceptable solutions to the problem of providing a notation system that will identify common components in each basic document.

Using the notation system depicted in Figure 5-4, the following arrangement might be found on part of a page in a *scope and sequence document:*

Curriculum area: .01 English
Grade level or course title: .01.01 Reading—Grade 1

units or topics	*generalizations*
.01.01.01	.01.01.01.01
Word Attack Skills	Reading expertise is facilitated when learners first master simple, one-syllable words and then move on to more complex words of two or more syllables.

Grade-level program plans and course plans will include more than just the four key areas from the scope and sequence document (curriculum area, grade-levels or course titles, unit or topic titles, and generalizations). However, each of these four areas must be noted in some way. The following notation scheme might be featured on a page of a *grade level plan:*

.01.01.01 Unit One—Word Attack Skills
Rationale: To develop learners' independence, the teacher should introduce the idea of context early. Furthermore, learners must be
exposed to the grapheme-phoneme correspondences that fur-
nish the most reliable cues for decoding words for which they
have not already developed an instant recognition capacity.
Key Concepts: phonic analysis, context cues, structural analysis, sight
vocabulary

generalizations	*instructional procedures*	*evaluation procedures*
.01.01.01.01 Reading expertise is facilitated when learners first master simple, one-syllable words and then move on to more complex words of two or more syllables.	(This section includes general discussion of instructional procedures recommended to help learners grasp the generalizations.)	(This section includes general discussion of evaluation procedures recommended to help learners grasp the generalizations.)

Note that specific information is not provided in this example regarding either the curriculum area or the grade level. These are indicated
only by the notation. Recall that the first two digits denote the curriculum
area, and the second two digits indicate the grade level. From the master
notation system given in Figure 5-4, the curriculum area is English and
the grade level is grade 1.

Instructional unit plans include more specific details for teachers
than do grade level or course plans. As is the case in grade-level and
course plans, the four key areas from the general scope and sequence document are referenced using the adopted notation system.

Using the notation system explained in Figure 5-4, the following
scheme might be featured on a page of an *instructional unit plan:*

.01.01.03 Unit Three—Comprehension Skills
.01.01.03.03 Generalization—Deriving meaning from written language
depends on mastery of specific compre-
hension skills.
Performance Objective 1—The learner will identify the main idea of a
story. The objective will be mastered by learn-
ers who answer correctly 5 of 6 m/c items on a
test.

Sample Instructional Strategy

O (emphasizing objectives)	—Talk about what the word *idea* means. Write a simple definition of the term on the board. Tell members of the class that they are going to learn how to recognize the main idea of a story.
M (motivating learning)	—Ask, "Who likes stories?" Then, tell learners they will be able to hear a story "right now."
R (recalling previous learning)	—Point out again the meaning of the word *idea*. Tell members of the class to listen carefully to get the main idea from this simple story, "Tip Likes to Hide."
P (presenting new information)	—Read "Tip Likes to Hide" to the class.
KP (recognizing key points)	—Remind members of the class that the main idea is the most important idea in the story. Ask someone in the class to explain the main point in this story.
APP (applying new information)	—Ask class members to think about something that might happen to them that was similar to what happened to Tip. Ask them to explain how they might act.
ANL (assessing new learning)	—Read another simple story. Ask members of the class to tell you the main idea. Critique their answers.

Note how the notation system used in this abbreviated unit allowed the curriculum designer to tie performance objectives and the suggested instructional strategy to the guiding generalization, the unit title, the grade level, and the curriculum area.

A complete instructional unit usually includes some sections in addition to those illustrated in this abbreviated unit. For example, there may be sets of diagnostic tests, examples of questions to evaluate learners' progress, and titles and sources of materials teachers will find useful in teaching the unit content.

The notation system presented in these illustrations uses digits. Not all do. A variety of symbols can be employed. In recent years, however, there has been a tendency to use digits rather than letters of the alphabet or other symbols, because digital notations lend themselves easily to computer storage. The scheme depicted in Figure 5-4, for example, could be employed to generate curriculum documents that could be stored in part or in their entirety on a computer system.

Were this done, a central-office curriculum specialist could use the computer to generate a comprehensive report covering general purposes (or generalizations, or unit titles) for all programs in English, social studies, mathematics, science, or any other K-to-12 area. Such a computer-stored document set could also be used to generate more narrowly focused information. For example, all suggested instructional techniques for a given generalization could be displayed and printed. The opportunity that computer-stored curriculum documents affords for auditing and monitoring the curriculum suggests that the trend to feature digits in notation systems will probably continue.

SUMMARY

Curriculum documents express the curriculum in written form. They embrace many kinds, each with a special purpose. The contents and organization of individual curriculum documents reflect their orientation to the needs of a special audience. Some examples of curriculum documents include philosophy statements, general scope and sequence documents, curriculum guides, grade-level plans and course plans, instructional unit plans, and courses of study.

Curriculum developers consider a number of issues as they attempt to develop quality curriculum documents. These issues relate to the legitimacy of the documents, the credibility of developers, the nature of information provided about intended learners, the nature of information provided about educators who will use the documents, the scope of the documents, the clarity of format and organization, the internal and external consistency of the documents, and the quality of the editing and reproduction of the documents.

In some places, basic curriculum-document systems have been developed to help manage the entire instructional program. Often sets of interrelated documents are prepared that allow for the efficient auditing of programs to assure compliance with state and local policies. The formats used in these basic curriculum documents may be used to develop other documents in response to particular needs.

EXTENDING AND APPLYING CHAPTER CONTENT

1. Interview an associate superintendent for curriculum, a director of curriculum, or someone else having curriculum responsibilities. Ask this person about the kinds of curriculum documents that have been developed to facilitate smooth functioning and efficient auditing of the instructional programs. Inquire about how individual documents were developed,

particularly in terms of the people involved, and about how each is used. Share the results of the interview with your instructor and the class.

2. Look again at the issues related to curriculum-document quality that were raised in the chapter. Suppose you were asked to develop some criteria for each of the following characteristics of a curriculum document that could be used to rate its relative excellence:

   a. legitimacy
   b. credibility of developers
   c. specification of intended learners
   d. specification of document users
   e. specification of document scope
   f. clarity of format and organization
   g. internal and external consistency
   h. evidence of professional editing/reproduction

   What kinds of standards would you adopt for each of the above categories? What indicators would you look for in each category? Develop a rating scale that you might use to assess a document in terms of at least four of the above categories. Define rating points clearly. (For example, if you developed a five-point scale, what would a document look like that merited a rating of "4" on the characteristic "legitimacy"?) Share your rating scale with others in the class.

3. Obtain a copy of an existing curriculum document or look at one of the microfiched documents in the Kraus Curriculum Development Library. Think about some of the issues related to curriculum-document quality that were introduced in the chapter. Write a paper in which you make a general assessment of this document's strengths and weaknesses in terms of some of these issues. Submit your paper to your instructor for review.

4. An example of a notational system that might be used in a basic curriculum document system was introduced in this chapter. This particular system provided notations that identified (a) curriculum area, (b) grade-level or course title, (c) unit or topic titles, and (d) generalizations. Suppose you were asked to develop a notation scheme for a basic curriculum document system of your own design. What elements would you wish to identify with your notations? What would your notation system look like? To illustrate your responses to these questions, develop a sheet that provides information along the lines of that introduced by Figure 5-4.

5. Curriculum documents are not universally admired. Instructional unit plans, in particular, have sometimes been attacked as infringements on a teacher's academic freedom. Some people holding this view have suggested that instructional unit plans place unwarranted restrictions on what teachers can do in the classroom. Others have argued that the plans simply provide a format for writing down decisions about how content will be treated, and that the plans, themselves, place no important restraints on teachers. They point out that teachers must follow certain

state and local mandates whether they work with instructional unit plans or without them.

Think about some of the issues raised about curriculum documents. Then, prepare a position paper in which you argue a case for or against the proposition that curriculum documents in general, and instructional unit plans in particular, represent a threat to teachers' academic freedom.

BIBLIOGRAPHY

Armstrong, David G. and Robert E. Shutes. 1981. "Quality in Curriculum Documents: Some Basic Criteria." *Educational Leadership* (December 1981): 200–202.

Beane, James A., Conrad F. Toepfer, and Samuel J. Alessi, Jr. 1986. *Curriculum Planning and Development.* Boston: Allyn and Bacon.

Berelson, Bernard and Gary A. Steiner. 1967. *Human Behavior: An Inventory of Scientific Findings.* New York: Harcourt Brace Jovanovich.

Bruner, Jerome S. 1960. *The Process of Education.* Cambridge, MA: Harvard University Press.

Bruner, Jerome S., Jacqueline J. Goodnow, and George Austin. 1962. *A Study of Thinking.* New York: Science Editions.

Foshay, Arthur W., ed. 1980. *Considered Action for Curriculum Improvement.* 1980 ASCD Yearbook. Alexandria, VA: Association for Supervision and Curriculum Development.

Fraenkel, Jack R. 1980. *Helping Students Think and Value,* 2d ed. Englewood Cliffs, NJ: Prentice-Hall.

Glatthorn, Allan A. 1987. *Curriculum Leadership.* Glenview, IL: Scott, Foresman and Company.

Hunkins, Francis P. 1980. *Curriculum Development: Program Improvement.* Columbus, OH: Charles E. Merrill.

Martorella, Peter H. 1962. *Concept Learning: Designs for Instruction.* Scranton, PA: Intext Educational Publishers.

Posner, George and Alan N. Rudnitsky. 1982. *Course Design: A Guide to Curriculum Development for Teachers,* 2d ed. New York: Longman.

Taba, Hilda. 1962. *Curriculum Development: Theory and Practice.* New York: Harcourt, Brace, and World.

Wulf, Kathleen M. and Barbara Schave. 1984. *Curriculum Design.* Glenview, IL: Scott, Foresman and Company.

CHAPTER 6

General Scope and Sequence Documents

This chapter introduces information to help the reader

1. point out some purposes of general scope and sequence documents.
2. recognize that general scope and sequence documents can be formatted in different ways.
3. describe how notation systems introduced in general scope and sequence documents can be used to identify common elements that appear in other documents in a basic set of interrelated curriculum documents.
4. suggest reasons why a school district or large private-sector training organization might wish to develop general scope and sequence documents.
5. describe purposes of various sections of a sample general scope and sequence document.

INTRODUCTION

General scope and sequence documents provide directions that can be used to guide curriculum development at different levels of specificity. They are often used when a decision has been made to establish a set of interrelated curriculum documents. In such cases, general scope and sequence documents lay out and explain certain common elements that are reflected in all other documents. For example, in a three-tiered document set such as that introduced in Chapter 5, certain features introduced in the general scope and sequence document also appear in grade-level plans and course plans and in instructional unit plans.

The nature of the information that is introduced in the general scope and sequence document and then repeated within subordinate documents varies depending on situational needs. Often there is a description of the function of each document type in the basic set, which points out its purposes and categories of content.

The general scope and sequence document often provides information to establish the credibility of all curriculum documents in the set. Frequently, it identifies the individuals who have participated in the curriculum development efforts, citing their academic degrees and relevant qualifications. Sometimes there will be mention of the school district or other authority that sanctioned development of the document.

Another common feature of general scope and sequence documents is a discussion of the notation system that will be used throughout the entire document set. Often this explanation includes examples that illustrate different applications of the notation system. This information helps potential users understand how the notation system will be used to denote common elements as they occur in different documents in the set.

As noted in Chapter 5, general scope and sequence documents in school settings tend either to reference the entire grades K-to-12 program or to be split into two parts. When the document is split, usually one part focuses on the elementary program, grades K to 6, while the other focuses on the secondary program, grades 7 to 12. General scope and sequence documents in nonschool settings may be configured in a number of ways depending on needs.

REASONS FOR DEVELOPING INTERRELATED DOCUMENTS

Not all school districts and nonschool educational settings have general scope and sequence documents. For example, in some school districts, curriculum guides, documents that contain information related to only a single major component of the school curriculum (e.g. science, social studies, mathematics, English), are developed quite independently of any general scope and sequence document. When this is done, the organizational features of guides for different curriculum areas may have little in common. In some settings, this arrangement works well. The individual curriculum guides are used as bases for subsequent curriculum development in their area. For example, the curriculum guide in science would be useful in the development of science courses and the preparation of instructional units.

The decision to prepare general scope and sequence documents often is made when it is considered desirable to achieve a common curriculum design framework that can be used, perhaps with some modifications, in all curriculum areas. Such a decision might be made for several reasons.

There may be relatively few people in a school district with curriculum-development expertise. In such a case, trained curriculum people could develop a general scope and sequence document that would provide a common point of departure for curriculum development in all subject areas. This approach might be more efficient than asking the small number of trained curriculum people to help others develop different designs for curriculum guides in each of the major curriculum areas.

Another reason for developing general scope and sequence documents is to provide for the development of curricula that can be easily monitored. At the local level, a school board may have mandated that certain kinds of content be included within large numbers of courses. A general scope and sequence document can help in assuring that this material has been included in instructional programs, as required.

At a higher level, in many parts of the country state legislatures and state departments of education are identifying specific information to be included in school programs. School districts may even be audited by state officials to assure that mandated content is present in courses and grade levels as required by law and regulation. A general scope and sequence document, together with related subordinate documents, can be used by school officials to keep track of how these state requirements are being met in a district's programs. Some educators fear that a decision to follow guidelines contained in a general scope and sequence document will impose a restrictive, top-down pattern of curriculum development on schools and teachers. This need not be the case.

Ordinarily, general scope and sequence documents identify major categories of content that must be taught. Individuals who play major roles in designing courses and instructional units, predominantly teachers, still have great latitude in determining how major categories of required content will be approached. Furthermore, mandated content typically represents only a fraction of the total content included within courses and units. Curriculum developers enjoy considerable freedom in identifying, organizing, and sequencing the majority of content included in grade-level plans, course plans, and instructional unit plans.

SELECTING COMMON CONTENT ELEMENTS

The general scope and sequence document introduces some features that will reappear in all related documents. First, the general scope and sequence document establishes a pattern for the introductory pages that is followed in all other documents in the set. For example, curriculum developers might decide that the beginnings of all documents will include a table of contents, a general introduction to the document, and a listing of people who participated on the curriculum development team.

In addition to establishing a format for the opening pages of each document, the general scope and sequence document serves as a repository of basic information about all programs that will be described in more detail in related subordinate documents. In a public school district, this means that a general scope and sequence document will have some information about programs at all grade levels covered by the document (K to 12, K to 6, or 7 to 12). In a corporate training setting, a general scope and sequence document will feature basic information about every instructional program managed by top-level training and development officers.

The kinds of basic information about instructional programs contained in general scope and sequence documents varies from situation to situation. For example, developers of a general scope and sequence document might decide that central office program leaders ought to have ready access to certain information: (1) the names of all curriculum areas included in the overall program, (2) the names of grade-level programs in all subject areas (relevant only if the general scope and sequence document is concerned with elementary-school programs) and of all courses taught in the program, (3) the titles of instructional units related to each grade-level program or course, and (4) the generalizations or general purposes related to each grade-level program or course and to each instructional unit.

A general scope and sequence document that included information related to the four categories above would be huge. For a large and complex school district program, such a document might fill a number of large volumes. Because of the need to provide information related to so many subject areas, grade levels, and courses, the general scope and sequence document does not provide information guidelines for teaching content and evaluating learners. There simply is not enough room. This kind of information is provided in subsequent, more narrowly focused documents such as grade-level plans, course plans, and instructional unit plans.

A general scope and sequence document usually is not completed in its entirety by curriculum developers brought together specifically for this purpose. It is too big a job to be done centrally. For example, it would be an almost impossible task for a single group to gather together data representing the four categories of information previously noted for every single instructional program.

Curriculum developers charged with preparing a general scope and sequence document often restrict themselves to identifying content that is mandated by law. For example, they may develop unit titles and generalizations for topics required by state law or by local policies, and include this information once they have established a basic format for the general scope and sequence document. The initial job of the general scope and sequence team is over once the initial framework is established and the basic required content is included.

Information in this abbreviated version of the general scope and sequence document provides useful guidelines for developers of grade-level plans, course plans, and instructional units, who can begin their work by including the content, required by law or policy, mentioned in the general scope and sequence document. They can then develop new content that they determine to have value for learners, and when finished, add the new nonmandated unit titles and generalizations to the general scope and sequence document.

In summary, the general scope and sequence document establishes a basic framework. It includes, initially, only information about content that must be included in the programs. Subsequently, information about nonmandated content can be added, often after such content has been identified by developers of grade-level plans, course plans, and instructional units.

The following sections elaborate on kinds of information that might be found in a general scope and sequence document that featured: (1) names of curriculum areas, (2) names of grade-level programs or courses, (3) instructional unit titles, and (4) generalizations or general purposes.

CURRICULUM AREA NAMES

The general scope and sequence document might list names of all curriculum areas offering courses. These curriculum areas include the names of basic subject or program divisions. For a public school, some titles in a general scope and sequence document might include the following:

English (includes Reading, Language Arts)
Science
Mathematics
Social Studies
Music
Art
Vocational Education
Health
Physical Education
Music
Gifted and Talented Education
Special Education

GRADE-LEVEL PROGRAMS OR COURSES

This information will identify individual subject areas taught by grade level or names of courses. In school settings, grade-level programs will be used to denote different aspects of the elementary program. Course names will be used to identify content taught at the secondary level. The following are some examples of names of grade-level programs or courses that might be found in a general scope and sequence document prepared for use in a school district:

Kindergarten, Social Studies
Grade 1, Social Studies
Grade 1, Art
Grade 5, Gifted and Talented
Grade 6, Music
American History, Grade 7
American History, Grade 11
Biology I
Biology II
English Literature
Spanish, 1st Year
Spanish, 2nd Year
Auto Mechanics

INSTRUCTIONAL UNIT TITLES

Instructional unit titles are subdivisions of major subjects taught at individual grade levels or of courses. The number of unit titles will vary, but in general, there are more units in elementary programs than in secondary. This is true because elementary school units characteristically take less time to teach; some may last only one or two weeks. Units designed for secondary school students or for adult learners sometimes last four weeks or more.

GENERALIZATIONS

Scope and sequence documents often identify a limited body of required information to which learners must be exposed. This information can be introduced in a variety of ways, sometimes in the form of generalizations or general-purpose statements. (Generalizations are described in some detail in Chapter 5.)

Recall that generalizations are succinct statements of relationships among concepts. Note this example that might be found in a high school geography program: "Innovations spread unevenly across the earth's surface; they tend to be adopted first in large urban centers and to only gradually be adopted in smaller cities, towns, and rural areas."

Some curriculum developers prefer to work with general-purpose statements rather than generalizations. General-purpose statements tend to convey the same information as generalizations, but they are formatted differently. General-purpose statements are rather loosely worded descriptions of what learners are to understand at the conclusion of instruction. This is an example of a general-purpose statement that treats the same ideas as the preceding generalization: "Learners will appreciate that innovations begin first in large cities and spread across the earth in an uneven pattern such that some time passes before they are adopted by people in smaller cities, towns, and rural areas."

Individuals who favor using general-purpose statements suggest that they are relatively easy for instructors to use as beginning points for developing more precise instructional objectives. Instructional objectives are statements that indicate what observable behaviors can be expected of learners at the conclusion of instruction to verify they have mastered a specific body of information. (One approach to preparing instructional objectives is introduced in Chapter 8.)

FLEXIBILITY AND THE NOTATION SYSTEM

An example of a notation system was introduced in Chapter 5 (pages 114 to 117). This scheme allows for a good deal of flexibility. Recall that the following basic arrangement was used to identify individual content components:

Curriculum Area

   .00 Interdisciplinary
   .01 Mathematics
   .02 Social Studies
   .03 English
   .04 Art
   etc.

Grade-Level Programs or Courses

   .02 Social Studies
      .00 Kindergarten
      .01 Grade 1
      .02 Grade 2
      .
      .

.15 Economics
.16 World Geography
etc.

Instructional Unit Titles

.02 Social Studies
.16 World Geography
.01 Foundations of Geography
.02 Earth's Basic Patterns
.03 Anglo-America

.

.11 The Urban World
etc.

Generalizations

.02 Social Studies
.16 World Geography
.11 The Urban World
.01 Innovations in agriculture that allowed one person to grow enough food for many people allowed people to move off their individual farms and gather together in clustered settlements that, in time, became cities.

.07 Large cities generate a demand for certain kinds of specialized talent that cannot be supported in rural areas and small towns.
etc.

This scheme allows a great deal of information to be referenced by a single line of notation. For example, the line of notation reading .02.16.11.01 tells us that the curriculum area is social studies, the subject is world geography, the instructional unit is the urban world, and the generalization is the one related to conditions needed for the initial formation of cities. As noted in Chapter 5, this information can be stored in a computer to permit a comprehensive review of the entire curriculum program once all information has been initially entered.

The line of notation .02.16.11.01 illustrates a situation where a generalization refers only to a single unit. What if a generalization relates to more than a single unit? This problem is solved by a procedure known as *notation stacking*. Suppose that generalization .07 has relevance for the unit titled "Earth's Basic Patterns," as well as the one titled "The Urban World." This situation can be notated as follows:

.12.16.02.07

.12.16.11.07 Large cities generate a demand for certain kinds of specialized talent that cannot be supported in rural areas and small towns.

Observe that these notations establish the connection of this generalization to both Unit 2 ("Earth's Basic Patterns") and Unit 11 ("The Urban World"). This system can easily be expanded to deal with occasional situations when a single generalization may relate to an even larger number of unit titles. If a single generalization summarized content taught in three units, there would be a stack of three lines of notation.

In addition to its flexibility in handling situations where a single generalization may reference content taught in several units, this notational system is easily expanded to include special kinds of content elements. In some places, curriculum developers may find it necessary to devise a notation system that includes references to more categories than curriculum areas, grade-level programs or course titles, unit or topic titles, and generalizations. For example, in states that require specific content to be included in certain courses, curriculum developers may find it useful to develop a special category for this mandated content. An example of how a notation scheme might accommodate this situation follows:

Curriculum Area

> .00 Interdisciplinary
> .01 Mathematics
> .02 Social Studies
> .03 English
> .04 Art
> etc.

Grade-Level Programs or Courses

> .02 Social Studies
> > .00 Kindergarten
> > .01 Grade 1
> > .02 Grade 2
> >
> > .
> > .
> >
> > .15 Economics
> > .16 World Geography
> > etc.

State-Mandated Content Elements

> .02 Social Studies
> > .16 World Georgraphy

.01 Relative Locations of Nations of the World
.02 Distributional Patterns of Ethnic and Cultural Groups
.03 Patterns of Evolution of Cities
etc.

Instructional Unit Titles

.02 Social Studies
.16 World Geography
.03 Patterns of Evolution of Cities
.01 Foundations of Geography
.02 Earth's Basic Patterns
.03 Anglo-America

.

.

.11 The Urban World
etc.

Generalizations

.02 Social Studies
.16 World Geography
.03 Patterns of Evolution of Cities
.11 The Urban World
.01 Innovations in agriculture that allowed one person to grow enough food for many people allowed people to move off their individual farms and gather together in clustered settlements that, in time, became cities.

.

.

.07 Large cities generate a demand for certain kinds of specialized talent that cannot be supported in rural areas and small towns.
etc.

The line of notation reading .02.16.03.11.01 references social studies as the curriculum area, world geography as the course, the state-mandated content relating to patterns of city development, the unit on the urban world, and the generalization having to do with conditions needed for initial development of cities.

AN EXAMPLE OF A GENERAL SCOPE AND SEQUENCE DOCUMENT

An example of a general scope and sequence document is provided on the following pages. Note the comments in the left-hand margins about various features of this document.

There is no intent to suggest that all general scope and sequence documents ought to be formatted in this way. Certainly the needs of individual school districts and nonschool instructional settings vary tremendously, and many other formats for general scope and sequence documents can be and have been developed that work very well. This example is provided to stimulate thought about problems associated with developing general scope and sequence documents.

COMMENTS

GENERAL SCOPE AND SEQUENCE DOCUMENT

Note that this document is designed for use in grades K to 6. Scope and sequence documents may also be designed for grades 7 to 12 or for grades K to 12.

This document includes information relating to all subjects taught in the elementary program, grades kindergarten through six inclusive.

Harris Center Public School District
Harris Center, Texas

Note date of the revision. These documents must be updated frequently.

Revision of Spring, 1989

COMMENTS

Note that this is a partial table of contents. It focuses only on the first parts of the scope and sequence document where the basic set of interrelated documents and the notation system are introduced.

A table of contents facilitates ease of use of a curriculum document. It provides a brief overview of document contents and makes it possible for people to find particular information quickly. It is especially important to have in longer documents.

TABLE OF CONTENTS
(a partial listing)

Foreword
Explanation of Document Types and
      Identification of Primary Users
Developers of Curriculum Documents
Explanation of Notation System
Explanation of a Line of Notation
Sample Layout Page

COMMENTS

FOREWORD

This material provides a very general introduction to the set of interrelated documents. It provides some very basic information about the individuals who were involved in preparation of the materials. It introduces potential users to some of the district's guiding assumptions.

As directed by the Board of Education of the Harris Center Public School District, a series of curriculum documents has been prepared. This series consists of a set of interrelated curriculum documents. They include general scope and sequence documents for grades K to 6 and for grades 7 to 12. Other documents include grade-level plans, course plans, and instructional unit plans. Collectively, these documents describe a coordinated and sequenced program for all learners in the school district.

All documents in this basic document system employ a common notational system. This system allows for easy cross-referencing of program elements that are described in more than one document type.

Programs reflected in these written materials are the product of many hours of difficult work. Large numbers of the district's teachers and administrators were involved. As appropriate, experts in instructional design and in various academic specialties were involved. There was also input from students, from parents, and from other dedicated school patrons.

These documents will be periodically augmented and revised to keep programs responsive to the changing needs of learners in our district. Only through a process of change and adaptation can we hope to keep pace with changes in the knowledge base of our courses, changes in our learner population, and shifts in national, state, and local educational priorities.

Signatures of the superintendent and the president of the school board help to establish the documents' credibility.

_____

Joaquin S. Solandares, Superintendent
Harris Center Public School District

_____

Jane F. LaVitte, President
Board of Education, Harris Center Public
School District

_____

COMMENTS

Information in this section introduces each document type. This basic information is repeated in every document in the system. For example, it will reappear in all grade-level plans and in all instructional unit plans. This information ensures that a person who is unfamiliar with the system and who happens to encounter one document type by accident will realize that there are other documents available. Some of these may be more relevant to an individual's needs than the one first discovered. For example, a teacher who happens upon a grade-level plan may find it only mildly interesting, but this same teacher might have a great deal of interest in seeing some of the instructional unit plans.

EXPLANATION OF DOCUMENT TYPES AND IDENTIFICATION OF PRIMARY USERS

From time to time, many individuals may wish to look over individual documents in this set. As part of the Harris Center Public School District's established program of study, these documents are to be available for inspection by interested citizens as well as professional employees of the district. In their day-to-day work, some members of the professional staff may find certain of these documents more useful than others. This section briefly introduces each of the major document types and suggests individuals who might logically be thought of as primary users of each.

The General Scope and Sequence Document

The general scope and sequence document in this set provides an overview of all subjects taught from kindergarten through grade 6. (Please note that another scope and sequence and related documents are available covering instructional programs for grades 7 through 12.) The general scope and sequence document provides some very basic information about content to be covered in each subject area at each grade level. Specifically, there is information related to each curriculum area, each K-to-6 grade level, titles of units to be taught in each subject at each grade level, and generalizations that are related to each unit to be taught in each subject at each grade level. In addition, the general scope and sequence document introduces a notation system that will be used throughout all other documents in the basic document set.

Primary Users. This document will be of primary interest to individuals who have responsibilities spanning the breadth of the entire K-to-6 instructional program. It is designed to help them verify that any general policies related to courses and content are being followed. Central-office associate and assistant superintendents for instruction and district-level curriculum supervisors and specialists are among individuals who may find the general scope and sequence document to be of particular interest. At times, individual subject area specialists, principals, and teachers may wish to work with this document. In most cases, their needs will be better served by other documents in the set.

The Grade-Level Plan

This document provides a general framework for one subject area at one grade level of the elementary school program. (A similar document called a course plan is used to describe basic components of individual courses in grades 7 to 12.) The grade-level plan includes all unit titles for a given subject at a given grade level—for example, Grade 6 Science. In addition to unit titles, the document includes rationales supporting the selection of each unit, generalizations related to each unit, and major concepts to be introduced. There are also rather general descriptions of suggested instructional approaches and evaluation procedures.

Primary Users. This document type is of primary interest to individuals seeking information about basic content to be covered within a given academic area at a particular grade level. Primary users might include subject-area supervisors at the district level, building principals, and teachers who are responsible for coordinating instruction within a single subject in a building or within a given grade level in a building. Individual classroom teachers may find this document useful to provide them with a general overview of content to be covered in a particular subject area at the grade level they teach. Suggestions for day-to-day approaches to teaching the content will be much more detailed, however, in the instructional unit plans.

The Instructional Unit Plan

This document provides a detailed outline of each unit to be taught in each subject at each grade level. It includes such elements as the unit title, generalizations related to the unit, major concepts to be taught, performance objectives to be mastered, ideas for diagnosing learner characteristics, detailed suggestions for introducing the content, complete sets of evaluation procedures, and a list of materials to be used. As appropriate, there are also suggestions for organizing the classroom and managing learners and materials. A procedure for cross-referencing relationships among generalizations, concepts, performance objectives, and learning materials is also included.

Primary Users. The instructional unit plan is of primary interest to teachers and paraprofessionals who work with learners in the classroom. The level of detail regarding instructional procedures that is provided goes beyond the needs of most central-district administrators and building principals. The instructional unit document is not meant to establish a rigid, prescriptive set of procedures for the teacher. Its purpose is to provide some ideas that teachers may or may not use and to suggest a framework for teachers to use in independently developing instructional units of their own.

DEVELOPERS OF CURRICULUM DOCUMENTS

Information included in this section is provided to help establish the credibility of programs described in the documents in the interrelated document set. Often this is done by reporting information about the kinds of individuals who were involved (teachers, administrators, outside experts, and

Large numbers of people participated in the development of the curriculum documents in this system. Initial leadership was provided by district-level specialists in curriculum. Teachers played a very important part in this activity. There was representation from every elementary school in the district. Building administrators also participated directly in all phases of program development and document preparation.

Our schools belong to our community. Hence, it is entirely appropriate for community members' views to be heard as school programs are being planned. A number of parents and other school patrons participated in the curriculum activities that resulted in the preparation of these documents, and they made many important contributions.

From time to time, groups of individuals involved in various phases of program development and revision had need of specialized assistance. As

COMMENTS

so forth). Note in this example the special attention given to educational qualifications of the district's central-office curriculum staff.

needed, subject-matter specialists and other experts were invited to contribute to the curriculum-development activity. Their assistance was helpful in the effort to assure that developed programs were as up-to-date and as consistent with state-of-the-art knowledge as possible.

General leadership of the curriculum development activities resulting in the development of these documents was provided by the following people:

Dianna Basco, Associate Superintendent for Instruction: B.S., Secondary Education; M.S., Educational Administration; Ph.D., Curriculum and Instruction.

Peter F. B. Johnson, Curriculum Director: B.S., Elementary Education; M.S., Curriculum and Instruction; Ed.D., Curriculum and Instruction.

LaShawn C. Birdwhistle, Associate Curriculum Director—Elementary: B.S., Elementary Education; M.S., Curriculum and Instruction.

EXPLANATION OF NOTATION SYSTEM

There are many ways to organize a notation system. Specific elements to be included are selected according to needs in settings where curricula are developed. The symbols used to denote various program components often differ from setting to setting. The scheme used here lends itself nicely to computerized program management.

Curriculum Area

  .01 English (includes Reading, Language Arts)
  .02 Mathematics
  .03 Science
  .04 Social Studies
  .05 Music
  .06 Art
  .07 Physical Education
  .08 Health
  .09 Industrial Education

  .   (Same pattern continues for other areas.)

Grade-Level or Course Title

  .01 English
  .02 Mathematics
  .03 Science
    .00 Science, Grade K
    .01 Science, Grade 1
    .02 Science, Grade 2
    .
    .
    .06 Science, Grade 6
  .04 Social Studies
    .00 Social Studies, Grade K
    .01 Social Studies, Grade 1

  .   (Same pattern continues for all other areas.)

Unit or Topic Titles

  .01 English
  .02 Mathematics
  .03 Science
    .06 Science, Grade 6
      .01 Introduction
      .02 Our Living World
      .03 Our Physical World
      .04 Earth and Space

Generalizations

  .03 Science
    .06 Science, Grade 6
      .01 Introduction
        .01 Productive work in science depends, in part, on knowledge of basic laboratory safety procedures.

COMMENTS   .05 The Human Body

.
.   (Same pattern continues to
       display unit or topic titles for
       all curriculum areas and
       grade levels or courses.)

This notation ordinarily is displayed as a line. The line of notation provides a kind of shorthand that identifies various parts of the program in symbolic form. For example, the notation line reading .03.06.01.01 references a generalization related to the importance of knowledge of basic scientific processes and safety procedures to the first unit in the grade 6 program of the district's curriculum in science. For a more complete explanation of a line of notation, see the information below.

It is very important that a clear explanation of the notation system be provided. If this information is lacking, document users will find the notation very confusing. When the same notation is used in different documents, each document should repeat the information that explains the basic notation system.

EXPLANATION OF A LINE OF NOTATION

.03.06.01.01

Curriculum Area _____| | | |___ Generalization
Grade-Level/Course Title _____| |_____ Unit or Topic Title

This notation system is used in all curriculum documents in the basic set of interrelated documents, including the general scope and sequence document, the grade-level program plans or course plans, and the instructional unit plans. In this system, each cluster (a set of numerals bounded on both sides by periods) refers to a particular component. In the line of notation above, the first cluster (.03) refers to the curriculum area. The second cluster (.06) refers to the grade-level or course title. The third cluster (.01) refers to the unit or topic title. The fourth cluster (.01) identifies a specific generalization.

This is how the line of notation at the top of the page should be interpreted:

The first cluster	.03	This indicates the curriculum area is science.
The second cluster	.06	This indicates the science program in grade 6.
The third cluster	.01	This indicates the first unit taught at grade 6. It is a unit titled simply "Introduction."
The fourth cluster	.01	This indicates the first generalization related to the first unit in the grade 6 science program. It focuses on the importance of content related to basic scientific processes and to safety.

This layout is simply an example of how information might be displayed in a scope and sequence document. There are certainly other functional alternatives.

Because general scope and sequence documents embrace information from all curriculum areas, they may become very lengthy. For practical purposes, often they are printed as separate documents for each curriculum area.

SAMPLE LAYOUT PAGE

Curriculum Area: .03 Science
    Grade-Level or Course Title: .03.06 Science, Grade 6

Unit or Topic Title	*Generalizations*
.03.06.01 Introduction	.03.06.01.01 Productive work in science depends, in part, on knowledge of basic laboratory safety procedures.
(Pattern continues for other unit or topic titles.)	(Pattern continues for other generalizations.)

The pattern established above would be repeated for all unit or topics in the grade 6 science program and for all related generalizations.

SUMMARY

The general scope and sequence document provides a basic organizational framework for an interrelated set of documents. It details certain common elements of information that will appear, in some form, in each document within the set. Often a common notation system is introduced in the general scope and sequence document that will be used to denote these common elements as they appear throughout the entire document set. For example, if a decision has been made to develop course plans, grade-level plans, and instructional unit plans, the notation system might be used to identify major curriculum areas, names of courses or grade-level designations, unit or topic titles, and generalizations.

The general scope and sequence document also provides information about content categories that will be displayed in each document type included in the interrelated set. This information alerts individuals to features of other documents that are particularly suited to their needs.

A general scope and sequence document can be formatted in many ways. The example provided in this chapter represents one approach. Specific formatting should reflect needs peculiar to the setting where the general scope and sequence document and others related to it are developed.

In some places, stringent requirements mandate that certain kinds of content be taught at specific grade levels and in specific courses. A general scope and sequence document and its accompanying related documents can be useful to central office curriculum specialists and administrators as they monitor programs to establish their compliance with these legal mandates.

EXTENDING AND APPLYING CHAPTER CONTENT

1. Prepare a paper on present trends in mandated content for school programs. Review professional literature on education in your library for articles dealing with state requirements in various parts of the country about content to be taught within specific courses and at specific grade levels. If possible, cite examples of required content. Does your state require some content to be taught? If so, how would you reference this content in a general scope and sequence document?

2. Examine a number of curriculum documents used to describe instructional programs in a school district or a private-sector training setting. To what extent do you find evidence that individual documents are parts of a larger interrelated set? What evidence is there that a common notational system has been used throughout? Do you infer that these documents have been prepared after a general scope and sequence document delineating the basic program structure has been developed? Or, do these documents tend to be "freestanding"?

3. There are many approaches to formatting general scope and sequence documents. Suppose you were in charge of organizing curriculum development activities in a setting with which you are familiar. Suppose, further, that you felt it would be useful to develop a general scope and sequence document. Decide on elements you would include, a notational system, and a format. Develop your ideas in the form of a model general scope and sequence document to present to your instructor.

4. Interview someone who has been responsible for overall curriculum development and management in a large school district or private-sector training operation. Ask specifically about his or her needs to assure that certain kinds of content are included. To what extent are general scope and sequence documents used to gather together in one place information about key elements of content? If such documents are not in use, does the person interviewed believe they might have value in his or her work? Share your findings with class members in the form of an oral presentation.

5. Not all school districts and private-sector training operations have general scope and sequence documents. Write a position paper in which you support or attack this statement: "A general scope and sequence document acts as an impediment to responsible, creative program development." Your instructor may wish to use varying responses on this assignment as a basis for a class discussion.

BIBLIOGRAPHY

Armstrong, David G. and Robert E. Shutes. 1981. "Quality in Curriculum Documents: Some Basic Criteria." *Educational Leadership* (December): 200–202.

Candlin, C. 1985. "Curriculum and Syllabus Design." 1985. *ELT Journal* (April): 101–108.

Gallini, J. K. and A. D. Fisk. 1986. "An Information Processing Approach to Instructional System Design." *Educational Technology* (April): 24–26.

Glatthorn, Allan A. 1987. *Curriculum Leadership.* Glenview, Ill.: Scott, Foresman.

Holt, Maurice. 1983. *Curriculum Workshop: An Introduction to Whole Curriculum Planning.* New York: Methuen.

Tanner, Daniel and Laurel N. Tanner. 1980. *Curriculum Development: Theory into Practice,* 2d ed. New York: Macmillan.

Wales, Charles E. and Robert A. Stager. 1987. *The Guided Design Approach.* Englewood Cliffs, N.J.: Educational Technology Publications.

CHAPTER 7

Grade-Level Plans and Course Plans

This chapter provides information to help the reader

1. **distinguish between the purposes of grade-level plans and course plans.**
2. **identify primary users of grade-level plans and course plans.**
3. **develop grade-level plans or course plans following a format that allows them to be closely tied to other documents in a basic curriculum document set.**
4. **recognize that grade-level plans and course plans can be successfully developed using different formats.**
5. **describe some content elements that frequently appear in grade-level plans or course plans.**

INTRODUCTION

Grade-level plans describe major elements of instruction that occur within a given subject at a given grade level. For example, there may be grade-level plans for grade 1 reading, for grade 3 social studies, and for grade 6 science. Grade-level plans ordinarily are used to organize content delivered in elementary school instructional programs.

Course plans are used to organize content in individual subjects taught in secondary schools, in higher education settings, and in private-sector and governmental training programs of many kinds. Course plans may have such diverse titles as World Geography, Algebra I, Choral Music, Basics of Arc-Welding, Safe Driving Practices, and Advanced Topics in Topology.

Though there are differences in the age levels of learners for which programs described in grade-level plans and course plans are intended, the types of information contained in each are similar. School districts often find that the same basic design format can be used for the grade-level plans developed for the elementary program and the course plans developed for the secondary program.

Grade-level plans and course plans seek to provide a great deal of specific information about contents to be covered within each grade-level subject and each course. The designs of these documents vary from place to place, but most contain descriptions of how content to be covered will be organized. Frequently grade-level plans and course plans include listings of the major units or topics to be covered and the information to be emphasized in each.

Sometimes these documents contain general suggestions about how teachers and instructors might introduce content and assess learners' progress toward mastery. However, they tend not to include extremely specific, step-by-step instructions. The highly detailed information of interest to a teacher new to the described content is not the province of grade-level plans or course plans, but of the instructional unit plan documents.

Grade-level plans and course plans occupy a middle ground between the general scope and sequence document and the instructional unit plans. They are of particular interest to building principals, training-and-development program administrators, grade-level coordinators in individual buildings, and department heads in secondary schools. Teachers and instructors, too, may have some interest in the contents of grade-level plans and course plans. However, they often find that instructional unit plans have information more responsive to their needs.

RELATIONSHIPS TO THE BASIC SET
OF INTERRELATED DOCUMENTS

Sometimes grade-level plans and course plans are developed that have no ties to other document types. For example, in some settings no general scope and sequence document exists; yet, there are established needs for grade-level plans and course plans. In other cases, information provided in grade-level plans may be sufficiently detailed to meet the needs of all potential users. Hence, no instructional unit plans are prepared.

Often, though, grade-level plans and course plans are developed as part of a system that also includes these other document types. When a decision has been made to produce a number of different but related documents, the nature of these relationships needs to be noted in each document in the set. In the three-document system that has been introduced in this text, the ties of grade-level plans and course plans to the general scope and sequence document and to related instructional unit plans must be explained.

Information that highlights interrelationships among documents sometimes is placed in the opening pages of grade-level plans and course plans. Material in this section reemphasizes information about the document set that was first developed with the preparation of the general scope and sequence document.

This information needs to be repeated because document developers do not know whether a potential user of a grade-level plan or course plan will have had an opportunity to see the general scope and sequence document. If the grade-level plan or course plan is the first document the person sees, he or she needs to be made aware of the entire document system and the kinds of contents included in each document type. For example, a teacher new to a district who discovered the grade-level plan for grade 6 music might be interested in knowing that instructional unit plans were available that provided more specific guidance regarding how topics might be introduced to learners.

The notational system introduced in the general scope and sequence document also needs to be explained again at the beginning of the grade-level plan or course plan. This common notation functions as "glue" to cement together all the documents in the system. Because much space will be required in grade-level plans and course plans to describe unit generalizations, concepts to be taught, and other information, often references to curriculum area and grade-level or course title will be made by notation alone.

COMPONENTS OF GRADE-LEVEL PLANS OR COURSE PLANS

There are many schemes for organizing grade-level plans or course plans. Entire books are devoted to promoting particular approaches to preparing courses. The suggestions included here are not necessarily better or worse than others; they are introduced to provide functional examples that curriculum developers can adapt as they respond to specialized local requirements. The grade-level plan in this chapter is linked to related instructional unit plans and to a general scope and sequence document.

FRONT MATTER OF THE DOCUMENT

The first pages of the grade-level plans and course plans repeat much of the information from the general scope and sequence document. This information serves two purposes: First, it helps to establish the credibility and the legitimacy of the document by citing the names of qualified individuals who were involved in the program-development activity; and, second, it signals the existence of a basic set of interrelated documents that share certain common features.

In addition to the names of individuals with general responsibilities for planning all instructional programs, there is usually a listing of persons who were directly involved in the preparation of the grade-level plan or course plan. This information helps potential users to recognize that qualified people were involved in the curriculum-development process.

Information may be included regarding the curriculum area, the grade level and course, the unit or topic titles, and the generalizations that will provide the focus for instruction. If a common notational system is used, these elements may be introduced, along with an explanation of that system.

GRADE-LEVEL OR COURSE OVERVIEW

Grade-level plans and course plans often feature an overview of the content to be covered. This section gives curriculum developers an opportunity to comment on the general nature of the content and on their assumptions about how information should be introduced. Ordinarily, the overview is brief.

UNIT OR TOPIC SEQUENCE AND DESCRIPTION

Often a suggested sequence for units or topics is included. The need for this information varies with the subject matter being treated. Some subjects demand a very specific sequence, as when one topic must precede another topic if learners are to have a reasonable chance of mastering the material. In other situations, where individual topics or units are more or less freestanding, developers of grade-level plans or course plans may not mention a suggested sequence.

Whether or not the issue of sequence is addressed, it is very common for grade-level plans and course plans to include a brief description of each unit or topic to be covered. Ordinarily, a short paragraph suffices in providing this background information. Sometimes these documents also include brief rationale statements that defend the decisions made to include each selected unit or topic.

GENERALIZATIONS AND CONCEPTS

Often grade-level plans and course plans will list the generalizations that will be used to guide instruction. Sometimes key concepts related to each generalization will be listed, as well, such that their relationship to a particular generalization is made clear.

SUGGESTED INSTRUCTIONAL APPROACHES

Frequently, grade-level plans and course plans will suggest instructional approaches. Developers may choose to provide a general discussion of this issue toward the beginning of the document, followed later by more specific suggestions tied to individual unit or topic titles.

The recommendations regarding the instructional approach, however, are not richly detailed. Instead, their purpose is to provide teachers and instructors with basic ideas, which they may choose to incorporate in their instructional plans. More specific attention to the instructional approach is provided in instructional unit plan documents.

SUGGESTED EVALUATION PROCEDURES

As with suggested instructional approaches, ideas for evaluating learning are kept rather general in grade-level plans and course plans. The beginning of the document may contain a short discussion of evaluation procedures as they relate to the entire grade-level program or course, and developers may also choose to include somewhat more detailed recommendations for individual units or topics and their related generalizations. However, much more specific information about evaluation is found in the instructional unit plan documents.

FORMAT

Developers of grade-level plans and course plans must devise ways to display the decisions they have made. Formats vary tremendously. Whatever format is adopted, it must be introduced and explained fairly early in the document. A discussion of format often follows immediately after the pages introducing the basic curriculum document scheme, the personnel involved, and the notation system. An explanation of format need not be lengthy or complex. A single page illustrating how the material will be presented in the subsequent pages of the document will suffice.

AN EXAMPLE OF A GRADE-LEVEL PLAN

An example of a grade-level plan for grade 6 science is provided on the pages that follow. The same approach that was used to display the general scope and sequence document in Chapter 6 has been followed, with comments in the column to the left of the document.

Again, the design of this particular grade-level plan is not intended as a formula for "what ought to be done." There are many other ways to organize grade-level program and course materials. The approach reflected in this grade-level plan offers one response.

Individuals interested in preparing grade-level plans and course plans can find many periodical articles and books that provide useful guidelines. Though these sources and the model introduced here should prove helpful, the designs that are adopted will undoubtedly incorporate features that respond to information needs peculiar to the setting where curriculum development takes place and where the designed program will be implemented.

GRADE-LEVEL PLAN: SCIENCE, GRADE SIX

This document includes information regarding
the science program taught at the sixth-grade level.

Harris Center Public School District

Revision of Spring, 1989

COMMENTS

TABLE OF CONTENTS
(a partial listing)

*The same pattern
follows for units
three, four, and five.*

COMMENTS

FOREWORD

The material included in the next several pages is identical to that contained in the general scope and sequence document. This information is repeated in each document in the basic set. It seeks to orient individuals to the document system and its contents, regardless of which document type is encountered first.

As directed by the Board of Education of the Harris Center Public School District, a series of curriculum documents has been prepared. This series consists of a set of interrelated curriculum documents. They include general scope and sequence documents for grades K to 6 and for grades 7 to 12. Other documents include grade-level plans, course plans, and instructional unit plans. Collectively, these documents describe a coordinated and sequenced program for all learners in the school district.

All documents in this basic document system employ a common notational system. This system allows for easy cross-referencing of program elements that are described in more than one document type.

Programs reflected in these written materials are the product of many hours of difficult work. Large numbers of the district's teachers and administrators were involved. As appropriate, experts in instructional design and in various academic specialties were involved. There was also input from students, from parents, and from other dedicated school patrons.

These documents will be periodically augmented and revised to keep programs responsive to the changing needs of learners in our district. Only through a process of change and adaptation can we hope to keep pace with changes in the knowledge base of our courses, changes in our learner population, and shifts in national, state, and local educational priorities.

Joaquin S. Solandares, Superintendent
Harris Center Public School District

Jane F. LaVitte, President
Board of Education, Harris Center Public
School District

EXPLANATION OF DOCUMENT TYPES AND
IDENTIFICATION OF PRIMARY USERS

From time to time, many individuals may wish to look over individual documents in this set. As part of the Harris Center Public School District's established program of study, these documents are to be available for inspection by interested citizens as well as professional employees of the district. In their day-to-day work, some members of the professional staff may find certain of these documents more useful than others. This section briefly introduces each of the major document types and suggests individuals who might logically be thought of as primary users of each.

The General Scope and Sequence Document

The general scope and sequence document in this set provides an overview of all subjects taught from kindergarten through grade 6. (Please note that another scope and sequence and related documents are available covering instructional programs for grades 7 through 12.) The general scope and sequence document provides some very basic information about content to be covered in each subject area at each grade level. Specifically, there is information related to each curriculum area, each K-to-6 grade level, titles of units to be taught in each subject at each grade level, and generalizations that are related to each unit to be taught in each subject at each grade level. In addition, the general scope and sequence document introduces a notation system that will be used throughout all other documents in the basic document set.

Primary Users. This document will be of primary interest to individuals who have responsibilities spanning the breadth of the entire K-to-6 instructional program. It is designed to help them verify that any general policies related to courses and content are being followed. Central-office associate and assistant superintendents for instruction and district-level curriculum supervisors and specialists are among individuals who may find the general scope and sequence document to be of particular interest. At times, individual subject area specialists, principals, and teachers may wish to work with this document. In most cases, their needs will be better served by other documents in the set.

The Grade-Level Plan

This document provides a general framework for one subject area at one grade level of the elementary school program. (A similar document called a course plan is used to describe basic components of individual courses in grades 7 to 12.) The grade-level plan includes all unit titles for a given subject at a given grade level—for example, Grade 6 Science. In addition to unit titles, the document includes rationales supporting the selection of each unit, generalizations related to each unit, and major concepts to be introduced. There are also rather general descriptions of suggested instructional approaches and evaluation procedures.

Primary Users. This document type is of primary interest to individuals seeking information about basic content to be covered within a given academic area at a particular grade level. Primary users might include subject-area supervisors at the district level, building principals, and teachers who are responsible for coordinating instruction within a single subject in a building or within a given grade level in a building. Individual classroom teachers may find this document useful to provide them with a general overview of content to be covered in a particular subject area at the grade level they teach. Suggestions for day-to-day approaches to teaching the content will be much more detailed, however, in the instructional unit plans.

The Instructional Unit Plan

This document provides a detailed outline of each unit to be taught in each subject at each grade level. It includes such elements as the unit title, generalizations related to the unit, major concepts to be taught, performance objectives to be mastered, ideas for diagnosing learner characteristics, detailed suggestions for introducing the content, complete sets of evaluation procedures, and a list of materials to be used. As appropriate, there are also suggestions for organizing the classroom and managing learners and materials. A procedure for cross-referencing relationships among generalizations, concepts, performance objectives, and learning materials is also included.

Primary Users. The instructional unit plan is of primary interest to teachers and paraprofessionals who work with learners in the classroom. The level of detail regarding instructional procedures that is provided goes beyond the needs of most central-district administrators and building principals. The instructional unit document is not meant to establish a rigid, prescriptive set of procedures for the teacher. Its purpose is to provide some ideas that teachers may or may not use and to suggest a framework for teachers to use in independently developing instructional units of their own.

DEVELOPERS OF CURRICULUM DOCUMENTS

Large numbers of people participated in the development of the curriculum documents in this system. Initial leadership was provided by district-level specialists in curriculum. Teachers played a very important part in this activity. There was representation from every elementary school in the district. Building administrators also participated directly in all phases of program development and document preparation.

Our schools belong to our community. Hence, it is entirely appropriate for community members' views to be heard as school programs are being planned. A number of parents and other school patrons participated in the curriculum activities that resulted in the preparation of these documents, and they made many important contributions.

From time to time, groups of individuals involved in various phases of program development and revision had need of specialized assistance. As

COMMENTS   needed, subject-matter specialists and other experts were invited to contribute to the curriculum-development activity. Their assistance was helpful in the effort to assure that developed programs were as up-to-date and as consistent with state-of-the-art knowledge as possible.

General leadership of the curriculum development activities resulting in the development of these documents was provided by the following people:

Dianna Basco, Associate Superintendent for Instruction: B.S., Secondary Education; M.S., Educational Administration; Ph.D., Curriculum and Instruction.

Peter F. B. Johnson, Curriculum Director: B.S., Elementary Education; M.S., Curriculum and Instruction; Ed.D., Curriculum and Instruction.

LaShawn C. Birdwhistle, Associate Curriculum Director—Elementary: B.S., Elementary Education; M.S., Curriculum and Instruction.

DEVELOPERS OF GRADE-LEVEL PLAN FOR
SIXTH GRADE SCIENCE

Information in this part of the document seeks to establish the credibility of the material by identifying people from a number of district schools and by citing, briefly, their academic qualifications.

Rodney F. Lu, Director of Elementary Science, Harris Center Public School District; B.A., Elementary Education; M.Ed., Educational Curriculum and Instruction.

C. F. Appleton, Assistant Director of Secondary Science, Harris Center Public School District; B.S., Biology; M.Ed., Educational Curriculum and Instruction.

Carmen Barrera, Principal, Altos Elementary School, Harris Center Public School District; B.S., Elementary Science Education; M.Ed., Educational Administration.

Thalia Jean Pharr, Sixth Grade Teacher, Watkins Middle School, Harris Center Public School District; B.A., Liberal Arts; M.Ed., Educational Curriculum and Instruction.

Penny Q. Johannsen, Sixth Grade Teacher, Lohasset Middle School, Harris Center Public School District; B.A., Elementary Science Education; M.Ed., Educational Curriculum and Instruction.

C. Charles McNeese, Sixth Grade Teacher, Triana Middle School, Harris Center Public School District; B.S., Geology; M.Ed., Educational Curriculum and Instruction.

Joe Ray Travis, Sixth Grade Teacher, Vista Oaks Middle School, Harris Center Public School District; B.A., Elementary Education; M.Ed., Educational Curriculum and Instruction.

COMMENTS

EXPLANATION OF NOTATION SYSTEM

Information provided on this page and the one that follows duplicates that included in the general scope and sequence document. This helps the potential user who encounters this document without first having seen the general scope and sequence document. This notation scheme will be used throughout this grade-level plan to identify key elements of content.

Curriculum Area

.01 English (includes Reading,
      Language Arts)
.02 Mathematics
.03 Science
.04 Social Studies
.05 Music
.06 Art
.07 Physical Education
.08 Health
.09 Industrial Education
  .

  .   (Same pattern continues for
     other areas.)

Grade-Level or Course Title

.01 English
.02 Mathematics
.03 Science
  .00 Science, Grade K
  .01 Science, Grade 1
  .02 Science, Grade 2
  .
  .
  .06 Science, Grade 6
.04 Social Studies
  .00 Social Studies, Grade K
  .01 Social Studies, Grade 1
  .

  .   (Same pattern continues for
     all other areas.)

Unit or Topic Titles

.01 English
.02 Mathematics
.03 Science
  .06 Science, Grade 6
    .01 Introduction
    .02 Our Living World
    .03 Our Physical World
    .04 Earth and Space
    .05 The Human Body

  .
  .   (Same pattern is continued
     to display unit or topic titles
     for all curriculum areas and
     grade levels or courses.)

Generalizations

.03 Science
  .06 Science, Grade 6
    .01 Introduction
      .01 Productive work in sci-
        ence depends, in part,
        on knowledge of basic
        laboratory safety pro-
        cedures.

This notation ordinarily is displayed as a line. The line of notation provides a kind of shorthand that identifies various parts of the program in symbolic form. For example, the notation line reading .03.06.01.01 references a generalization related to the importance of knowledge of basic scientific processes and safety procedures to the first unit in the grade 6 program of the district's curriculum in science. For a more complete explanation of a line of notation, see the next page.

EXPLANATION OF A LINE OF NOTATION

.03.06.01.01

Curriculum Area_____⌋ ⌋ ⌋_____Generalization
Grade-Level/Course Title_____⌋ ⌋_____Unit or Topic Title

This notation system is used in all curriculum documents in the basic set of interrelated documents, including the general scope and sequence document, the grade-level program plans or course plans, and the instructional unit plans. In this system, each cluster (a set of numerals bounded on both sides by periods) refers to a particular component. In the line of notation above, the first cluster (.03) refers to the curriculum area. The second cluster (.06) refers to the grade-level or course title. The third cluster (.01) refers to the unit or topic title. The fourth cluster (.01) identifies a specific generalization.

This is how the line of notation at the top of the page should be interpreted:

The first cluster   .03   This indicates the curriculum area is science.
The second cluster .06   This indicates the science program in grade 6.
The third cluster   .01   This indicates the first unit taught at grade 6. It is a unit titled simply "Introduction."

The fourth cluster   .01   This indicates the first generalization related to the first unit in the grade 6 science program. It focuses on the importance of content related to basic scientific processes and to safety.

DESCRIPTION OF THE
GRADE SIX SCIENCE PROGRAM

Information in this part of the document provides users with a general overview of the sixth grade program. Its purpose is simply to communicate a very general view of the program to readers.

The sixth grade science program seeks to introduce learners to many basic scientific concepts. Content is drawn primarily from the discipline of biology, physics, geology, and mathematics. Units have been organized to provide for a systematic accretion of knowledge of important scientific concepts. Furthermore, there has been an effort throughout the program to develop learners' abilities to use scientific modes of thought and to apply rational thinking skills to real-life problems that are logically connected to science.

Development of important scientific performance skills is an important program objective. Among important process skills that are emphasized in the program are (1) observation, (2) measurement, (3) classification, (4) communication, (5) prediction, (6) experimentation, and (7) interpretation of recorded data.

Note the attention here to the issue of flexibility. Users are informed that they

The course has been broken into a number of units. Each unit "packages" a specific component of the course and highlights key elements of content to be mastered. A description of the units is provided in the section beginning on the next page. The sequence of units that has been suggested

COMMENTS

need not teach units in the order in which they are presented. This helps users to feel that the program will not be placing severe limits on their freedom to sequence content for their own learners.

Material in this part of the grade-level plan goes beyond a general course description to provide more explicit information about what learners will experience in each unit.

Developers of this grade-level plan have chosen to organize the total year's work in science into only five units. This means that the amount of instructional time devoted to each unit will be large. Other developers might have identified larger numbers of units,

made sense to the program developers. However, users of the program may find other sequences to be preferable, and they should feel free to alter the order in which the units are taught so long as all are covered by the end of the school year.

DESCRIPTION OF UNITS

Unit One: Introduction

Learners will review scientific processes, procedures, skills, methods, and laboratory safety. Further, they will be provided opportunities to apply what they have learned in solving problems. They will be required to pass a basic laboratory safety test with a score of 100 percent. In this unit, they will learn steps of the scientific method; measure objects to determine length, volume, and mass; record data; and communicate results of experiments in writing. They will design and conduct a scientific investigation.

Unit Two: Living Things

Living things are all around us. They are found on land, in air, and water. Learners will discover that the cell is the basic unit of life. They will be introduced to plant and animal cells, and they will learn how to differentiate between the two types. The hierarchy of living things from simple to complex forms will be explained. They will learn how living things adapt so they can survive in their environments. Learners will become aware that each plant and animal needs certain basic environmental conditions if it is to survive.

Unit Three: Our Physical World

The physical world is made up of everything around us. The physical world consists of matter. This unit introduces learners to the topics of matter and energy. The nature of matter, the changes it undergoes, practical uses of light and electrical energy, and changing technologies are among issues stressed during this unit.

Unit Four: Earth and Space

Earth is our home. It supplies us with many materials that we call "resources." In this unit wise use of resources is stressed. Important concepts are "conservation" and "recycling." Learners are given opportunities to discuss changes that influence the earth's crust and other environmental features.

This unit also focuses learners' attention on wind and weather patterns. Learners are exposed to variables that go together to produce specific weather and general climatic patterns. They will collect data and engage in weather-predicting activities.

Finally, learners are introduced to environmental conditions that exist beyond the limits of our home planet. Practical results of space exploration efforts that have affected our lives are emphasized.

COMMENTS

each of which would require (on average) somewhat less instructional time than those in this five-unit design.

Unit Five: The Human Body

In this unit, learners are introduced to issues related to the human body. They learn about the body's control system and are introduced to patterns of human growth and development. There is an emphasis on how unique we human beings really are.

DESCRIPTION OF GENERAL INSTRUCTIONAL APPROACHES

This information provides some general background regarding suggested instructional approaches as they relate to the entire grade 6 science program. More specific suggestions are included in the instructional unit plan documents.

The sixth grade science program is process centered. Forty percent of each week's instructional time is devoted to hands-on, laboratory-type activities. Learners are encouraged to observe, measure, record observations, analyze and interpret data, and make conclusions.

Teachers provide a classroom routine that capitalizes on the prime learning time represented by the first fifteen minutes of each class period. Because learners' characteristics vary, instruction is flexible enough to accommodate individual needs. Periods of instruction are intended to be logically and sequentially organized, featuring an initial focus activity, teacher modeling, monitored practice, and evaluation. Learners are encouraged to enrich the program by sharing their own experiences and by bringing to class materials that pertain to content being studied.

Both inductive and deductive instructional approaches are encouraged. Demonstrations, laboratory activities, textbook assignments, discussions, research projects, brainstorming, and other individual and group assignments lend variety to the program. Instruction is particularly directed at providing learners with opportunities to apply what they have learned in settings beyond the classroom.

It is hoped that teachers will encourage high levels of learner interest by maintaining a flexible approach to instruction that maximizes learners' opportunities for active involvement. Other documents in this series provide more elaborate and specific suggestions for instruction. These are the instructional unit plans, one of which has been developed for each unit in the sixth grade science program. Additionally, subsequent sections of this document include some general suggestions related to instruction that are tied to specific elements of content.

DESCRIPTION OF GENERAL EVALUATION PROCEDURES

This section of the document introduces users to some very general perspectives on the issue of evaluation as it applies to the grade 6 science program. More spe-

Evaluation of a formative nature occurs daily within the grade 6 science program. Summative evaluation opportunities are provided at appropriate times as the individual units are taught. They provide learners with mechanisms to demonstrate what they have learned and teachers with a data source that can be analyzed to make judgments about their instructional effectiveness. Evaluation may take the form of assessments of learners' oral behavior, written work, or laboratory performance.

COMMENTS

cific suggestions related to individual content elements of the program are included elsewhere in the document.

Opportunities for oral assessment include times when learners are involved in discussions, laboratory activities, cooperative learning work, brainstorming sessions, and in other activities that allow teachers to listen and assess learners' verbal behavior. Written evaluation may include assessment of such things as learner composition, proficiency in preparing data tables, written reports, worksheets, graphs, formal tests, and special homework assignments. Among laboratory skills assessed are those related to using microscopes, constructing electrical devices, and using acid-base indicators.

More specific suggestions for evaluation are provided in each of the instructional unit plans that have been developed for the grade 6 science program. Subsequent sections of this document include some general ideas for evaluation that are tied to specific content elements of the program.

UNIT TITLES AND RELATED GENERALIZATIONS

Unit One: Introduction

Developers of this document chose to provide a complete listing of generalizations for each unit in the program. This enables users to identify all program generalizations quickly. These same generalizations will appear again in a subsequent section of the document. In this later reference, the generalizations will be listed, along with related concepts and with some ideas for teaching the content and for evaluating learners' progress.

Generalizations:
01 Productive work in science depends, in part, on knowledge of basic laboratory safety procedures.
02 Classification of variables is a component of scientific observation that allows data to be organized in a systematic way.
03 Utilization of the steps of the scientific method rationalizes and standardizes the process of problem-solving in science.
04 The metric system of measure allows easy conversions from linear measure to volume measure; hence, it has become a standard among scientists, even in nations where the system is not widely used by the general public.
05 Scientific advance depends on individuals' abilities to conceptualize, design, and implement their own experiments.

Unit Two: Our Living World

01 The ability to use the microscope enables investigators to study many phenomena that have contributed greatly to our understanding of the physical world.
02 An understanding of the basic cellular composition of organisms is an essential building block for more sophisticated learning in life-science related areas.
03 Living things and non-living things have different structural properties.
04 Survival of species depends upon their abilities to adapt to their environments.

Note: This same basic pattern continues for the remaining unit two generalizations and for generalizations related to units three, four, and five.

COMMENTS

This page provides information that cues document users to look for certain categories of information in specific places on subsequent pages.

EXPLANATION OF THE FORMAT USED
THROUGHOUT THE REMAINDER OF THE DOCUMENT

UNIT TITLE (The title of the unit will be displayed here.)

Rationale: (This section includes a brief rationale establishing the importance of the unit.)

Generalizations	Suggested Instructional Procedures	Suggested Evaluation Procedures
Generalizations related to the unit will be found in this column. *Concepts:* Concepts related to each generalization will be listed under the generalization to which they apply.	Suggestions for teaching content related to each generalization will be found in this column.	Suggestions for evaluating content related to each generalization will be found in this column.

COMMENTS

The notation in front of the unit title, "introduction," indicates that it is the first unit (.01) in grade 6 (.06) of the district's science program (.03).

.03.06.01 INTRODUCTION

Rationale: An introduction to basic scientific processes and methods, including a review of what has been introduced in previous years, provides a basic foundation of information needed for mastery of content developed in subsequent grade six science units.

Generalizations	Suggested Instructional Procedures	Suggested Evaluation Procedures
.03.06.01.01 Productive work in science depends, in part, on knowledge of basic laboratory safety procedures. *Concepts:* safety, safety equipment	Discuss basic safety rules. Identify basic safety equipment and make certain learners know what it is and how to use it.	Teacher observes while learners role-play emergency situations that could occur. Multiple-choice test focusing on appropriate safety measures. Teacher observes learners as they work on laboratory assignments to be sure that safety rules are being followed.
.03.06.01.02 Classification of variables is a component of scientific observation that allows data to be organized in a systematic way. *Concepts:* variable, manipulated variable, responding variable, control	Define the terms "variable," "manipulated variable," "responding variable," and "control."	Check on understanding by asking individual learners to explain their understanding of terms related to variables to the class. Ask individuals to cite examples of different variables.
	Discuss examples of experiments, and ask learners to identify and classify the variables.	In-class worksheet that asks learners to look at variables and to classify them by type.
	Conduct a class experiment in which learners identify the variables to be controlled.	Observe learners in laboratory sessions to determine whether they are controlling variables properly.

This notation refers to the first generalization for unit one of the grade 6 science program.

This notation refers to the second generalization for unit one of the grade 6 science program.

COMMENTS	Generalizations	Suggested Instructional Procedures	Suggested Evaluation Procedures
This notation refers to the second generalization for unit one of the grade 6 science program.	.03.06.01.02 (continued)	Ask learners to design experiments of their own that feature well-controlled variables.	Evaluate learner-designed experiments in terms of how well the variables are controlled.
This notation refers to the third generalization for unit one of the grade 6 science program.	.03.06.01.03 Utilization of the steps of the scientific method rationalizes and standardizes the process of problem solving in science *Concepts:* problem, hypothesis, experiment, materials, observations, procedures, conclusion	Review basic steps of the scientific method. Participate in laboratory activities. Develop a lab report that includes categories of the scientific method.	Assess abilities to solve problems in ways consistent with the scientific method. Assess appropriateness of the sequence of steps described in learners' lab reports. Written test asking learners to identify and define steps of the scientific method.
This notation refers to the fourth generalization for unit one of the grade 6 science program.	.03.06.01.04 The metric system of measure allows easy conversions from linear measure to volume measure; hence, it has become a standard among scientists, even in nations where the system is not widely used by the general public. *Concepts:* linear measure, volume measure, mass, liter, meter	Review with learners units of mass, length, and volume in the English system and the metric system. Provide opportunities for learners to use equipment designed to provide measures of various kinds in metric units.	Short-answer quiz focusing on metric-system measures. Assess learners' work on parts of experiments requiring them to express findings in terms of metric units.
This notation refers to the fifth generalization for unit one of the grade 6 science program.	.03.06.01.05 Scientific advance depends on individuals' abilities to conceptualize, design, and implement their own experiments. *Concepts:* data table, analysis	Provide opportunity for learners to identify research topics.	Meet with and provide feedback to each learner and assess his or her general ideas for an experiment.

COMMENTS

	Generalizations	Suggested Instructional Procedures	Suggested Evaluation Procedures
This notation refers to the fifth generalization for unit one of the grade 6 science program.	.03.06.01.05 (continued)	Describe components of a complete plan for conducting an experiment.	Evaluate written explanations of the planned experiment.
		Provide opportunities for learners to conduct their experiments.	Assess completed data tables and other information that accompanies learners' final reports of the results of their experiments.

The notation in front of the unit title, "our living world," indicates that it is the second unit (.02) in grade 6 (.06) of the district's science program (.03).

.03.06.02 OUR LIVING WORLD

Rationale: Living things are found everywhere in our world. However, not all living things are found in exactly the same kinds of places. This unit helps learners understand that environmental conditions place some constraints on living things. Content provides an introduction to how life forms of various kinds have adapted to different environments.

	Generalizations	Suggested Instructional Procedures	Suggested Evaluation Procedures
This notation refers to the first generalization for unit two of the grade 6 science program.	.03.06.02.01 The ability to use the microscope enables investigators to study many phenomena that have contributed greatly to our understanding of the physical world. *Concepts:* objective, diaphragm, field, ocular lens, magnification, nose piece	Review parts of the microscope with learners. Provide opportunities for learners to work with the microscope.	Formal quiz covering parts of the microscope. Observe and assess learners' abilities to use the microscope properly.
This notation refers to the second generalization for unit two of the grade 6 science program.	.03.06.02.02 An understanding of the basic cellular composition of organisms is	Introduce learners to parts of animal cells and parts of plant cells.	Evaluate learners' drawings of typical animal cells.

COMMENTS	Generalizations	Suggested Instructional Procedures	Suggested Evaluation Procedures
This notation refers to the second generalization for unit two of the grade 6 science program.	.03.06.02.02 (continued) an essential building block for more sophisticated understanding in life-science-related areas.	Involve learners in a laboratory experience focusing on cheek cells.	Critique drawings of cells in learners' lab reports.
	Concepts: cell, cytoplasm, nucleus, chromosomes, genes, plasma membrane, cell wall, nuclear membrane, protists, diatoms, bacteria, chlorophyll, chloroplasts	Involve learners in an onion cell laboratory experience.	Ask learners to draw what they observe, and evaluate their work.
		Discuss characteristics of protists with learners.	Critique drawings of examples of protists.
		Involve learners in a pond-water laboratory experiment	Look at learners' drawings of protists made during the experiment, and ask learners to describe what they observed.
This notation refers to the third generalization for unit two of the grade 6 science program.	.03.06.02.03 Living things and non-living things have different structural properties.	Lead a discussion focusing on learners' understanding of differences between living and non-living things.	Look at lists developed by learners of qualities processed by living things.

Note: The basic pattern reflected on this page and on the several that precede it is repeated for the remaining two generalizations and for each generalization in units three, four, and five.

SUMMARY

Grade-level plans and course plans often are formatted in the same way. The basic distinction between them lies in the audiences for whom the described programs are intended. Grade-level plans are used to organize academic subject content to be taught at the elementary school grade level. Course plans organize content to be covered within secondary school courses or courses that might be taught in colleges and universities, government programs, and private-sector training and development settings.

Grade-level plans and course plans have information of potential interest to large numbers of people. Those individuals most likely to benefit from the information they contain include middle-level administrators and managers such as school principals, grade-level leaders, department heads, and training and development directors. While teachers and instructors may derive some benefit from the information introduced in grade-level plans and course plans, usually they find instructional unit plans—documents that feature explicit information regarding how content is to be taught—to be more useful.

Sometimes grade-level plans and course plans are developed as part of an interrelated system of documents that might include a general scope and sequence document and instructional unit documents. In other cases grade-level plans and course plans may provide all the documentation needed to organize and manage an instructional program. In such a situation, other documents would not be needed.

The contents of grade-level plans and course plans vary. Elements often included are titles of units or topics to be taught, focusing generalizations, and concepts related to the generalizations. Sometimes there are also general suggestions regarding instructional procedures and evaluation methods. The specific contents are determined by local needs.

EXTENDING AND APPLYING CHAPTER CONTENT

1. Think about your own instructional situation. Then, develop some categories of content that you would include in a grade-level plan or a course plan. Provide a brief rationale for your decision to include each content category. Finally, prepare a table of contents (no page numbers needed) that refers to all key components of your document and the order in which they will appear.

2. A number of books and articles describe procedures for organizing courses. Skim two or three sources that take differing approaches to the task of course construction. Prepare a short paper in which you compare and contrast features of each. Which appeals to you the most? How would you modify this best approach to make it serve your own needs even more adequately?

3. Interview a curriculum director or another person who has been in charge of a project to produce a grade-level plan or a course plan. Leaders of such projects sometimes face an important political problem. The course that is developed will be more generally acceptable to teachers if there is representation from a high percentage of the district's schools. However, the people who are most qualified to participate in a curriculum preparation effort may be concentrated in only one or two schools. Ask the individual you interview how he or she has responded to this situation. Share your information with your instructor and others in the class.

4. With a group of others in the class, design and prepare a completed grade-level plan or course plan. Present it to the instructor. Then revise it in light of your instructor's suggestions.

5. In some places, grade-level plans and course plans are "stand-alone" documents, existing independent of any general scope and sequence document or instructional unit plans. In other places, grade-level plans and course plans are components of an interrelated curriculum document set. Prepare a short paper in which you discuss the relative advantages of conceiving of grade-level plans and course plans as both stand-alone documents and as parts of a larger, interrelated curriculum document set.

BIBLIOGRAPHY

Designing and Managing Instructional Programs. 1983. Columbia, Md.: GP Courseware.

McNeil, Jon D. 1976. *Designing Curriculum: Self-Instructional Modules.* Boston: Little, Brown.

Markle, Susan M. 1983. *Designs for Instructional Designers.* Champaign, Ill.: Stipes Publishing Company.

Posner, George J. and Alan N. Rudnitsky. 1981. *Course Design: A Guide to Curriculum Development for Teachers,* 2d ed. White Plains, N.Y.: Longman.

Robinson, Emma D. et al. 1982. *Course Development in Schools of Nursing.* New York: National League for Nursing.

Romiszowski, A. J. 1981. *Designing Instructional Systems: Decision-Making in Course Planning and Curriculum Design.* New York: Nichols Publishing Company.

Tracey, W. 1984. *Designing Training and Development Systems,* rev. ed. New York: AMACOM.

CHAPTER 8

Instructional Units

This chapter provides information to help the reader

1. point out the relationship of instructional units to grade-level plans and course plans.
2. describe components frequently found in instructional units.
3. identify primary users of instructional units.
4. recognize that instructional units can be prepared according to a variety of formats.
5. develop instructional units that are tied to other document types in a basic curriculum document set.

INTRODUCTION

Instructional units describe suggested procedures to be followed by teachers and instructors as they teach content associated with each unit in a grade-level plan or a course plan. They convey very specific information of practical value for individuals who work directly with learners in the classroom.

Sometimes instructional units may be prepared by curriculum teams for each unit in a grade-level plan or course plan. Other times curriculum development groups develop only one or two units as models. These models then stand as examples to be followed by teachers and instructors as they develop additional units on their own. Occasionally, no instructional unit models are provided in a basic curriculum document set. In such cases, instructors and teachers are expected to develop instructional units of their own design (not consistent with any established model) or to use other methods for organizing instruction.

There are many approaches to organizing content in instructional units, and specific designs must respond to local conditions. For example, a curriculum-development group might determine that teachers and instructors are not familiar with many sources of information related to topics to be covered in a new course. In response, developers might decide to provide instructional units with particularly detailed listings of learning resources.

In another setting, curriculum developers might find some teachers and instructors to be unfamiliar with potentially useful instructional techniques. This could lead to a decision to provide explicit information about when and how certain instructional procedures might be employed.

Good instructional unit documents respond to real needs of teachers and instructors, even though central office administrators, principals, department heads, and others may have some interest in their contents. Instructional units contain highly specific information about day-to-day instruction. The measure of their quality is the relevance teachers and instructors believe these units have in assisting them to improve classroom instruction.

The learners to be served, the resources available for instruction, and the personalities and backgrounds of teachers and instructors vary enormously from place to place. This is true even within a single school district or a large corporate employee-education program. Differences in the instructional environments faced by individual teachers impose important restrictions on the developers of instructional units, as not all of the potential users will be participating in the development process.

A unit developed by people who do not teach in a given instructional setting may not perfectly fit that setting. The written presentation of the unit, therefore, should contain language that recognizes this and invites individuals to adapt the unit's contents to local conditions. Otherwise, users may reject the entire unit as something that "is not practical" or "not responsive to my needs."

RELATIONSHIPS TO THE BASIC SET OF INTERRELATED DOCUMENTS

Sometimes it is useful to incorporate instructional units into a basic curriculum document set. For example, a state may require certain content to be taught and mastered at a given grade level. Developing instructional unit plans that are consistent with a school district's general scope and sequence document and with grade-level plans and course plans can help assure that prescribed content is being taught as mandated by law.

When an instructional unit document is prepared as part of a basic curriculum document set, the nature of the interrelationships should be described in the first part of the document. Some information in this section will be the same as that provided in the general scope and sequence document and in the grade-level plans and course plans. An important part of this explanation is a discussion of the notation system.

As explained in previous chapters, the notation system helps tie together all the documents in the system. Information in the instructional unit pertaining to instructional objectives, instructional strategies, evaluation procedures, and needed materials consumes a great deal of space. Hence, reference to other types of information, including the general curriculum area and grade-level or course title, may be made by notation alone.

COMPONENTS OF INSTRUCTIONAL UNIT PLANS

Numerous books and articles have been written on developing instructional units, and organizing instruction around selected units or topics within grade-level programs and courses has been a recommended procedure for decades. Over the years, many different approaches to organizing instructional units have been described, and there are important differences among some of these formats. Many, however, share certain common features.

The components described here and illustrated later in the abbreviated sample instructional unit plan are representative of those found in large numbers of guidelines for unit planning. This is not to suggest that an instructional unit that lacks some of these components or that includes some others not referenced here is necessarily deficient. The instructional unit is primarily a document prepared to meet a teacher's practical needs, and it is quite possible that individuals in certain settings have found other categories of content more useful than those introduced in this chapter.

The categories presented in the following subsections ought to be regarded as general suggestions. Properly, they should be modified to provide the kind of instructional assistance needed by those who will be the ultimate consumers of the finished product—the teachers and instructors.

GENERALIZATIONS AND CONCEPTS

Each instructional unit in a course must describe important generalizations and concepts that will be treated in that course. These generalizations and concepts then are used as a foundation for designing the remainder of the unit.

DIAGNOSTIC PROCEDURES

In instructional unit planning, diagnosis can be viewed from one of two major perspectives. On the one hand, diagnosis can be employed to determine whether learners have the basic prerequisite information needed for success with content associated with a new unit. On the other hand, diagnosis can be used to determine whether learners already know some of the content that will be introduced in the new unit.

When diagnosis is used to assess learners' mastery of prerequisites, it looks back at what they have already accomplished. The teacher gathers information about learners' understanding of the content they must have mastered before they can profit from instruction focusing on new material. This might involve checking samples of previous work, reviewing test performance, talking individually with learners, or developing and administering special tests.

When diagnosis is used to determine how much learners already know about content to be introduced in the new unit, the teacher or instructor develops ways of determining levels of understanding of this new content. These results might suggest that less instructional time be allocated to those areas of a new unit about which learners already know something than those areas that are totally unfamiliar to them. Pretests and interviews with learners often are used to gather diagnostic information of this type.

Sometimes teachers and instructors who are planning units will seek only one kind of diagnostic information. For example, teachers who have worked for most of the year with a group of students may feel they know a great deal about their students' mastery of basic knowledge and skills. For units to be taught late in the year, however, they may wish to diagnose only what students might or might not know about new content to be introduced.

After deciding what kind of diagnostic information to gather and gathering that data, developers often find it useful to prepare a visual display of the information. Diagnostic information can be portrayed in a way that allows teachers and instructors to identify patterns characterizing individual learners and the class as a whole. An example of a diagnostic profile chart that allows for a quick visual inspection of these patterns is provided in the sample instructional unit plan introduced later in this chapter.

INSTRUCTIONAL OBJECTIVES

Instructional objectives state what learners are supposed to be able to do as a result of their exposure to instruction. They provide a general framework for planning the instructional experiences to be included. The number and complexity of instructional objectives is a design decision to be made by the unit developers, and may vary from unit to unit. Among the variables often considered in making decisions related to instructional objectives are unit length, complexity of unit content, and age and developmental level of learners.

Unit developers sometimes use tables of specifications as aids in unit planning. (See Chapter 5 for a discussion of tables of specifications and their uses.) Tables of specifications help curriculum developers to identify and display the relative importance of major divisions of content that will be treated in the unit. For example, a table of specifications may suggest that some content is to be taught to the cognitive level of analysis, whereas other content is to be taught only to the level of knowledge.

Instructional objectives can be written that reference each of the major content areas included in the table of specifications. If there is an indication that learners should operate at the level of application when they have completed study of one of the major content components of the unit, then developers must write an instructional objective that demands an application-level performance. Reference to a table of specifications can help developers prepare instructional objectives that are consistent with the levels of learning expected for each content division of the unit.

The professional literature contains many sets of guidelines for preparing instructional objectives. In the *ABCD* approach, one functional format, each objective is supposed to include an *A* or *audience* component, a *B* or *behavior* component, a *C* or *condition* component, and a *D* or *degree* component.

The audience part of an instructional objective identifies the learner or group of learners who will be expected to demonstrate the cited behavior. The following examples show how the audience component might appear in an instructional objective:

> Each student . . .
> Every Music II learner . . .
> Manuel's group . . .

The behavior component of an instructional objective clearly expresses what the learner is to do to demonstrate mastery. Verbs used should express behavior in clearly observable terms. That is, verbs such as "appreciate," "understand," and "know," should be avoided in favor of verbs describing observable behaviors that can be used as indicators of appreciating, understanding, and knowing. For example, the verbs "select," "compare," "differentiate," "compute," "point out," and "describe" are among those favored by writers of instructional objectives. (A number of lists of good, observable verbs for use in instructional behaviors exist. One good source is Norman O. Gronlund's *Stating Objectives for Classroom Instruction.*)

The following are examples of the behavior component of an instructional objective:

> . . . cite examples of . . .
> . . . compare and contrast . . .
> . . . state . . .

The conditions components in this approach references the conditions of assessment, the specific approach to be used to gather data about the learner's proficiency on the stated behavior. This can be either a formal test or a less formal procedure. The following are examples of the behavior component of an instructional objective:

> . . . on an essay examination . . .
> . . . on a multiple-choice test . . .
> . . . in a one-on-one teacher-learner conference . . .

The degree component identifies the proficiency level expected of the student for the teacher or instructor to assume mastery. This may be indicated in terms of a percentage of test items that must be answered correctly, as a minimum required raw score, or by general references to categories of information that must be included in a response. The following are examples of how the degree component might be expressed in an instructional objective:

> . . . with 80 percent accuracy.
> . . . responding correctly to at least 15 of 18 items.
> . . . including specific references to (a) economic causes, (b) political causes, and (c) social causes.

The following examples of completed objectives include each of the required ABCD components:

> Each student, on a matching test, will identify outcomes of important World War II battles with 80 percent accuracy.
> Each learner will compare and contrast *Huckleberry Finn* and *The Last of the Mohicans* on an essay examination. Specific references must be made to (a) imagery, (b) general prose style, (c) plot development, and (d) characterization.
> Each management trainee will recognize appropriate fiscal-management procedures by responding correctly to 12 of 15 multiple-choice questions.

SEQUENCING INSTRUCTION

Instructional units often include suggestions for sequencing instruction that indicate general directions regarding what should be done first, second, third, and so forth, as teaching related to a given objective goes forward. The general idea is that some sequences will produce better learning outcomes than others. This position has long historic standing.

The ancient Hebrews and Spartans placed a high value on learners memorizing certain critical information. Teachers developed a four-part sequence that seemed to work well for most learners: (1) present material to be learned; (2) require learners to think about the material; (3) repeat the material and work with learners until they believe they have it memorized; (4) ask learners to recite the material (Posner, 1987).

Centuries later, Jesuit schools developed another standard set of guidelines for students. The Jesuit sequence included these features: (1) present new information slowly enough for learners to take notes; (2) pause periodically to explain challenging parts; (3) relate new material to other subjects; (4) ask learners to memorize the material; (5) assign monitors to check on the accuracy of learners' presentations of memorized material; (6) follow this phase with a discussion or interpretation of the meaning of the new material; (7) reward the best students as an incentive for further learning (Posner, 1987).

In the nineteenth century, the learning theorist Johann Friederich Herbart formulated his theory of *apperception*. This theory suggested that learning occurred when ideas already in the mind contacted new ideas. If there was a logical relationship between existing ideas and new ideas, the new information would more easily become part of a person's store of knowledge. This position provided an important rationale for diagnosing learners by determining which ideas they already knew and how consistent they were with new content to be taught.

Herbart devised a five-part sequence of instruction designed to provide experiences consistent with his view of how learning occurred. These steps were (1) preparation, (2) presentation, (3) association (tying new information to old information), (4) generalization (stating broad applications of knowledge), and (5) application (Meyer, 1975).

Though apperception has been displaced by more contemporary learning theories, Herbart's sequence is still influential. In part this is true because the steps make sense in terms of many more modern views of learning as well as the apperceptionist position from which they were originally developed.

Suggested instructional sequences continue to be developed. One that has been widely disseminated was introduced by Hunter and Russell in 1977. It suggests that instruction should follow a pattern involving these seven basic steps: (1) anticipatory set (taking action to get learners to focus their attention on the instruction to follow); (2) objective and purpose (making clear to learners what they will be able to do as a result of their exposure to what will be taught); (3) instructional input (transmitting relevant content to learners); (4) modeling (providing examples to learners of what they should be able to do as result of instruction); (5) checking for understanding (acting to assure that learners are absorbing new information needed to accomplish objectives); (6) guided practice (monitoring learners as they begin work on assigned tasks); and (7) independent practice (assigning learners to work without the benefit of direct teacher assistance) (Hunter and Russell, 1977; pp. 86–88).

Another framework for sequencing, based on the work of Gagne and Briggs (1974), was introduced by Denton, Armstrong, and Savage (1980). The Denton, Armstrong, and Savage sequence includes these steps: (1) emphasizing objectives (letting learners know what will be expected of them as a consequence of their exposure to the instructional sequence); (2) motivating learning (establishing a desire for or an interest in the content to be presented); (3) recalling previous learning (establishing a connection between previous learning and the new material); (4) presenting new information (introducing the new content); (5) recognizing key points (helping learners distinguish between critical and less critical information); (6) applying new information (giving learners opportunities to use new knowledge); and (7) assessing new learning (evaluating and providing feedback to learners regarding their performances).

There are commonalities among many of these suggested instructional sequences. For example, the emphasis on having learners apply new information they have learned is a recurring theme. The idea that teachers should monitor learners' performances to check for understanding is also common to several sequencing models.

When using one of these models, a different model, or some blend of several models to suggest sequences in instructional units, curriculum developers must observe several cautions. First, sequencing ideas should be clearly identified as suggestions. As professionals, many teachers resent being presented with a canned program that tells them they must do this first, that second, that third, and so forth. Instead, such ideas should be introduced as possibilities for teachers to think about in light of their own instructional needs.

Sometimes, whether intended or not, people who look over an instructional sequence in an instructional unit document conclude that it must be accomplished during a single class period. If an instructor believes that that is the intention of the developers, he or she is likely to reject the sequencing suggestions. Too many variables affect instructional pacing for teachers to accept an admonition to accomplish a given sequence within one class period. Presentations of ideas about instructional sequences, therefore, should make clear that there are no assumptions that all tasks will occur within a narrowly defined time limit.

EVALUATION

Instructional units often include evaluation procedures for determining whether or not learners have mastered unit objectives. In this case, examples of the assessment types referenced in the conditions component of each instructional objective should be provided. For example, if various objectives call for multiple-choice tests, matching tests, and essay tests, then these should be developed and included in the instructional unit.

Evaluation tools provided should be described as suggestions for teachers and instructors to use or modify to meet their own needs. They are included in the unit to stimulate thought about evaluating learner performances as described in the unit objectives. Some teachers and instructors may wish to use these assessment tools exactly as they are printed. Others may choose to modify them or to develop new ones of their own. Such modifications should be encouraged. However, unit developers should emphasize that evaluations, if developed independently, should be consistent with the instructional objectives.

For example, if a given objective cues learners to expect a matching test, they should be given a matching test and not an essay test (whether the one provided in the unit or devised by the teacher is not important). If teachers and instructors have serious objections to the kinds of evaluations called for in the conditions components, they should modify the language of the objectives. This way, learners will be assessed in a manner consistent with their expectations, as those expectations are reflected in the conditions component of the instructional objective.

MATERIALS AND EQUIPMENT

Instructional units often identify learning materials and equipment. This information can be organized as either a general listing for the entire unit or as separate listings related to each instructional objective. This latter arrangement has an advantage in that it allows unit users to review materials and equipment needs at the same time they are planning instruction tied to a given objective.

Lists of materials and equipment are not intended to be comprehensive. Individual teachers and instructors will want to exercise some personal choice. The lists are intended instead as a beginning point for planning.

CROSS-REFERENCING GENERALIZATIONS, CONCEPTS, INSTRUCTIONAL OBJECTIVES, AND MATERIALS AND EQUIPMENT

Developing a complete instructional unit involves the manipulation and organization of many separate pieces of information. It is easy to overlook some critical information and to leave some sections of the unit incomplete.

To avoid this situation, curriculum developers sometimes use a system of cross-referencing generalizations, concepts, instructional objectives, and materials and equipment. This can take the form of a page that displays each of these basic unit components, an inspection of which will reveal whether there has been a failure to provide instructional objectives relating to some important unit concepts. An example of such a cross-referencing scheme is provided in the sample instructional unit in the next section of this chapter.

AN EXAMPLE OF AN INSTRUCTIONAL UNIT

An instructional unit designed as part of a grade 6 science program is provided on the following pages. It follows the same general scheme used for the presentation of the examples of the general scope and sequence document and the grade-level plan. Note that comments have again been included in the column to the left of the document.

This example reflects one approach to unit design. Certainly others might do an equally good job of organizing and displaying content. Publishers of commercial textbook programs for schools often provide prototype units, and articles and books on the subject are also widely available.

This unit suggests one approach to the task of preparing an instructional unit that has a relationship with other documents in an interrelated set. Note, for example, the continued use of the notation scheme first introduced in the general scope and sequence document.

INSTRUCTIONAL UNIT: UNIT I—"INTRODUCTION"

An instructional unit featuring content taught in
the first unit of the grade 6 science program.

Harris Center Public School District

Revision of Spring, 1989

TABLE OF CONTENTS

COMMENTS

FOREWORD

The material included on this page of the document and on the next several pages is identical to that contained in the general scope and sequence document and the grade-level program document for grade 6 science. Repetition of this basic information is provided because it is impossible to predict which document a user will first encounter. Users need to understand that this document is part of an interrelated set of documents.

As directed by the Board of Education of the Harris Center Public School District, a series of curriculum documents has been prepared. This series consists of a set of interrelated curriculum documents. They include general scope and sequence documents for grades K to 6 and for grades 7 to 12. Other documents include grade-level plans, course plans, and instructional unit plans. Collectively, these documents describe a coordinated and sequenced program for all learners in the school district.

All documents in this basic document system employ a common notational system. This system allows for easy cross-referencing of program elements that are described in more than one document type.

Programs reflected in these written materials are the product of many hours of difficult work. Large numbers of the district's teachers and administrators were involved. As appropriate, experts in instructional design and in various academic specialties were involved. There was also input from students, from parents, and from other dedicated school patrons.

These documents will be periodically augmented and revised to keep programs responsive to the changing needs of learners in our district. Only through a process of change and adaptation can we hope to keep pace with changes in the knowledge base of our courses, changes in our learner population, and shifts in national, state, and local educational priorities.

Joaquin S. Solandares, Superintendent
Harris Center Public School District

Jane F. LaVitte, President
Board of Education, Harris Center Public
School District

EXPLANATION OF DOCUMENT TYPES AND IDENTIFICATION OF PRIMARY USERS

From time to time, many individuals may wish to look over individual documents in this set. As part of the Harris Center Public School District's established program of study, these documents are to be available for inspection by interested citizens as well as professional employees of the district. In their day-to-day work, some members of the professional staff may find certain of these documents more useful than others. This section briefly introduces each of the major document types and suggests individuals who might logically be thought of as primary users of each.

The General Scope and Sequence Document

The general scope and sequence document in this set provides an overview of all subjects taught from kindergarten through grade 6. (Please note that another scope and sequence and related documents are available covering instructional programs for grades 7 through 12.) The general scope and sequence document provides some very basic information about content to be covered in each subject area at each grade level. Specifically, there is information related to each curriculum area, each K-to-6 grade level, titles of units to be taught in each subject at each grade level, and generalizations that are related to each unit to be taught in each subject at each grade level. In addition, the general scope and sequence document introduces a notation system that will be used throughout all other documents in the basic document set.

Primary Users. This document will be of primary interest to individuals who have responsibilities spanning the breadth of the entire K-to-6 instructional program. It is designed to help them verify that any general policies related to courses and content are being followed. Central-office associate and assistant superintendents for instruction and district-level curriculum supervisors and specialists are among individuals who may find the general scope and sequence document to be of particular interest. At times, individual subject area specialists, principals, and teachers may wish to work with this document. In most cases, their needs will be better served by other documents in the set.

The Grade-Level Plan

This document provides a general framework for one subject area at one grade level of the elementary school program. (A similar document called a course plan is used to describe basic components of individual courses in grades 7 to 12.) The grade-level plan includes all unit titles for a given subject at a given grade level—for example, Grade 6 Science. In addition to unit titles, the document includes rationales supporting the selection of each unit, generalizations related to each unit, and major concepts to be introduced. There are also rather general descriptions of suggested instructional approaches and evaluation procedures.

Primary Users. This document type is of primary interest to individuals seeking information about basic content to be covered within a given academic area at a particular grade level. Primary users might include subject-area supervisors at the district level, building principals, and teachers who are responsible for coordinating instruction within a single subject in a building or within a given grade level in a building. Individual classroom teachers may find this document useful to provide them with a general overview of content to be covered in a particular subject area at the grade level they teach. Suggestions for day-to-day approaches to teaching the content will be much more detailed, however, in the instructional unit plans.

The Instructional Unit Plan

This document provides a detailed outline of each unit to be taught in each subject at each grade level. It includes such elements as the unit title, generalizations related to the unit, major concepts to be taught, performance objectives to be mastered, ideas for diagnosing learner characteristics, detailed suggestions for introducing the content, complete sets of evaluation procedures, and a list of materials to be used. As appropriate, there are also suggestions for organizing the classroom and managing learners and materials. A procedure for cross-referencing relationships among generalizations, concepts, performance objectives, and learning materials is also included.

Primary Users. The instructional unit plan is of primary interest to teachers and paraprofessionals who work with learners in the classroom. The level of detail regarding instructional procedures that is provided goes beyond the needs of most central-district administrators and building principals. The instructional unit document is not meant to establish a rigid, prescriptive set of procedures for the teacher. Its purpose is to provide some ideas that teachers may or may not use and to suggest a framework for teachers to use in independently developing instructional units of their own.

DEVELOPERS OF CURRICULUM DOCUMENTS

Large numbers of people participated in the development of the curriculum documents in this system. Initial leadership was provided by district-level specialists in curriculum. Teachers played a very important part in this activity. There was representation from every elementary school in the district. Building administrators also participated directly in all phases of program development and document preparation.

Our schools belong to our community. Hence, it is entirely appropriate for community members' views to be heard as school programs are being planned. A number of parents and other school patrons participated in the curriculum activities that resulted in the preparation of these documents, and they made many important contributions.

From time to time, groups of individuals involved in various phases of program development and revision had need of specialized assistance. As

needed, subject-matter specialists and other experts were invited to contribute to the curriculum-development activity. Their assistance was helpful in the effort to assure that developed programs were as up-to-date and as consistent with state-of-the-art knowledge as possible.

General leadership of the curriculum development activities resulting in the development of these documents was provided by the following people:

Dianna Basco, Associate Superintendent for Instruction: B.S., Secondary Education; M.S., Educational Administration; Ph.D., Curriculum and Instruction.

Peter F. B. Johnson, Curriculum Director: B.S., Elementary Education; M.S., Curriculum and Instruction; Ed.D., Curriculum and Instruction.

LaShawn C. Birdwhistle, Associate Curriculum Director—Elementary: B.S., Elementary Education; M.S., Curriculum and Instruction.

DEVELOPERS OF GRADE-LEVEL PLAN FOR SIXTH GRADE SCIENCE

Rodney F. Lu, Director of Elementary Science, Harris Center Public School District; B.A., Elementary Education; M.Ed., Educational Curriculum and Instruction.

C. F. Appleton, Assistant Director of Secondary Science, Harris Center Public School District; B.S., Biology; M.Ed., Educational Curriculum and Instruction.

Carmen Barrera, Principal, Altos Elementary School, Harris Center Public School District; B.S., Elementary Science Education; M.Ed., Educational Administration.

Thalia Jean Pharr, Sixth Grade Teacher, Watkins Middle School, Harris Center Public School District; B.A., Liberal Arts; M.Ed., Educational Curriculum and Instruction.

Penny Q. Johannsen, Sixth Grade Teacher, Lohasset Middle School, Harris Center Public School District; B.A., Elementary Science Education; M.Ed., Educational Curriculum and Instruction.

C. Charles McNeese, Sixth Grade Teacher, Triana Middle School, Harris Center Public School District; B.S., Geology; M.Ed., Educational Curriculum and Instruction.

Joe Ray Travis, Sixth Grade Teacher, Vista Oaks Middle School, Harris Center Public School District; B.A., Elementary Education; M.Ed., Educational Curriculum and Instruction.

COMMENTS

DEVELOPERS OF THE INSTRUCTIONAL UNIT FOR UNIT I, "INTRODUCTION"

Note the provision of information about primary developers of the unit. Often different individuals will be assigned to prepare different units that are described in the grade-level plan.

C. Charles McNeese, Sixth Grade Teacher, Triana Middle School, Harris Center Public School District; B.S., Geology; M.Ed., Educational Curriculum and Instruction.

Florine L. Nesmith, Sixth Grade Teacher, Watkins Middle School, Harris Center Public School District; B.A., Elementary Science Education; M.Ed., Educational Curriculum and Instruction.

Other grade six teachers in the district critiqued work of the developers. Their suggestions were incorporated into the design presented in this document.

EXPLANATION OF NOTATION SYSTEM

Information provided on this page and the one that follows duplicates that included in the general scope and sequence document and the grade-level plan.

Curriculum Area
.01 English (includes Reading, Language Arts)
.02 Mathematics
.03 Science
.04 Social Studies
.05 Music
.06 Art
.07 Physical Education
.08 Health
.09 Industrial Education
.
.   (Same pattern continues for other areas.)

Grade-Level or Course Title
.01 English
.02 Mathematics
.03 Science
   .00 Science, Grade K
   .01 Science, Grade 1
   .02 Science, Grade 2
.
.
   .06 Science, Grade 6
.04 Social Studies
   .00 Social Studies, Grade K
   .01 Social Studies, Grade 1
.
.   (Same pattern continues for all other areas.)

Unit or Topic Titles
.01 English
.02 Mathematics
.03 Science
   .06 Science, Grade 6
      .01 Introduction
      .02 Our Living World
      .03 Our Physical World
      .04 Earth and Space
      .05 The Human Body

Generalizations
.03 Science
   .06 Science, Grade 6
      .01 Introduction
         .01 Productive work in science depends, in part, on knowledge of basic laboratory safety procedures.

COMMENTS

.

. (Same pattern is continued
to display unit or topic titles
for all curriculum areas and
grade levels or courses.)

This notation ordinarily is displayed as a line. The line of notation provides a kind of shorthand that identifies various parts of the program in symbolic form. For example, the notation line reading .03.06.01.01 references a generalization related to the importance of knowledge of basic scientific processes and safety procedures to the first unit in the grade 6 program of the district's curriculum in science. For a more complete explanation of a line of notation, see the information below.

EXPLANATION OF A LINE OF NOTATION

.03.06.01.01

Curriculum Area_____⌡   ⌊___Generalization
Grade-Level/Course Title_____⌡   ⌊___Unit or Topic Title

This notation system is used in all curriculum documents in the basic set of interrelated documents, including the general scope and sequence document, the grade-level program plans or course plans, and the instructional unit plans. In this system, each cluster (a set of numerals bounded on both sides by periods) refers to a particular component. In the line of notation above, the first cluster (.03) refers to the curriculum area. The second cluster (.06) refers to the grade level or course title. The third cluster (.01) refers to the unit or topic title. The fourth cluster (.01) identifies a specific generalization.

This is how the line of notation at the top of the page should be interpreted:

The first cluster	.03	This indicates the curriculum area is science.
The second cluster	.06	This indicates the science program in grade 6.
The third cluster	.01	This indicates the first unit taught at grade 6. It is a unit titled simply "Introduction."
The fourth cluster	.01	This indicates the first generalization related to the first unit in the grade 6 science program. It focuses on the importance of content related to basic scientific processes and to safety.

.03.06.01 INTRODUCTION

UNIT OVERVIEW

Information in this section provides some basic details regarding the substance of what is to be taught in this unit. It also provides an opportunity for curriculum developers to suggest

This unit is designed to introduce the grade 6 science program to learners. Typically, learners will be exposed to this material after having been away from school and science instruction for about three months. For this reason, part of the unit content involves review and extended applications of content

COMMENTS
*a rationale for the
importance of this
content.*

*The notation in front
of the unit title,
"introduction,"
indicates that this is
the first unit (.01) in
grade 6 (.06) of the
district's science
program (.03).*

elements introduced in the grade 5 program. Among ideas introduced at grade 5 and extended in this "Introduction" unit are basic classification skills, basic writing skills, basic computational skills, and basic approaches to conducting scientific experiments.

The grade six program places particularly heavy emphases on laboratory experiences. For this reason, a major component of the "Introduction" unit focuses on laboratory safety issues. The intent is to familiarize learners with safe laboratory procedures so that they will be able to operate in a hazard-free manner that will enable them to maximize their learning from the many hands-on experiences that will be provided throughout the entire grade 6 program.

As a result of their involvement in laboratory activities, students will be introduced to many important concepts associated with the scientific method and scientific experimentation. The intent is to build a solid basis of preparation for the secondary school program and to assist learners to think scientifically about problems they confront today and will continue to confront as adult citizens. The "Introduction" unit is designed to begin building some of these important scientific-thinking abilities.

.03.06.01 INTRODUCTION

DIAGNOSING LEARNERS: SOME COMMENTS

This section is designed to provide teachers with some general ideas about how the task of diagnosing learners might be approached.

The "Introduction" unit provides the first formal instruction in science most learners will have had since leaving the fifth grade. While content of this unit does reinforce some grade-5 content, developers have made some general assumptions about competencies these learners should have. Because success in this unit depends, in part, on the accuracy of these assumptions, it may be desirable to do some diagnostic work at the beginning of the term to determine whether any learners might be deficient in some of the areas where they are assumed to be knowledgeable.

The science program in the fifth grade provides learners with experiences designed to help them sort information into meaningful categories. They will be required to apply these basic sorting skills in the "Introduction" unit. Hence, it may be a good idea to prepare some activities, design some simple tests, or take some other action to determine how proficient learners are on sorting tasks before beginning instruction on the new unit.

The fifth grade program also provides learners with opportunities to develop written descriptions of what they have observed. They will be expected to do a great deal of laboratory-report writing in grade 6. Some diagnostic activities directed toward assessing learners' abilities to prepare coherent observation reports may be desirable.

The mathematics program at grade 5 places a heavy emphasis on the metric system. Learners are taught to convert English-system linear and volume measure to metric-system equivalents. Further, they are taught relationships between linear and volume measure within the metric system.

COMMENTS

*Because teachers'
situations vary
tremendously from
setting to setting, it is
a good idea to leave
many decisions
regarding kinds of
diagnostic informa-
tion to be gathered to
the individual
teacher.*

Learners will be required to work extensively with the metric system in the "Introduction" unit. It may be desirable to develop some diagnostic procedures to assess their abilities to work with metric-system measures.

The "Introduction" unit and subsequent units will include a good deal of information presented in prose form. Learners who have deficient reading skills may experience difficulty with some of the provided learning materials. Teachers may wish to identify these individuals early so they can provide some supplementary learning experiences for these learners to assist them in mastering the content. Some diagnostic information focusing on learners' reading abilities might be appropriately gathered as a prelude to begining instruction on unit one, "Introduction."

Because individual teachers' situations vary tremendously from setting to setting, some teachers may have needs for quite different kinds of diagnostic information than those suggested here. Further, the sources of such information may be different from place to place. For example, in some schools, reading specialists may have excellent information regarding reading-proficiency levels of individual learners. In others, teachers may wish to develop reading proficiency procedures of their own (for example cloze tests) to develop some feel for how their learners will fare with reading materials to be used in the science program. Teachers should feel free to gather kinds of diagnostic information they believe to be appropriate and to use means that are appropriate for their individual circumstances.

Regardless of which diagnostic information is needed and how it is gathered, it makes sense to develop a means of organizing diagnostic data. One procedure that some teachers have found to be useful is the *diagnostic profile chart*. This allows teachers to make a quick visual inspection of diagnostic information for an entire class. It permits quick identification of individual learners who are having problems in certain areas, as well as of some general areas of weakness that characterize a high percentage of the class. This latter kind of information is particularly important. For example, were diagnostic information to reveal that large numbers of students were weak in terms of their ability to work with the metric system, this would suggest the desirability of some extended direct instruction on this topic as part of the unit work. An example of a diagnostic profile chart is provided on the next page.

COMMENTS   **AN EXAMPLE OF A DIAGNOSTIC PROFILE CHART**

Student	Metric-System Measure (Linear)	Metric-System Measure (Volume)	Sorting Skills	Writing to Describe	Basic Reading Skills
C. Ariola		x			
R. Bates					
F. Bolin	x	x			x
L. Carr					
G. Chu					
L. Cullen		x		x	x
W. Day					
A. Eisen	x	x	x	x	x
D. Ewenson		x			
H. Finucci		x	x		
T. Garza					
P. Hymes				x	x
R. Jones	x	x			
W. Jones		x			
F. Li					
P. Larsen		x	x	x	x
B. Monk					
N. Nielsen					
E. O'Keeffe		x			
F. Potts		x			
I. Sakamura					
T. Smith		x	x		
N. Thomas					
Q. Wenck					
S. Wilson		x	x		
K. Yates					
D. Yonce		x			
Totals	3	14	5	4	5

Note how the diagnostic profile chart allows a teacher to identify areas of weakness associated with individual learners as well as general patterns of weakness characterizing many people in the class.

The x's denote learners identified to have weaknesses in the category where they appear. Note that this system allows identification of particular problem areas experienced by each learner. For example, A. Eisen was found to be weak in all five major categories. The class, as a whole, seems to be fairly well grounded in all of the areas except for metric-system (volume). Fourteen of the twenty-seven people in this class were found to be deficient in this area. Such a finding might well prompt the teacher to provide some direct instruction related to volume measure in the metric system at the beginning of unit one, "Introduction."

COMMENTS

Note the use of the notation system. The notation for the first generalization indicates that it is from the curriculum area of science (.03), associated with the grade 6 program (.06), related to the first unit in that program (.01), and that it is the first generalization related to that unit (.01).

Sometimes developers of instructional units choose to note the cognitive levels of the provided cognitive domain objectives. Developers of this particular unit chose not to do so.

In this unit, the developers chose not to tie the instructional objectives directly to the basic notational system. They have simply used the designations "unit instructional objective 1," "unit instructional objective 2," and so forth. Other developers might have chosen to tie the notation indicating the instructional objectives to the basic notational system used throughout the set of interrelated documents. In such a case, "unit instructional objective 2" might have been identified by this notation: .03.06.01.04.02. This would mean that the

Five generalizations guide instruction to this unit. For each, at least one cognitive instructional objective has been developed. Additionally, there is an affective objective that relates to the unit as a whole and that encompasses all unit generalizations. The unit generalizations (and related concepts) and associated instructional objectives follow:

.03.06.01.01 Productive work in science depends, in part, on knowledge of basic laboratory safety procedures.
Concepts: safety, safety equipment
Unit Instructional Objective 1: Each learner will recognize appropriate laboratory safety procedures by responding correctly to at least 11 of 13 items on a multiple-choice quiz.

.03.06.01.02 Classification of variables is a component of scientific observation that allows data to be organized in a systematic way.
Concepts: variable, manipulated variable, responding variable, control
Unit Instructional Objective 2: Each learner will differentiate among control, manipulated, and responding variables by responding correctly to at least 10 of 12 questions on a true-false test.

.03.06.01.03 Utilization of the steps of the scientific method rationalizes and standardizes the process of problem-solving in science.
Concepts: problem, hypothesis, experiment, materials, observation, procedures, conclusion
Unit Instructional Objective 3: Each learner will identify the sequence of steps in the scientific method by responding correctly to at least 18 of 20 worksheet items.

.03.06.01.04 The metric system of measure allows easy conversions from linear measure to volume measure; hence, it has become a standard among scientists, even in nations where the system is not widely used by the general public.
Concepts: linear measure, volume measure, liter, meter, gram, mass
Unit Instructional Objective 4: Each learner will differentiate among symbols used to indicate mass, volume, and linear measurement by responding correctly to 8 of 10 matching items.
Unit Instructional Objective 5: Each learner will use metric laboratory equipment 90 percent of the time while performing laboratory work associated with this unit with little or no help from the teacher.

.03.06.01.05 Scientific advance depends on individuals' abilities to conceptualize, design, and implement experiments on their own.
Concepts: data table, analysis

COMMENTS

program area was science (.03), the grade-level was grade 6 (.06), the unit was the first in the sequence (.01), the generalization was the fourth in this unit (.04), and that this was the second instructional objective related to this generalization (.02).

Unit Instructional Objective 6: Each learner will design and implement an investigation that includes a variable and a control group. Then each will explain the design orally to the class in such a way that variables are properly labeled and procedures explained in sufficient detail that another person in the class could conduct the same experiment.

One affective objective has been developed for this unit. It is not tied to a specific unit generalization. Rather, it relates to the unit as a whole.

Unit Instructional Objective 7 (affective domain): On average, students in the class will rate their interest in science higher on an attitude inventory given at the conclusion of the unit than on a similar attitude inventory given at the beginning of the unit.

INSTRUCTIONAL OBJECTIVES, SUGGESTED INSTRUCTIONAL APPROACHES, SUGGESTED EVALUATION, AND NEEDED MATERIALS

Note the special notation used in the "suggested instructional approaches" section. Developers of this unit have used a sequencing scheme adapted from that introduced by Denton, Armstrong, and Savage. The letters at the beginning of each step are simply convenient abbreviations. This is what each means:

O—Provide Objective

M—Provide for initial Motivation

R—Recall previous learning

P—Present new information

KP—Emphasize Key Points

APP—Provide learners opportunities to Apply new learning

This section of the instructional unit identifies instructional procedures recommended for helping learners master each objective. Additionally, there are examples of assessment devices suitable for testing for mastery. Finally, there are lists of some basic materials recommended for use as content related to each objective is introduced.

03.06.01 Introduction
.03.06.01.01 Productive work in science depends, in part, on knowledge of basic laboratory safety procedures.
Concepts: safety, safety equipment
Unit Instructional Objective 1: Each learner will recognize appropriate laboratory safety procedures by responding correctly to at least 11 of 13 items on a multiple-choice test.
Suggested Instructional Approaches (for Unit Instructional Objective 1)
O— The teacher paraphrases the objective orally in a manner that communicates its intent to learners.
M— The teacher stimulates learner interest by drawing attention to special safety equipment arranged on a table.
R— The teacher engages the class in a general discussion of other kinds of safety equipment they might know about (welders' goggles and so forth).
P— The teacher carefully explains the function of each item of equipment.
KP— The teacher assigns learners to groups. Each group is asked to role play a specific laboratory-safety problem

COMMENTS

ANL—Assess New Learning and provide feedback to learners.

Developers clearly could have used other sequencing schemes to frame their suggestions. For example, they might well have used the seven-step model introduced by Hunter and Russell (1977).

This quiz is provided simply as an example of one that might be used to test learners' mastery of content associated with unit instructional objective 1. Individual teachers may well wish to develop assessment tools of their own.

.03.06.01 Introduction (continued)

.03.06.01.01 Productive work in science depends, in part, on knowledge of basic laboratory safety procedures (continued).

situation. They are asked to indicate the specific safety equipment they would use. In the follow-up discussion, the teacher reiterates key information about each piece of equipment.

APP— Brainstorming activity. Learners are asked to name 10 potential laboratory safety problems and to suggest ways of dealing properly with each.

ANL— The teacher asks questions about laboratory safety to randomly selected members of the class to determine general levels of understanding of laboratory safety.

Suggested Evaluation (for Unit Instructional Objective 1)

Multiple-Choice. Write the letter of the correct answer in the blank provided. There is only one correct answer for each question.

_____ 1. When mixing an acid with water, you should
  a. add the water last.
  b. add the acid last.
  c. mix both together at the same time.

_____ 2. The *most* important of our grade 6 science rules is for you to
  a. always write with black ink.
  b. listen carefully to the teacher and follow instructions.
  c. wear your lab apron.

_____ 3. When mixing chemicals in the lab, you should
  a. do only what the teacher says.
  b. mix several things to see what happens.
  c. taste things to see what they are.

_____ 4. The first thing you should do if something gets in your eye is
  a. try to remove it with a toothpick.
  b. put a bandage on your eye.
  c. send for the teacher and go to the eye-wash station.

_____ 5. The gas jets in the laboratory
  a. should be turned on at all times.
  b. should be turned on only when needed in a laboratory activity.
  c. are of a new design that has removed all potential danger.

_____ 6. When you heat something in a test tube, you should
  a. hold the test tube so it points straight up.

.03.06.01 Introduction (continued)
    .03.06.01.01 Productive work in science depends, in part, on knowl-
        edge of basic laboratory safety procedures (continued).
    Suggested Evaluation (for Unit Instructional Objective 1) (contin-
    ued)

        b. look down into the test tube to see what
          is happening.
        c. hold the test tube at a slight angle pointing
          away from you and others.

_____ 7. If your lab partner's clothes caught on fire, the best thing to
        do would be to
        a. use a fire extinguisher to put it out.
        b. run and get help.
        c. grab the fire blanket and wrap it around your lab partner.

_____ 8. In a lab, when you do not understand something, you
        should
        a. ask your lab partner.
        b. skip what you do not understand and do something else.
        c. ask your teacher.

_____ 9. Which of the following is safe to do in a laboratory?
        a. Mix two unknown chemicals.
        b. Wear safety goggles.
        c. Ask your lab partner for directions if you didn't under-
          stand the teacher.

_____ 10. If some paper or other material catches fire at your table, you
        should
        a. move to another table to work.
        b. send for the teacher and use the fire extinguisher.
        c. pour water on it.

_____ 11. Which of the following is the *correct* procedure to follow at
        the end of a laboratory period?
        a. Do not clean up your table because the next class may
          learn from your work.
        b. Clean up your lab equipment and your lab table.
        c. Avoid washing your hands for at least an hour after the
          lab ends.

_____ 12. The first thing you should do if you smell a gas leak is to
        a. leave the laboratory room.
        b. tell your teacher.
        c. write this information in your lab report.

_____ 13. You should wear safety goggles
        a. when using heat, but not when using chemicals.
        b. when using chemicals, but not when using heat.
        c. when using either heat or chemicals.

COMMENTS

NEEDED MATERIALS (FOR INSTRUCTIONAL
UNIT I, "INTRODUCTION")

Materials listed in this section are not intended to be all inclusive. Teachers may well use many additional resources as they work with learners on this material. These materials are simply among those that, to the unit developers, seem especially important to support instruction related to this content.

The following materials are among those needed to support instruction related to Unit Instructional Objective 1:

safety goggles
eyewash station, including all needed equipment
fire extinguisher
fire blanket
booklet: *Safety in the Elementary Science Classroom* (Washington,
D.C.: National Science Teachers Association)

Note: A similar format is followed to explain suggested instructional procedures, evaluation, and materials for every instructional objective developed for the remaining unit generalizations. There are a total of six cognitive objectives for the five generalizations related to Unit I, "Introduction." Hence, the format presented above for the objective related to the first unit generalizations will be repeated for each of the five remaining unit instructional objectives.

MASTER LIST OF MATERIALS NEEDED FOR UNIT I, INTRODUCTION (.03.06.01)

Not all instructional units include a master list of all materials needed for the unit. However, it is a feature that some teachers appreciate as they begin planning the entire block of instruction related to content in a given instructional unit.

A. safety goggles
B. eyewash station (and all associated equipment)
C. fire extinguisher
D. fire blanket
E. Buscocopters
F. paper clips
G. scissors
H. glycerin
I. alcohol
J. water
K. crayfish
L. bullfrog tadpoles
M. plastic trays
N. eyedroppers
O. food coloring
P. beakers
Q. triple-beam balance
R. meter sticks

S. graduated cylinders
T. kilogram scales
U. metric tape measures
V. graham crackers
W. marshmallows
X. Hersey bars
Y. toilet paper (4 brands)
Z. Booklet. *Safety in the Elementary Science Classroom.* (Washington, D.C.: National Science Teachers Association)
AA. Schafer, Larry E. "Buscocopter Science," *Science and Children*, April 1982.
BB. "Galileo: Challenge of Reason." Sound 16 mm film. (28 minutes) (New York: Audio Associates)

UNIT I, INTRODUCTION (03.06.01): CROSS-REFERENCED CONCEPTS, UNIT INSTRUCTIONAL OBJECTIVES, NEEDED MATERIALS

This cross-listing was helpful to the developers of the unit in determining whether instructional objectives and materials had been prepared and identified for all important unit concepts. Where materials are noted as lacking, teachers will be required to provide appropriate information of their own design. The chart further helps teachers to identify concepts for which only a few materials suggestions have been provided. This information can be used as a beginning point for selecting additional resources to supplement instruction related to certain unit concepts.

Major Unit Concepts	Unit Instructional Objective Numbers	Needed Materials
analysis	3, 6	K, L, Y
conclusion	3, 6	. . .
control	2, 6	E, F, G, H, I, J, K, L, Y, AA
data table	3, 6	E, F, H, I, J, M, Q, R, S, Y
experiment	3, 6	E, K, L, Y, AA, BB
gram	4, 5	Q, V, W, X
hypothesis	3, 6	E, K, L, Y, AA, BB
linear measure	4, 5	R, U, X
liter	4, 5	J, M, P, S
manipulated variable	2, 6	E, F, G, H, I, J, K, L, Y, AA
mass	4, 5	T, V, W, X, Y
materials	3, 6	E, F, G, H, I, J, K, L, M, N, O, P, Q, R, S, T, U, V, W, X, Y
meter	4, 5	K, L, R, U, Y
observation	3, 6	E, K, L, Y, AA, BB
problem	3, 6	E, K, L, Y, AA, BB
procedures	3, 6	. . .
responding variable	2, 6	E, F, G, H, I, J, K, L, Y, AA
safety	1	A, B, C, D, Z
safety equipment	1	A, B, C, D, Z
variable	2, 6	E, F, G, H, I, J, K, L, Y, AA
volume measure	4, 5	H, I, J, M, N, P, S

Note: Needed materials are identified by the letter designations used on the master list of unit materials that appears on the previous page.

SUMMARY

Instructional units are documents that are specifically designed to meet the needs of teachers and instructors. They tend to provide much more detailed treatment of issues related to presentation of content, learner evaluation, and instructional support materials than do general scope and sequence documents, grade-level plans, and course plans. They provide suggestions of a practical nature to individuals who will teach the described material.

There are many designs for organizing content into units. The sample provided in this chapter incorporates features that are frequently found in instructional units. This format includes a number of focus generalizations, with one or more instructional objectives developed, for each generalization, a suggested instructional sequence for introducing content related to each objective, and a list of materials that might be used as unit content. The sample unit also includes a notation system that helps to tie this document to others in the basic document set.

Because teachers' instructional settings vary, many developers of instructional units take care to advise teachers that they are free to modify unit suggestions. This is particularly important regarding ideas for introducing content and for evaluating learners. Though in some places state and local requirements may require teachers to focus on certain unit topics, generalizations, and concepts, almost nowhere are teachers required to use identical instructional strategies and evaluation procedures.

EXTENDING AND APPLYING CHAPTER CONTENT

1.   In recent years, there has been much discussion in the professional literature of education about various models for sequencing instruction. Identify one approach, for example, the one introduced by Hunter and Russell (1977), and read several articles that discuss its strengths and weaknesses. Prepare a short paper in which you summarize points made by individuals who have evaluated this approach to instructional sequencing.

2.   Instructional objectives (known also by such labels as "behavioral objectives," "learning objectives," and "performance objectives") are very common features of instructional units. Such objectives generally use verbs indicating observable behaviors to identify what learners should be able to do as a result of their exposure to unit content. Supporters of instructional objectives say they help unit developers focus clearly on their expectations for learners. Critics suggest that the need to express instructional objectives in observable terms restricts the kinds of learning experiences that unit developers will want to include. The debate over this issue can be framed by this question: "Do instructional objectives restrict the range of learning experiences curriculum developers will want to include in instructional units?" Prepare a position on one side of this issue and volunteer to debate another student who prepares a contrary position.

3.   Interview several teachers about their reactions to instructional units that have been developed by others. What have been their general reac-

tions? What features have they particularly liked? What have they felt to be the most common failings of such units? Share your findings with others in your class.

4. There are many formats for preparing instructional units. Read some articles or look at some books focusing on this issue. With a team of other students, identify two or three examples. Prepare a chart that displays features of each in such a way that similarities and differences can be easily seen. Use this chart as part of an oral presentation you make to the entire class.

5. Develop a framework for preparing an instructional unit of your own design. Specify components to be included and suggest how they will be ordered. Prepare a rationale supporting the design features you have included. Submit your design and accompanying rationale to your course instructor for comments.

BIBLIOGRAPHY

Connell, W. F. 1987. "History of Teaching Methods." *The International Encyclopedia of Teaching and Teacher Education*. Edited by Michael J. Dunkin. Oxford, England: Pergamon Press.

Denton, Jon J., David G. Armstrong and Tom V. Savage. 1980. "Matching Events of Instruction to Objectives." *Theory into Practice* (Winter): 10–14.

Dick, Walter and Lou Carey. 1985. *The Systematic Design of Instruction*, 2d ed. Glenview, Ill.: Scott, Foresman.

Gagne, Robert M. and Leslie J. Briggs. 1974. *Principles of Instructional Design*. New York: Holt, Rinehart, and Winston.

Gronlund, Norman O. 1985. *Stating Objectives for Classroom Instruction*, 3d ed. New York: Macmillan.

Hunter, Madeline and Douglas Russell. 1977. "How Can I Plan More Effective Lessons?" *Instructor* (September): 74–75; 86–88.

Kemp, Jerrold E. 1985. *The Instructional Design Process*. New York: Harper & Row.

Meyer, Adolphe E. 1975. *Grandmasters of Educational Thought*. New York: McGraw-Hill.

Posner, George S. 1987. "Pacing and Sequencing." *The International Encyclopedia of Teaching and Teacher Education*. Edited by Michael J. Dunkin. Oxford, England: Pergamon Press, pp. 266–272.

CHAPTER 9

Implementing Curriculum Change

This chapter introduces information to help the reader

1. recognize the important role that individual school learners and central office leaders play in curriculum implementation.
2. identify some contextual barriers to curriculum change.
3. understand the need to explain to potential users of an innovation what they must do to implement it properly.
4. describe several ways to assist individuals who will be asked to implement a curriculum change.
5. point out how levels of concern can be used to plan inservice and staff development activities.
6. recognize the need to tailor staff development training to the demonstrated needs of individuals.

INTRODUCTION

New programs that represent modest deviations from present practices and involve few people are relatively easy to implement, particularly when the people called upon to teach the innovations have been members of the curriculum development team. These people naturally have a good grasp of the rationales supporting the changes, and their knowledge of the new structure is thorough. Often, too, they will have developed a sense of pride and "ownership" in the new program. Many of them will have no need for special training before they begin teaching the new material.

The situation is quite different when a new curriculum is introduced to large numbers of people who were not involved in its development. For example, a new English curriculum for grades 7, 8, and 9 in a large school district will have to be implemented by dozens of teachers who may have played little or no part in its preparation. Initially, many of these people may know very little, even about the reasons change is being proposed. Some may be unconvinced that change is needed. Others may admit the need but be suspicious of changes they see as being imposed by outsiders.

Curriculum professionals have long recognized that people who have not been directly involved in a curriculum-development project often find the results less ideal than those who have participated. Bradley suggested that new programs do not fail so much because of inadequacy of design as because of poor implementation, noting that "the curriculum world is full of good planners and initiators. Where curriculum development is falling short is in the implementation process" (Bradley, 1985; p. 11).

Successful implementation of a new program demands effective leadership and a staff of informed teachers who are committed to the change and understand exactly what they are to do. The section that follows introduces some information regarding the importance of leadership. Subsequent sections focus on issues related to winning teachers' support for change.

LEADERSHIP AND SUCCESSFUL CURRICULUM CHANGE

Curriculum change is facilitated when leaders are committed to it and when potential users recognize this commitment. McLaughlin and Marsh (1978) found three levels of leadership to be important: principals, central office leadership, and curriculum project leaders.

PRINCIPALS

Principals play a critical role in shaping the nature of academic programming at their schools. A principal is a highly influential individual, and many teachers are heavily influenced by his or her opinions. If a principal is known to be supportive of cooperative efforts between and among teachers, an innovation such as team teaching is much more likely to win teachers' support than if the principal has no such commitment.

The school principal also tends to establish the professional atmosphere of the building. If this atmosphere is an open one where teachers feel free to discuss general problems, to develop and try proposed solutions, and to be mutually supportive, prospects for an innovation's being accepted are good. On the other hand, if the principal rules with an iron hand and teachers are afraid to admit the existence of problems out of a fear they will be thought failures, curriculum change has less of a chance to take root.

CENTRAL OFFICE LEADERSHIP

Personnel in the central administrative offices of schools and private firms with training and development divisions exercise an important influence over implementation of curriculum change. This influence may be expressed in several ways. For example, if an innovation requires new or different instructional materials, a commitment by central office administrators to supply these materials in appropriate quantities suggests to teachers that the innovation is backed with the full faith of top leaders. Their support gives credibility to the proposed change.

Curriculum changes often require teachers to change existing patterns of behavior or to play unfamiliar roles. Special training may be required to provide them with this needed expertise. Action by central office administrators to allocate funds to pay for inservice training opportunities indicates that top leadership is serious about the changes and willing to spend money to prepare instructional personnel to implement them effectively.

CURRICULUM PROJECT LEADERS

Individuals who lead curriculum development projects have a great influence on how well the changes are implemented. First, they must earn the confidence and respect of the teachers who will be asked to implement the changes. Then they must articulate a project's general goals effectively and, at the same time, provide concrete, practical information to teachers about how the changes will affect the teachers' instructional practices (McLaughlin and Marsh, 1978).

TEACHERS AND SOME CONTEXTUAL BARRIERS TO CHANGE

How teachers view themselves has much to do with their reactions to change. A hallmark of a professional is an ability to weigh alternatives and to make a personal choice to commit or not to commit to an option. Education's literature and its development programs for newcomers have long sought to convince teachers that they are, indeed, professionals.

One side effect of this effort has been to encourage the view that teaching is very much a matter of personal judgment.

Individuals with this perspective are not inclined to commit immediately to instructional program changes suggested by others. This does not mean that teachers will not change. It does suggest, however, that something must be done to win their commitment. Consider the situation described in Figure 9-1.

It is not always easy for curriculum professionals to demonstrate a compelling need for change. Teachers recognize that many curricular innovations result from political motives. Pressure groups can influence school boards to adopt programs that may serve certain interests well but that are not unequivocally good for everyone. Sometimes waves of enthu-

---

FIGURE 9-1 "I Want to Do It My Way!"

Recently, these comments by a teacher were overheard in a faculty lounge:

> "I've been teaching chemistry for twenty years. My people have always done extremely well on the advanced-placement chemistry SAT tests. I feel like I know what I'm doing, and I think the results bear me out.
>
> "Now some genius at our state office has pushed through a regulation that 40 percent of my students' time is to be spent doing laboratory work. I think that's way too much. If I do it, I'm afraid my students' test scores will go down.
>
> "They've scheduled an inservice meeting for us Friday afternoon. We are supposed to learn how to implement the 40 percent requirement. I'll go, but I tell you I am going to fight this thing with everything I've got."

Suppose you are a curriculum leader in this teacher's district. It is your responsibility to convince this individual to abide by the new requirement. Identify at least three different approaches you might take:

1. _____
   _____
2. _____
   _____
3. _____
   _____

After you have completed this chapter, review your responses. Are there changes you would like to make? Are there some additional approaches you would like to add?

---

siasm give a certain aura to an innovation, and every school district feels it has to have it. In the 1960s and into the early 1970s, for example, there was a great rush to embrace team teaching. Yet little association between team teaching and achievement was demonstrated in the research literature (Armstrong, 1977). Even so, there was a general feeling that team teaching was good.

The research base pointing to effective instructional practice has grown tremendously in recent years. However, teachers recognize that many innovations continue to be supported more by enthusiasm than by logic. So long as this continues to happen, a good number of teachers will be suspicious of innovations. Curriculum specialists will be pressed to build a case for change that teachers can endorse on professional, not emotional, grounds.

Educational institutions are not highly independent; schools are creatures of a watchful public. Even in the private sector, schools are responsible to boards of directors who must give some attention to the desires of their paying clients. In industrial settings, educational training and development operations must not deviate from corporate guidelines.

Given the nature of educational institutions, it is little wonder that teachers may view proposals for change suspiciously. Commenting on this situation, Stiles and Robinson stated "education professionals, by the nature of their employment, are enslaved to the status quo; they are not free to advocate change, except of course to keep schools aligned with majority changes within the society itself" (Stiles and Robinson, 1973; p. 259). A teacher who identifies with a change that later proves to be unacceptable to the community controlling the schools may find his or her position in jeopardy.

This situation has interesting implications for curriculum developers who are concerned about securing commitment of a large number of teachers to a curricular change. The younger, less experienced teachers whom one might suspect to be less rooted in present practices than their older colleagues are sometimes extremely resistant to change. Untenured individuals also sense themselves to be vulnerable. They may be little inclined to do anything that might possibly draw negative administrative or community attention. Curriculum leaders often find it a better strategy to work with older, tenured teachers. Once these more experienced teachers commit to a new program, newer teachers feel more secure about endorsing the change.

THE IMPORTANT ISSUE OF INNOVATION CLARITY

Researchers have demonstrated that many teachers asked to accept a curriculum understand neither the substance of the innovation nor how they are supposed to implement it (Fullan and Pomfret, 1977). Sometimes developers of a new program provide teachers with only very general descriptions of what has been prepared. As a result, teachers may not understand rationales lying behind the innovation and specific role changes that will be required of them as they implement it.

There is a strong connection between the explicitness of the explanation to potential users and the degree of implementation of a curriculum change. Fullan and Pomfret diagrammed this relationship, as follows:

Low explicitness → User confusion → Low degree of
                   Lack of clarity   implementation*
                   Frustration

The failure to communicate clearly may result from time constraints and from unwarranted assumptions that potential users can fill in the gaps themselves. Curriculum leaders and others who have been directly involved in a curriculum-development project sometimes are so familiar with all aspects of a new program that they fail to recognize the problems of potential program users who have not benefited from participation in the curriculum-development effort.

Proper implementation of a new program will not occur unless individuals who will be using it are provided opportunities to learn about their special responsibilities. They cannot be expected to commit to the innovation without a sound understanding of their own roles. As Czajkowski and Patterson commented, "To the extent that some written or otherwise established curriculum has become internalized in a school's people, things, and interactions, it is likely to make a difference; to the extent that it hasn't become so, its value to that particular school is at best unrealized" (Czajkowski and Patterson, 1980; p. 162).

Provision of specific information alone will not assure a commitment of all teachers to a curriculum innovation. Individual instructors have varying needs and views about program changes. A variety of approaches may be necessary to secure commitment to an innovation from a large number of teachers. The section that follows introduces some general approaches.

SOME GENERAL WAYS OF ENCOURAGING A PERSON TO CHANGE

A number of years ago, Guba, a noted expert in curriculum and evaluation, suggested a variety of approaches that might be taken to encourage a person to adopt an innovation (Guba, 1968). Some ideas derived from Guba's thinking are introduced in the following subsections.

---

* M. Fullan and A. Pomfret. "Research on Curriculum and Instruction Implementation." *Review of Educational Research*, 1977, 47, 369. Copyright © 1977, American Educational Research Association.

THE TRAINING APPROACH

One way to view a potential user of an innovation is as someone who would use the innovation if he or she knew how, the premise being that ignorance is the barrier to change. The response, then, is to provide the individual with the background and expertise needed in order to implement the innovation. Inservice training, workshops, and one-on-one counseling with teachers are reflective of things curriculum specialists do who are motivated by the training argument.

THE MODELING APPROACH

The modeling approach is a specific variation of the training approach. This approach presumes that teachers will be more willing to adopt a program change if they see it being used successfully in their own building by a teacher they know and respect.

Where the modeling approach is used, it is typical for well-respected and talented teachers from each building where a new program is to be implemented to serve on the curriculum-revision team. These individuals are involved in all aspects of development of the new program. Often such people become strongly committed to the change, and many will become enthusiastic users once it is developed. They can then serve as models for others in their buildings, providing specialized assistance and, as importantly, encouragement to others. Their commitment can help "sell" the new program.

THE LOGIC APPROACH

The logic approach presumes that a person who has not adopted or who has not decided to adopt a new curriculum innovation does not understand the change. Since he or she is presumed to be acting out of ignorance, the prescription is thought to be rational argument in support of the innovation. Curriculum specialists convinced that the difficulty is a lack of basic understanding build strong, data-backed cases that support the efficacy of the proposed change.

THE BUREAUCRATIC APPROACH

Educational institutions are bureaucracies in which some individuals have authority over others. Those with authority have the power to dispense certain favors to those who behave "properly" and to impose certain sanctions against those who do not. If a teacher proves reluctant to adopt a given curricular change that has been duly authorized by constituted authority, the curriculum leadership in a school district may seek

FIGURE 9-2   Influential Professional Organizations and the Curriculum

Professional groups within education often take stands regarding the kinds of experiences learners should get in school. Teachers who are members or supporters of these organizations may be influenced by their perspectives. When an organization supports a particular curriculum change, this information can be used by curriculum leaders as evidence that the change has support at the national level.

Suppose that a new social studies program had been designed that included lessons that were divided about equally between those intended to build an appreciation for and loyalty to the United States and those intended to point out some of our country's problems and shortcomings. The following statement from the Report of the National Council for the Social Studies Task Force on Scope and Sequence might help curriculum leaders to win support for the change:

> It is assumed that teachers will be sensitive to the dual—and often contradictory—thrusts of social studies education in a democratic society; namely, *socialization* and *social criticism*. A degree of social cohesiveness is needed in order to allow a society to function; yet, it must not be such as to repress necessary dissension, which on occasion may be unpleasant and not socially acceptable. The challenge to education in a democratic society is to steer a course that will ensure necessary socialization of citizens and foster that spark of social criticism that has kept the lamp of liberty ignited for over two centuries.

Source: "In Search of a Scope and Sequence for Social Studies," *Social Education, 48* (April 1984): 253.

the help of the principal and the teacher's department head. These individuals will be asked to do what they can to influence the teacher to adopt the approved change.

The bureaucratic approach depends for its success upon school leaders who, themselves, are committed to change. It also has the danger of alienating the teacher. There may be token compliance, but it may not result in enthusiastic teacher endorsement of the change.

THE AFFILIATION APPROACH

Many teachers are members of professional groups in education. Some of these are large national organizations embracing teachers in all subject areas and at all grade levels, while others serve narrower interests of teachers who work with certain categories of learners (elementary, secondary, gifted and talented, and so forth) or with specific academic subjects. Sometimes the journals of professional organizations and their influential members take a stand in favor of a particular kind of program organization or a particular instructional procedure. If teachers' professional organizations and their influential members support changes similar to those included in a given curriculum revision project, curriculum specialists may urge teachers to embrace the change because leaders in the field support it. Note the example of a position statement adopted by the National Council for the Social Studies in Figure 9–2.

In the real world of curriculum change, many avenues must be tried in the effort to gain wide acceptance for the innovation. Strategies adopted by curriculum leaders often will include several of the basic approaches just discussed.

Over the years, many individuals have studied the problem of implementing change. One general scheme that has been much discussed involves the use of change agents.

CHANGE AGENTS AND IMPLEMENTATION OF NEW CURRICULA

Rogers writes that "a change agent . . . [is] a person who attempts to influence an adoption decision in a direction that he feels is desirable" (Rogers, 1962; p. 254). The change agent works as a liaison between those who prepared a new curriculum and those who must use it. He or she may be the curriculum specialist who directed the project, although this is not necessarily so. The basic requirement for a change agent is that he or she be highly credible with individuals who are being asked to change familiar ways of doing things to embrace something new.

Change agents do not all approach their tasks in the same way. The subsections that follow describe approaches that some change agents have found fruitful.

CONSIDERING TEACHERS' PAST EXPERIENCES

Generally, the more profound the change demanded by an innovation the more difficult it is to sell. Successful change agents, recognizing this fact, attempt to capitalize on features of the change that represent little, if any, break with practices familiar to the teacher.

For example, suppose that a new program in state geography and history divided the state into five regions for purposes of study. The old program may have divided the state into four regions. Insightful change agents recognize that teachers have files of materials, including tests and map exercises, designed around the assumption of there being four regions. The change agent might ask for samples of some of these materials. Then, he or she might show the teacher how these items could be used in the new program with only minor modification.

Teachers who have been teaching certain content for a long time in a certain way may take some natural pride in what they have been doing. A proposed innovation, if it is not introduced with care, may be taken as a negative comment on the existing program. Change agents must take time to point out how the new change builds on some very real strengths of the old. Any suggestion that the previous program was weak or "bad" is likely to produce hostility, so careful change agents work hard to avoid this implication.

CONSIDERING WHY THE TEACHER SHOULD WANT A CHANGE

Though individuals involved in a curriculum-development project may see an obvious need for change, many teachers who are asked to implement it may feel otherwise. Successful change agents are often people who can help initially reluctant teachers perceive the need for modifications included within a program revision.

Sometimes this will require an indirect approach, as an attempt to sell the new program may run into a wall of resistance. Some teachers, however, may be quite willing to discuss general problems they are having with the existing program. Prompted by appropriate questions, these individuals may be willing to elaborate on a number of weak areas in their present programs, such as dated materials, inappropriate readability levels, or deficient materials for evaluating students.

A discussion of this kind can result in a teacher generating quite a list of "like to haves," which can then be used by the change agent as he or she begins to suggest how the revised curriculum responds specifically to each need cited by the teacher. This approach moves the discussion away from the general desirability of the new program to a more specific focus on how it might respond to particular teacher needs. Many change agents have found that this kind of needs-based discussion will lead initially reluctant teachers to adopt an innovation.

CONSIDERING THE IMPACT OF OPINION LEADERS

Within every instructional setting, some teachers are leaders. They usually do not owe their status to any official standing within the school, but this by no means undermines their very real status and considerable influence.

Sometimes this status accrues to teachers who have been teaching in a building for a long time. Other times the leaders are people who are active in professional organizations. Still others are people who have gained respect because of a willingness to serve on committees and to work with student activities of various kinds.

These individuals' opinions tend to be given great credence by other members of the instructional staff. They are listened to in faculty lounge discussions. Their advice is sought, and their counsel is often taken. Consequently their views on a curriculum revision can be of critical importance. When such individuals support a change, its implementation is smoothed; when they do not, other teachers, too, are likely to find fault with the new program.

Change agents often try to identify opinion leaders within schools where a new curricular program is to be introduced. This usually requires spending time in the faculty lounge and in classrooms visiting informally with teachers. District and school administrative organization charts do not reveal teacher opinion leaders. A change agent must get to know the teachers themselves before he or she can appreciate the informal deference paid to the views of these unofficial leaders.

When opinion leaders are identified, change agents make concerted efforts to win their support. This may require a great deal of work, but in the long run, will probably provide a shortcut to achieving the smooth implementation of a change. Once the opinion leaders are convinced, often other teachers will begin to find favor with the innovation. Hence, a successful discussion with one opinion leader may take the place of a dozen conversations with other less influential teachers.

CONSIDERING UNINTENDED CONSEQUENCES OF AN INNOVATION

The implementation of a curriculum program may have an impact that reaches beyond the teachers responsible for teaching it. For example, teachers in a new program may be provided with new texts, new supplementary teaching materials, and other useful instructional aids. This can breed resentment among other teachers in a building who may have to limp along with old and inadequate learning resources.

The new materials situation can be both positive and negative. On the one hand, reluctant adopters of the innovation may be encouraged to embrace the change because if they do, they will have new materials with which to work. On the other hand, teachers in other curricular areas may resent the expenditure of money on instructional resources to support a revision of a school program in which they are not personally involved. Consequently, relationships between teachers associated with the new program and those who are not may become strained.

To guard against this possibility, change agents must consider the attitudes of all teachers in a building where a new program is to be implemented. To the extent possible, they need to work with principals and central office administrators to provide some meaningful indication to teachers not involved in the new program that they are important. For example, inservice programs and new materials purchases should be directed at a broad spectrum of teachers, not just at those individuals in subject areas to be served by a new program. Such a policy will encourage an appreciation among teachers that the district is sensitive to all of their needs and that program improvement in one area reflects credit on them all. Consider the situation posed in Figure 9-3.

FIGURE 9-3   Side Effects of a New Program

The following news article recently appeared in a local newspaper:

New Physics Program Up and Running

After three years of waiting, the new physics program is "on line" at Central High School. Each teacher in the building has received 45 clock hours of training. For this purpose, local engineering firms contributed funds to bring in Dr. Hans Mueller from M.I.T. This summer, teachers received special state funding to attend summer seminars at M.I.T. and at selected other institutions in the Northeast.

New textbooks and approximately 60,000 dollars' worth of new laboratory equipment have been distributed to physics teachers in the building. Two new physics consultants have been hired to assist teachers in implementing the program.

At midyear, participating teachers will be guests at a National Science Foundation seminar. The new program will be reviewed at this time. Superintendent Miller noted that 35,000 dollars is being held back in anticipation of program improvement needs that may be evident after teachers have had one semester to "shake down" the new program.

Suppose you are a curriculum leader in this school district. How would you respond to the following?

1. Concerns of physics teachers at other high schools that their needs are being overlooked in favor of teachers at the administration's "favorite" school, Central High.
2. Comments of teachers in other subject areas that the district fails to appreciate the importance of what they are doing.
3. Worries that the "costly" physics program will delay curriculum improvement in other areas.

INNOVATIONS: TEACHERS' CONCERNS AND LEVELS OF USE

Fuller found that individuals preparing for careers as teachers had different concerns about their training needs at different points in their professional preparation program. She found that these concerns followed a predictable sequence. In the phase of the teacher preparation program prior to student teaching, she found that most students were characterized by an attitude of "nonconcern" about student teaching. During early phases of student teaching, there was a shift to "concerns about self." This period was characterized by students questioning their ability to control learners and to manage the many tasks that must be accomplished to get through the school day. Only during the latter part of student teaching did students develop "concerns about pupils and begin to worry about the impact of their instruction on learners" (Fuller, 1969).

Fuller's work was expanded by researchers at the Research and Development Center for Teacher Education when it was located at the University of Texas. The idea that concerns change developmentally was applied to educational innovations in general. Implications of this finding for program implementation were reflected in the Concerns-Based Adoption Model (CBAM) (Hall, Wallace, and Dossett, 1973; Hall, George, and Rutherford, 1977; Hall and Loucks, 1978).

The CBAM model focused on two general areas. The first, stages of concerns (SoC), looked at the issue of teachers' personal concerns related to an innovation. The second, levels of use (LoU), investigated the way teachers were using an innovation.

STAGES OF CONCERN

Seven stages of concern about an innovation have been identified, described, and tested by researchers of the CBAM model (Hall, Wallace, and Dossett, 1973; Hall and Rutherford, 1976; Hall and Loucks, 1978; James, 1981). These stages and descriptions of each are provided in Figure 9–4.

These stages are important for individuals charged with overseeing implementation of curriculum changes. Curriculum specialists and others who have been closely associated with a curriculum development effort may be very interested in how this change will affect learners. Indeed, the whole impetus for the curriculum project may have been a feeling that the present program was not serving learners' needs well.

The CBAM model suggests that, initially, impact-on-learners issues may not be high on the list of concerns of teachers who will be asked to use a new program. Therefore, the temptation to sell an innovation to prospective teachers on the grounds that it will be "good for the students" may not always be the most productive approach.

Some research suggests that even teachers who have some experi-

FIGURE 9-4   Stages of Concern

0 *Awareness:* Little concern about or involvement with the innovation is indicated.

1 *Informational:* A general awareness of the innovation and interest in learning more detail about it is indicated. The person seems to be unworried about himself/herself in relation to the innovation. She/he is interested in substantive aspects of the innovation in a selfless manner such as general characteristics, effects, and requirements for use.

2 *Personal:* Individual is uncertain about the demands of the innovation, his/her inadequacy to meet those demands, and his/her role with the innovation. This includes analysis of his/her role in relation to the reward structure of the organization, decision making, and consideration of potential conflicts with existing structures or personal commitment. Financial or status implications of the program for self and colleagues may also be reflected.

3 *Management:* Attention is focused on the processes and tasks of using the innovation and the best use of information and resources. Issues related to efficiency, organizing, managing, scheduling, and time demands are utmost.

4 *Consequence:* Attention focuses on impact of the innovation on students in his/her immediate sphere of influence. The focus is on relevance of the innovation for students, evaluation of student outcomes, including performance and competencies, and changes needed to increase student outcomes.

5 *Collaboration:* The focus is on coordination and cooperation with others regarding use of the innovation.

6 *Refocusing:* The focus is on exploration of more universal benefits from the innovation, including the possibility of major changes or replacement with a more powerful alternative. Individual has definite ideas about alternatives to the proposed or existing form of the innovation.

Source: Reprinted by permission of the publisher from Hall & Loucks, "Teacher Concerns as a Basis for Facilitating and Personalizing Staff Development," in Lieberman & Miller, eds. — *Staff Development: New Demands, New Realities, New Perspectives* (originally published as *Teachers College Record*, Vol. 80, No. 1, September 1978). (New York: Teachers College Press, © 1979 by Teachers College, Columbia University. All rights reserved.), 41.

ence with an innovation have other concerns that are much more intense than those associated with its impact on learners. Hall and Rutherford (1976), in a study involving the innovation of team teaching, found that teachers who had not used it were overwhelmingly more concerned with informational, personal, and management issues (stage 1, 2, and 3 concerns) than with other concerns. Those teachers who had had an opportunity to use the innovation for one, two, or three years were most concerned about managing it in the classroom (stage 3). Impact on learners (stage 4), concerns about working with others in using the innovation (stage 5), and ideas about modifying the innovation (stage 6) were lower priorities than management concerns even for teachers with two, three, or four years' experience in using the innovation.

These findings suggest that information responding to teachers' personal and management concerns about an innovation should be a very high priority for those facilitating implementation. In planning for presentations of an innovation to teachers who are unfamiliar with it but who will be asked to use it, an information checklist can be quite useful. The checklist consists of questions that prompt the organization of information to be included in the presentation. The checklist should be designed so as to place heavy emphases on teachers' personal and managerial concerns. Items such as the following might well be included:

_____ How will a teacher's personal day be changed by the innovation?

_____ How much additional preparation time will the innovation require?

_____ How much paperwork will be involved in implementing and monitoring the innovation?

_____ How will the innovation "fit in" to the content to which learners have already been exposed?

_____ What kinds of teacher resource materials will be provided?

_____ Will resource materials be in each teacher's room, in a separate room in the school, at the central administration building, or at some other location?

_____ What kinds of new learning materials will be provided for learners?

_____ Are reading levels and other characteristics of these materials clearly appropriate for learners to be served?

_____ What patterns of teacher-learner interaction will be demanded?

_____ Will any required instructional procedures demand teaching techniques teachers have not already mastered?

_____ What kinds of inservice training will be provided?

_____ What is the relationship of the innovation to standardized tests learners must take?

_____ What allowances are there going to be for possible declines in standardized test scores resulting from an instructional program new to teachers and learners alike?

_____ What are implications of the new program for classroom management?

_____ How strong is the central district administration's commitment to the support of the new program?

_____ To what extent are principals familiar with elements of the new program and able to assist teachers in implementing it?

_____ Who, specifically, can be called upon for help if there are problems regarding implementation of the innovation?

_____ Will this person be willing to visit individual classrooms?

_____ What school library and media resources are there to support the new program?

_____ To what extent do parents know about and support the new program?

_____ What are the implications of the new program in terms of classroom management?

Items on this checklist are just examples of those that might be developed to ensure that teachers' personal and management concerns are addressed. When they are, teachers are more likely to commit to a curriculum innovation.

LEVELS OF USE

The success of an innovation depends not only on convincing people to adopt it, but on how the adoption works once it is in place. The levels of use developed by researchers in the Concerns-Based Adoption Model project can provide important insights for curriculum leaders. These levels are depicted in Figure 9-5.

Levels of use are important because judgments of an innovation's worth tend to assume that it has been implemented as designed. Some research suggests a reality that is quite different. Even though individuals have been provided with identical information and similar training, teachers tend to modify the innovation to meet their own needs. Furthermore, some individuals will be able to take full advantage of an innovation's potential, while others will go mechanically through the steps minimally necessary to be in compliance with an administrative mandate to follow the new program.

One important study that looked at behaviors of a large number of teachers found that fully one-fifth of those who were supposed to be using an innovation were "nonusers" (Hall and Loucks, 1977). In a related study, 63 percent of teachers who had not been introduced to an innovation featuring individualized instruction were, in fact, using individualized instruction in their classrooms (Hall and Loucks, 1977).

This information points out some difficulties associated with examining the real impact of educational innovations. To provide a fair assessment, it is imperative that curriculum specialists have some information

FIGURE 9-5   Levels of Use of an Innovation

Level of Use	*Definition of Use*
0 Non-use	State in which the user has little or no knowledge of the innovation, no involvement with the innovation, and is doing nothing toward becoming involved.
1 Orientation	State in which the user has recently acquired or is acquiring information about the innovation and/or has recently explored or is exploring its value orientation and its demands upon user and user system.
2 Preparation	State in which the user is preparing for first use of the innovation.
3 Mechanical	State in which the user focuses most effort on the short-term, day-to-day use of the innovation with little time for reflection. Changes in use are made more to meet user needs than client needs. The user is primarily engaged in a stepwise attempt to master the tasks required to use the innovation, often resulting in disjointed and superficial use.
4a Routine	Use of the innovation is stabilized. Few, if any, changes are being made in ongoing use. Little preparation or thought is being given to improving innovation use or its consequences.
4b Refinement	State in which the user varies the use of the innovation to increase the impact on clients within the immediate sphere of influence. Variations are based on knowledge of both short- and long-term consequences for clients.
5 Integration	State in which the user is combining own efforts to use the innovation with related activities of colleagues to achieve a collective impact on clients within their common sphere of influence.
6 Renewal	State in which the user reevaluates the quality of use of the innovation to achieve increased impact on clients, examine new developments in the field, and explore new goals for self and the system.

Source: Adapted from Gene E. Hall and Susan F. Loucks. "A Development Model for Determining Whether the Treatment Is Actually Implemented." *American Educational Research Journal, 14* (Summer, 1977): 263–276. Copyright © 1977, American Educational Research Association.

about how an innovation is being implemented (See Chapter 10 for a more detailed treatment of this issue). Furthermore, if a comparison is to be made between users and nonusers, there must be some assurance that those labeled "nonusers" are not incorporating many features of the innovation in their own instruction.

Loucks, Newlove, and Hall (1975) developed a focused interview to ask users of an innovation about how they were using it. Responses were used to assign teachers to one of the levels of use depicted in Figure 9–5.

Whether they use a formal interview schedule or some less formal means, individuals responsible for curriculum development and adoption need to develop means of determining how each user is working with an innovation. The specific level of use can then provide guidelines for individual staff development, with the goal of helping as many teachers as possible to use the innovation properly.

Because teachers' levels of use have been found to vary so much, little is to be gained by forcing all of them to go through the same staff development program. Differentiated program planning keyed to individuals' particular levels of use makes good sense. An exercise focusing on developing differentiated staff training is provided in Figure 9–6.

FIGURE 9-6   Staff Development and Levels of Use

In a school district that has been using a curricular innovation for one or two years, different teachers are likely to be at different levels of use. Individuals at different levels will need different kinds of inservice training. The objective is to help as many teachers as possible to use the innovation as it was designed.

Identify an innovation. Then, suggest kinds of inservice activities that might be appropriate for teachers found to be at each of the following levels of use.

Innovation _____

Levels of Use	*Proposed Staff Development Activity*
0 Non-use	
1 Orientation	
2 Preparation	
3 Mechanical	
4a Routine	
4b Refinement	
5 Integration	
6 Renewal	

Research on teachers' levels of use of innovations has revealed that levels change over time. There is a tendency for teachers to move beyond level 3, mechanical use, to higher levels over a period of years (Hall and Loucks, 1977; 271). An important implication of this finding is that innovations take time to take root. Curriculum leaders need to work with administrators and others to give teachers adequate time to become familiar and comfortable with an innovation. If there is an attempt to assess the value of an innovation too soon, the results may not provide a fair measure of its worth.

ANALYSIS OF PROGRAM USE AND INSERVICE PLANNING

The degree to which a given teacher feels comfortable with an innovation is not always a reliable indicator that the innovation is being properly delivered. All instructors must take some action to fit an instructional program to their own classroom settings. In many cases this does not interfere with the integrity of the innovation. Sometimes, though, these changes may alter a component so critical to the innovation that its basic character is altered. Curriculum leaders have a responsibility to see that this does not happen. (If it does, their ability to assess the innovation's worth will again be impaired.)

Hall and Loucks (1981) suggest that every innovation has certain *essential* components and certain *related* components. The essential components are those that cannot be changed without undermining the nature of the innovation itself. For example, in team teaching, the feature of sharing of planning and instructional responsibilities is essential. Without it, there can be no team teaching.

On the other hand, there are some practices that individuals who use an innovation may choose or choose not to incorporate. For example, the number of large group and small group sessions in a given semester may vary from one team teaching program to another. This kind of discretionary difference that does not alter the basic nature of team teaching is referred to as a related component of the innovation.

To plan inservice activities to support a new innovation, curriculum leaders need information regarding several key issues. First, they must identify clearly the essential components of the innovation. Second, they need to ascertain the degree to which these essential components are included in what teachers using the program are doing in the school. Third, they need to plan inservice activities for individual teachers that emphasize essential components found to be absent from these teachers' own instructional programs. A three-step process, adapted and simplified from a proposal developed by Hall and Loucks (1981), is introduced here.

STEP 1: IDENTIFY THE ESSENTIAL
COMPONENTS OF THE INNOVATION

As a first step, the essential components of the innovation must be identified. To do this, curriculum specialists and other experts involved in the development of the innovation need to be queried. Teachers who participated in the development of the innovation, who thoroughly understand it, and who are among those implementing it in the schools also need to be questioned. A number of prompt questions can be asked to elicit comments that will help to bring the innovation's critical components into focus. Some examples are: "What are the key features of the innovation?" "Are there some things that, if eliminated, would destroy the basic character of the innovation?" "What would a person always expect to see in classrooms where this innovation is in use?"

Analysis of these questions can lead to a short list of essential components. This list should be restricted as much as possible to those features without which the innovation loses its fundamental character.

STEP 2: DEVELOP AND
ADMINISTER CHECKLISTS

The essential components that have been identified can be used as a basis for preparing innovation checklists. These will be completed by all teachers who are using the innovation.

Suppose a school district had implemented a new component of the grade 11 social studies program involving an innovative treatment of the topic, "Immigration." Discussions with curriculum specialists, subject matter experts, and teachers who had participated in its development were held. Analyses of their comments led to the development of the following list of essential characteristics of the innovation.

- Learning resources were to be broadened beyond the textbook to include films, photographs, art prints, reproductions of late nineteenth-century journal articles, and selections from novels dealing with immigration.
- Instruction was to be organized in such a way that at least 60 percent of the instructional time would be composed of student-to-student interactions in small groups.
- Writing skills were to be emphasized, and each student was to provide at least one writing sample for each objective related to immigration.
- Speaking skills were to be emphasized, and each student was to make at least one short oral presentation related to each immigration objective.
- Tests were to be developed in such a way that individual items could be specifically tied to each objective related to immigration.

These essential components sort into five basic categories: (1) learning resources, (2) grouping and patterns of teacher-learner interaction, (3) development of writing skills, (4) development of speaking skills, and (5) testing procedures. These categories can be used to develop an innovation checklist. Under each heading, there should be opportunities for teachers to check patterns consistent with what developers of the innovations have described as essential as well as patterns that deviate from the "essential" ones. Figure 9-7 is an example of such a checklist.

FIGURE 9-7 Checklist to Determine Use of Essential Components of an Innovation

1. *Learning Resources*

   Place a check by each that you regularly use in your program.
   _____ films
   _____ textbooks
   _____ photographs
   _____ art prints
   _____ selections from novels
   _____ reproductions of journal articles
   _____ other (specify): _____
   _____

2. *Grouping and Patterns of Teacher-Learner Interaction*

   In the blank, indicate the approximate percentage of time you use each of the following arrangements:

   _____ teacher-to-student interaction when students are organized in a large group
   _____ teacher-to-student interaction when students are organized in a number of small groups
   _____ student-to-student interaction when students are organized in a number of small groups
   _____ other (please specify): _____
   _____

3. *Development of Writing Skills*

   Please check which of the following characterizes your classroom.

   _____ Students turn in at least one written assignment for each objective related to immigration.
   _____ Students turn in several written assignments, but not necessarily one for each objective related to immigration.
   _____ Students turn in one or more written assignments, but these are not related to any immigration objectives.
   _____ other (please specify): _____
   _____

(Continues)

FIGURE 9-7   *(Continued)*

4. *Development of Speaking Skills*

   Please check which of the following characterizes your classroom:

   _____ Students give one oral presentation for each objective related to immigration.

   _____ Students give several oral presentations, but not necessarily one for each objective related to immigration.

   _____ Students give one or more oral presentations, but these are not related to any immigration objectives.

   _____ other (please specify): _____

   _____

5. *Testing Procedures*

   _____ Tests are given so that all items relate to one or more immigration objectives.

   _____ Tests are given so that some items relate to one or more immigration objectives.

   _____ Tests are given, but they do not tie directly to any immigration objectives.

   _____ other (please specify): _____

   _____

STEP 3: ANALYZE CHECKLIST RESULTS AND PLAN INSERVICE PROGRAMS

Data gathered from a checklist, such as the example provided in Figure 9-7, can be used to plan inservice and staff development programs designed to promote effective use of an innovative program. These analyses will reveal the extent to which teachers are deviating from practices thought to be essential to the innovation. Furthermore, the specific essential components that are being ignored can be identified.

In some instances, these analyses may reveal that large numbers of teachers are failing to implement some key feature of a new program. There are many reasons that might explain why this feature of the innovation is not being implemented. For example, if large numbers of teachers were found not to be using extracts from novels, photographs, or art prints, the possibility exists that, for some reason, these learning resources were not made available to them.

It is the responsibility of the curriculum leader to determine the reason for a teacher's failure to use an essential program component. This inquiry may reveal a need for additional inservice and staff development work. When large numbers of individuals are experiencing a common difficulty, sessions can be planned on scheduled inservice days. In this event, invitations should be generally restricted to teachers who have been identified as not using an essential feature of the innovation. Invitations to others who are doing a perfectly acceptable job may breed resentment. No one appreciates being taught again how to do what he or she is already doing.

In cases where analyses reveal some problems to be restricted to small numbers of teachers, remediation can take the form of individual conferences with teachers in their respective buildings. This can be done unobtrusively and comfortably in a nonthreatening setting.

The basic idea behind the checklist procedure is to enable curriculum leaders to tailor inservice development to the demonstrated needs of individuals. This procedure conserves scarce inservice and staff development resources by concentrating on individuals with clearly identified needs. It also has the potential to further emphasize the essential components of an innovation. When these essentials are adhered to, there is a much better probability that a fair assessment of the innovation will result. In addition when curriculum specialists focus on a very restricted number of innovation essentials they convey the message that, beyond these essentials, teachers are free to make whatever adaptations are needed to make the program a success with their own learners.

SUMMARY

Generally, the larger the number of people who must work with an innovation, the more challenges posed to curriculum leaders charged with overseeing its implementation. This particularly tends to be true when large numbers of users have not been directly involved in developing the innovation.

A number of key individuals play important roles in smoothing the way for curriculum implementation. Building principals are especially important. Their comments in behalf of teachers who will be adopting a change provide much needed psychological support. Central office personnel, through expressions of support and assurances of adequate supplies of needed resources, can also ease the transition to a new program. Finally, curriculum specialists who enjoy the confidence of teachers and who can speak clearly to teachers' concerns can help teachers commit to a curriculum change.

A number of contextual barriers make change in school settings difficult. For one thing, the professional culture of education tends to support the view that much of teaching is a matter of individual judgment. As a result, many teachers are predisposed to question changes suggested by others who lack the teachers' perspective on the unique nature of their instructional settings.

Teachers, too, are sensitive that some innovations are promoted for political, not professional, motives. Likewise since the schools operate within a political context, teachers may be wary of committing to an innovation that, at some future time, may be found objectionable by a new group of school board members. Untenured teachers particularly may resist changes that, in their view, make them vulnerable and, hence, may threaten their future employment security.

Teachers asked to implement curriculum innovations sometimes find that explanations of what they are to do lack clarity. Curriculum specialists and others who have been intimately associated with a curriculum-development project may make assumptions that others, who have not been involved, know as much about the change as they do. When teachers are not provided with highly specific information regarding their roles, there is a danger that they will fail to implement the change or that they will implement it improperly.

The change-agent approach is one that often has been used to smooth the transition between new and old instructional programs. Change agents take advantage of teachers' past experiences, utilize the influence of opinion leaders, and take other actions to facilitate adoption of an innovation.

The Concerns-Based Adoption Model project has focused on a number of processes associated with selected change. Researchers associated with the project have identified seven stages of concern associated with an innovation. An important implication of these stages for curriculum leaders is that, initially, many teachers are much more concerned with how an innovation is going to change their personal and professional lives than how it is going to affect learners. This suggests that initial inservice efforts place a heavy emphasis on teachers' personal concerns.

Other research has identified a number of levels of use of a curriculum innovation. One important finding of this research is that it takes time for a curriculum change to take root. Initially, many teachers go through the change in a mechanical way as they try to implement each component of an innovation. It may take several years for teachers to become truly comfortable with a changed set of procedures. This points out a need to allow innovations to function for some time before attempting to evaluate their worth.

Inservice activities that are directed toward specific needs of individual teachers are better suited to supporting change than those directed at all involved teachers. One procedure for establishing such inservice programs begins with identifying the critical elements of an innovation. Then teachers are surveyed to determine the extent to which they include these critical elements in what they are doing. Teachers who are not using one or more critical elements are identified, and inservice and staff development programs are developed that respond to the needs of these individuals.

EXTENDING AND APPLYING CHAPTER CONTENT

1. Suppose you had directed a large curriculum development project in a school district. Specifically, what actions would you take to assure that principals and central office administrators conveyed their support of the change to teachers? Prepare a plan of action in which you describe what you would do to accomplish these purposes:
    a. educating principals about the change and gaining their active support for it
    b. providing principals with strategies they might use to support teachers who will be teaching in the revised program
    c. obtaining a specific commitment from central office leadership that they will assure teachers that the district is solidly behind the change
    d. assuring that central office administrators will commit funds needed to buy materials needed to support the new program
    Present your plan to your class in the form of an oral report. Your instructor may wish to use this report as a basis for a classroom discussion focusing on the roles school and district leaders play in curricular change.
2. There are a number of contextual barriers to change that can impede implementation of a curriculum innovation. Organize a panel of curriculum specialists who have led large-scale curriculum revision projects. Ask them to comment on the specific actions they have taken to overcome these barriers. Ask them, too, to share their views regarding whether the kinds of barriers they faced tended to be specific to their own professional situations or whether they tended to be general sorts of obstacles faced by curriculum leaders everywhere.
3. Identify three curriculum innovations from the professional literature. Suppose you were in charge of an effort to implement these innovations. For each innovation, prepare as carefully worded a description as possible of precisely what teachers will have to do to implement the new program. Remember that teachers want very explicit information. Do not hesitate to provide plenty of details. Submit your descriptive information to the course instructor for review.
4. Identify a curriculum innovation that you, as a curriculum leader, might be interested in implementing in a school district. Share your innovation with your class. Explain the innovation carefully. Then, as a class, engage in a brainstorming activity in which you identify as many possible unintended results as you can that might be expected when the change

is implemented. Look over the list of possibilities that results from this activity. As a class, identify the five most serious potential problems. For each, decide upon a plan of action. Discuss alternatives as a class.

5. Interview a teacher who has been working with a new program for less than a year. From your interview, try to determine the nature of the teacher's concerns. Take notes. Bring these to class and share them with others. As a class decide which stage of concern is most clearly represented by the teacher's comments. Given this stage of concern, what kind of staff development activities might be appropriate for this teacher and why?

BIBLIOGRAPHY

Armstrong, David G. 1977. "Team Teaching and Academic Achievement." *Review of Educational Research, 47*, (Winter): 65–86.

Bradley, Leo H. 1985. *Curriculum Leadership and Development Handbook.* Englewood Cliffs, N.J.: Prentice-Hall.

Czajkowski, Theodore J. and Jerry L. Patterson. 1984. "Curriculum Change and the School." *Considered Action for Curriculum Improvement.* Edited by Arthur W. Foshay. 1980 ASCD Yearbook. Alexandria, Va.: Association for Supervision and Curriculum Development, pp. 158–175.

Fullan, Michael and Alan Pomfret. 1977. "Research on Curriculum and Instruction Implementation." *Review of Educational Research, 47*, (Summer): 335–397.

Fuller, Frances F. 1969. "Concerns of Teachers: A Developmental Conceptualization." *American Educational Research Journal, 6*, (March): 207–226.

Good, Thomas L. and Jere E. Brophy. 1987. *Looking in Classrooms*, 4th ed. New York: Harper & Row.

Guba, Egon C. 1968. "Diffusion of Innovations." *Educational Leadership, 25*, (January): 292–295.

Hall, Gene E., A. A. George, and William L. Rutherford. 1977. *Measuring Stages of Concern About the Innovation: A Manual for Use of the SoC Questionnaire.* Austin, Tex.: Research and Development Center for Teacher Education, The University of Texas.

Hall, Gene E., Shirley M. Hord, William L. Rutherford, and Leslie L. Huling. 1984. "Change in High Schools: Rolling Stones or Asleep at the Wheel?" *Educational Leadership, 41*, (March): 58–62.

Hall, Gene E. and Susan F. Loucks. 1977. "A Developmental Model for Determining Whether the Treatment Is Actually Implemented." *American Educational Research Journal, 14*, (Summer): 263–276.

Hall, Gene E. and Susan F. Loucks. 1978. *Innovation Configurations: Analyzing the Adaptations of Innovations.* Austin, Tex.: Research and Development Center for Teacher Education, The University of Texas.

Hall, Gene E. and Susan F. Loucks. 1981. "Program Definition and Adaptation: Implications for Inservice." *Journal of Research and Development in Education, 14*, (Winter): 46–58.

Hall, Gene E., Susan F. Loucks, William L. Rutherford, and Beulah W. Newlove. 1975. "Levels of Use of the Innovation: A Framework for Analyzing Innovation Adoption." *Journal of Teacher Education, 26*, (Spring): 52–55.

Hall, Gene E. and William L. Rutherford. 1976. "Concerns of Teachers About Implementing Team Teaching." *Educational Leadership, 34,* (December): 227–233.

Hall, Gene E., R. C. Wallace, Jr., and W. A. Dossett. 1973. *A Developmental Conceptualization of the Adoption Process Within Educational Institutions.* Austin, Tex.: Research and Development Center for Teacher Education, The University of Texas.

James, Robert K. 1981. "Understanding Why Curriculum Innovations Succeed or Fail." *School Science and Mathematics, 81,* (October): 487–494.

Joyce, Bruce R., Richard H. Hersh, and Michael McKibbin. 1983. *The Structure of School Improvement.* New York: Longman.

Loucks, Susan F., Beulah W. Newlove, and Gene E. Hall. 1975. *Measuring Levels of Use of the Innovation: A Manual for Trainers, Interviewers, and Raters.* Austin, Tex.: Research and Development Center for Teacher Education, The University of Texas.

McLaughlin, Milbrey W. and David G. Marsh. 1978. "Staff Development and School Change." *Teachers College Record, 80,* (September): 69–94.

Rogers, Everett. M. 1962. *Diffusion of Innovations.* New York: The Free Press.

Rutherford, William L. 1981. *Team Teaching—How Do Teachers Use It?* Rev. ed. Austin, Tex.: Research and Development Center for Teacher Education, The University of Texas.

Stiles, Lindley J. and Beecham Robinson. 1973. "Social Change in Education." *Processes and Phenomena of Social Change.* Edited by Gerald Zaltman. New York: John Wiley & Sons, pp. 257–280.

CHAPTER 10

Evaluating the Curriculum

This chapter introduces information to help the reader

1. describe early work in curriculum evaluation.
2. point out some contributions of Ralph Tyler to the field of curriculum evaluation.
3. suggest some criticisms that have been made of objectives-based evaluation.
4. identify some critical issues associated with program-improvement evaluation.
5. describe basic features of Daniel Stufflebeam's CIPP model.
6. point out some characteristics of Robert Stake's *responsive evaluation.*
7. indicate components of Malcolm Provus' *discrepancy evaluation* procedure.
8. describe purposes and characteristics of *adversary evaluation.*

INTRODUCTION

Evaluation is a judgmental process (Scriven, 1967). Measurement, on the other hand, is simply the gathering of information. Measurements of various kinds often are involved in evaluations, but they are not evaluations themselves. Evaluation requires an interpretive leap to an opinion that lies beyond the givens.

Because opinions are value laden, the same set of measurements may not always lead to the same evaluative conclusions. Different evaluators may make judgments based on quite different views as to what constitutes acceptable program performance. Evaluators differ regarding what should be judged, when it should be judged, and by whom it should be judged.

EARLY WORK IN CURRICULUM EVALUATION

The view that curriculum evaluation should focus specifically on learning objectives and the degree to which they have been mastered is less than sixty years old. Traditionally, educational evaluation often avoided any consideration of the specific subject matter being taught. Although subject matter tests occasionally were used, often they were little more than random collections of recall questions tied to information scattered throughout textbooks.

More frequently programs were evaluated on the basis of such variables as the numbers of books related to the subject area in the library or the academic qualifications of the teachers. Evaluators assumed a "trickle down" effect, resulting in better learning on the part of those learners attending schools with well-stocked libraries and well-prepared teachers.

EDUCATIONAL EVALUATION: THE WORK OF RALPH TYLER

Modern educational evaluation began with the work of Ralph Tyler in the 1930s (Stufflebeam and Shinkfield, 1985). Tyler observed that many program evaluations consisted of little more than learners' being asked random questions about the contents of their courses. During his work with the Progressive Education Association's Eight-Year Study (directed, among other things, at examining the impact on learners of teachers who taught specific problem-solving techniques), Tyler promoted the idea that specific learning objectives should be developed (Nowakowski, 1983).

Tyler wrote that "the process of evaluation begins with the objectives of the educational program" (Tyler, 1949; p. 110). He taught teachers to think about and articulate their instructional objectives, and he promoted the idea that evaluation properly seeks to ascertain the degree to which instructional objectives are mastered. Tyler is regarded as the father of modern educational evaluation.

SOME CONCERNS ABOUT TYING EVALUATION TO OBJECTIVES

During the late 1950s and into the 1960s, concerns began to emerge about objectives-based evaluation. One important question raised by critics focused on the selection of instructional objectives.

Within individual courses many possible objectives can be formulated. Some of these lend themselves more easily to formal measurement, or testing, than others. In particular, tests for less abstract kinds of content are easier to prepare than tests for more abstract kinds. (For example, in geography a test of the rather basic concepts *latitude* and *longitude* is less difficult to develop than one of more difficult concepts such as the *diffusion of innovations* or *chain migration.*)

Worries about the difficulty of constructing appropriate tests may encourage some teachers and instructors to develop objectives focusing on more concrete and, potentially, less important content. As a result, evaluation conceived of as measuring the achievement of objectives has the potential to diminish the intellectual rigor of instructional programs.

The growth of commercially produced standardized tests also has raised concerns about evaluation as mere measurement of establishment instructional objectives. Tyler, himself, emphasized developing objectives locally to fit specific teaching settings (Tyler, 1949). Widespread use of standardized tests has led to suspicions that some teachers, knowing their students will take these tests and that the scores will be examined by administrators and released to the public, will develop program objectives based on content reflected in the tests rather than on the real needs of local learners.

Another difficulty in developing objectives with a view to evaluating them with standardized tests involves how the results will be described. Many standardized tests yield only a single score. Even in the best of cases, only clusters of scores in certain subareas of the test, often called subscores, are reported. For example, in a standardized test on reading, there might be subscores on comprehension and reading rate.

This kind of reporting does not allow for fine-grained analysis. Tests prepared by teachers in light of personally developed objectives better lend themselves to item-by-item review. Then if a learner misses a single question, the test results can be used to pinpoint the specific content element that proved to be a problem.

Although Tyler emphasized the importance of developing objectives locally to meet the needs of specific learners, this is not always easy to do. It is particularly difficult when new, innovative programs are introduced. Often teachers, administrators, and others have only very general ideas about what kinds of objectives and degrees of proficiency should be established for learners. Consider some of the issues related to this activity that are introduced in Figure 10-1.

FIGURE 10-1   Selecting Objectives and Identifying Performance Standards for a Totally New Program

Identifying logical objectives for an innovative program is difficult. This is particularly true when the population to be served differs from that more typically found in regular school courses. For example, it is easier to identify objectives for typical grade 11 students in a United States history course than for a group of gifted students with hearing impairments who are enrolled in a special accelerated English course focusing on Chaucer.

Deciding how well students must perform on the tasks described in program objectives is also very difficult when innovative courses are being considered. No "track record" indicates what, on average, learners might logically be expected to do.

Suppose you were charged with developing objectives and describing expected performance standards for a new, innovative course. How would you respond to these questions?

1. How would you go about the task of identifying objectives?
2. How would you weigh opinions regarding what the objectives should be from such sources as (a) administrators, (b) teachers, and (c) learners?
3. What would you consider in identifying appropriate levels of expected performance for learners? How would you justify your decision to someone who might question your judgment?

Suppose, for example, a school district decided to develop a new course in economics for grade 10 students who had been selected on the basis of (1) their coming from homes where incomes were below a specified level, (2) their having measured reading abilities at least two years below grade level, and (3) their having earned grades of D or F in history and social science courses in grades 8 and 9. As an experimental program, what kinds of objectives should be established for this group? What kinds of expectations should there be? What kinds of test results would indicate that these students were making satisfactory progress?

The difficulty in answering these questions has led to concerns that evaluation limited to determining how well students master predetermined objectives is not appropriate for all instructional settings. A rigid decision to view evaluation in this way could even inhibit the development of innovative programs because of the difficulty of developing evaluation procedures appropriate to determining their effectiveness.

Another issue related to instructional objectives has to do with their appropriateness for *individual* learners within the group being taught.

Tyler's assumption is that needs analyses for a particular group of learners will lead program developers to prepare objectives appropriate for the learners to be served. This presumes that certain common patterns of needs will be found. If so, then objectives can be framed that will be generally suitable for all learners in a class.

Today, however, learners in classrooms are very diverse. Such laws as Public Law 94-142, the Education for All Handicapped Children Act—a law providing for *mainstreaming* learners (placing children with handicapping conditions in regular classrooms to the extent possible)—have greatly increased the range of learners found within individual classrooms. As a result, the needs of learners may be so diverse that teachers and instructors no longer should be expected to develop sets of objectives that apply to them all.

It may be necessary to develop special objectives for individual learners (indeed, in some cases this is now required by law) rather than to develop a set of objectives for a class as a whole. This changes the process of evaluation from one designed to examine the general impact of a common program on a class to a series of evaluations tied to the varying objectives developed for individuals and groups of individuals within a class.

In practice, evaluation that focuses on objectives and their mastery results in assessments that take place only at the end of a fairly long instructional sequence. A typical pattern involves the identification of objectives, the delivery of the program developed in support of these objectives, and the testing and other assessment procedures at the conclusion to find out how well the objectives were met. Results of such evaluation can confirm the excellence of a program, suggest the existence of alternative areas of strength or weakness, or suggest that procedures for delivering the instructional experiences are fundamentally flawed. What the results of these evaluations cannot do is reshape the program as it is being delivered. The evaluation occurs only after the instructional sequence has concluded.

As Scriven (1967) has argued, this practice posits a rather narrow view of evaluation by implying that it serves only the purpose of making a summary judgment about a program. Scriven has embraced a broader conception of evaluation. He contends that evaluation, in addition to its summary judgment role, also should be a vehicle for providing regular information to program developers as instruction is being delivered.

The idea behind this view is to provide feedback that can suggest ways to modify programs as they are being delivered in order to enhance their quality. Scriven has called this kind of ongoing feedback *formative evaluation*. Though Scriven has received a great deal of attention as the author of the term *formative evaluation*, he continues to emphasize the importance of final judgment, or what he terms *summative evaluation*, as well (Scriven, 1967; 43).

PROGRAM IMPROVEMENT EVALUATION: SOME CRITICAL ISSUES

Since the middle 1960s, curriculum evaluation specialists have professed an interest in program improvement as a key purpose of evaluation. Members of the Phi Delta Kappa National Study Committee on Evaluation noted that curriculum evaluation occurs before an instructional sequence begins, during its implementation, and at its conclusion (Stufflebeam et al., 1971).

A conception of curriculum evaluation as a facilitator of program improvement raises a number of critical issues. For example, how does a curriculum evaluator who must work intimately with program developers before and during implementation of an instructional sequence avoid being caught up in the enthusiasms of the program developers he or she is supposed to evaluate? This and other issues that continue to challenge curriculum evaluators are introduced in the subsections that follow.

WHAT CONSTITUTES EXCELLENCE?

Evaluation always requires judgments. And judgments are made in the light of specific criteria. A challenge for all educational evaluators is to ascertain which criteria are appropriate for a particular program being evaluated.

One difficulty relates to the scope of the program. Some evaluations will focus on rather brief instructional sequences, while others focus on complex programs involving dozens of teachers instructing learners in a wide variety of subject areas. The more sophisticated a program is structurally, the harder it is to develop a set of acceptable performance criteria. Indeed, probably no criteria will be acceptable to all people with a stake in the program. Curriculum developers must make choices, and in doing so, are bound to make some people unhappy.

It is hardly news that different people apply different criteria in making judgments about a program's effectiveness. For example, some professional educators not long ago took pride in improvements in the reading achievement of young people as measured by improvements in their scores on the National Assessment of Educational Progress Tests. At the same time, newspaper editorials were castigating the deterioration of school programs. The editorial writers were making judgments based on modest declines in Scholastic Aptitude Test (SAT) scores. The same school programs had produced the improved reading results and the slightly diminished SAT scores (Nowakowski, 1983). Depending on which criterion was applied, the schools were either doing a "better job" or a "poorer job" than they had done before. Sometimes efforts to raise SAT scores may have undesirable side effects. See Figure 10-2 for an example of such a situation.

FIGURE 10-2   One Way to Raise SAT Scores

At a recent school board meeting, a parent took members of the board to task for placing too much emphasis on raising SAT scores. Some of the parent's comments are summarized in the passage below:

> "I have no doubt that the board's new high school program will raise SAT scores. But if you think the scores will go up because of the more difficult programs, you are very much mistaken.
>
> "What *is* going to happen is just this. Your tough new academic requirements are going to result in a skyrocketing dropout rate. You have deliberately established a policy to push out the weaker students. One result, of course, will be that a generally more talented group of students will take the SAT test. Consequently, scores will go up. Is the good publicity you will get as a result worth the cost of denying a high school education to students who will not be able to handle the new, tougher graduation requirements? I don't think so."

Reflect on this statement. Then answer these questions.

1. How valid is the point made by the speaker?
2. Can standards be raised without "pushing out" some learners?
3. How do you think school board members responded?

This discussion of the quality of schools nationally raises another important question for the program evaluator. Should criteria of excellence be established in terms of national expectations? Or, should they be developed in terms of local conditions? If excellence is defined in terms of national standards, some districts may find criteria set too high for their students. Others may find them set too low. If they are set higher than an honest analysis of learners in the district suggests they should be set, even the best prepared and delivered instructional program will not produce results consistent with national norms. But, there may be political problems for school leaders if criteria of excellence are set below national standards. Some community members may publicly decry efforts to "water down" the school program.

Conversely, if a school district is blessed with a population of learners that tends to exceed national norms, an effort to establish criteria of excellence in terms of national standards may have regrettable results. In a few places, these criteria might be embraced by unethical school leaders as a vehicle for making the district's test scores look exceptionally good. There is also an accompanying danger that some influential community leaders will question what they may regard as an effort to undermine the rigor of the existing academic program.

WHAT ARE THE REAL NEEDS OF LEARNERS
TO BE SERVED?

The issue of serving the real needs of learners who will be consumers of instructional programs is closely associated with the issue of excellence. Ideally, criteria of excellence will be determined in light of the needs of the learners to be served. Regrettably, this is not always the case.

In developing a rationale for an instructional program, curriculum developers are often tempted to look to the professional research literature for guidance. For example, if considering a new gifted-and-talented program, they may review research reports on gifted-and-talented learners. If a new program is to serve disadvantaged students, there is an inclination for them to see what the research on disadvantaged students has to say.

This approach is laudable in its intent. However, results from national research reports are not always relevant to local populations of learners. There are enormous differences among a national group of learners identified as gifted and talented or as disadvantaged. Findings of research reports may speak clearly to characteristics of average learners in each of these groups, but at the local level the relatively small number of gifted and talented or disadvantaged learners (small in terms of the national total of such students) may have characteristics that differ substantially from these national averages.

It does not make much sense, therefore, to evaluate local programs for the gifted and talented or the disadvantaged on the basis of criteria that might be defensible when looking at the total national populations. Evaluators need to work closely with program developers to ascertain the real needs of the learners who are being served by the instructional program to be evaluated. The question should not be framed: "What are the needs of gifted and talented or disadvantaged learners?" Rather, it should be: "What are the needs of *our* gifted and talented or *our* disadvantaged learners?"

This kind of focus encourages program developers and evaluators to give some serious thought to the learners who will actually be served by the instructional program. Evaluation in light of the demonstrated needs of local learners makes more sense than schemes to assess progress in light of possibly irrelevant needs of national groups of similarly labeled learners.

HOW ARE PROGRAMS DELIVERED?

When an instructional program is evaluated, it is assumed to have been delivered as it was designed to be delivered. This assumption is something that evaluators cannot take for granted, particularly when the instructional program being assessed is large in scale and involves many teachers and instructors.

It is not enough to know that all teachers and instructors have been informed about what they are to do. Even the provision of workshops and training sessions is no assurance that the program is being delivered properly by all instructional personnel. Some people may have failed to understand certain directions provided during training sessions. Others may have missed some training sessions. Still others may have taken the training but found what they were being asked to do philosophically at odds with their own views of how certain content should be approached. For a variety of reasons, programs may not be consistently implemented as they are designed.

This situation poses problems for the evaluator. Unless he or she is sure that the instructional program is being delivered reasonably consistently, generalizations about overall program effectiveness are suspect. Evaluators, then, have an interest in looking at more than measures of learner performance. They also have to concern themselves with the issue of teacher-to-teacher consistency.

WHAT ARE THE IMPLICATIONS OF AN UNSATISFACTORY EVALUATION?

Since evaluation involves judgment, some instructional programs will be judged to be deficient in terms of at least some of the criteria that have been established. What will happen as a result of a negative evaluation can influence what the evaluators decide.

If evaluation is viewed as a summary judgment, a negative decision may well mean the discontinuance of a given program. For example, in a federally funded project, such a decision may "kill" a program at the end of the first year of a projected three-year program cycle. This possibility places very heavy pressure on the evaluator to find enough positives in a program to allow it to survive. Individuals responsible for program development also have an incentive to select evaluators thought to be generally sympathetic to program aims. Unless safeguards are built in, there is a possibility that the harsh consequences of a negative evaluation report may undermine the integrity of the evaluation process.

In addition to pressure from individuals having a stake in maintaining a given instructional program, evaluators asked to make summary judgments on programs also occasionally face another serious problem. Sometimes they are asked to make judgments about programs that have been in place only a very short time, perhaps only a single academic year. There is evidence that new programs require a certain settling-in period before they can function as designed, largely because teachers need to become thoroughly familiar with materials and weaknesses in the original program design need to be remedied. When summary evaluations are called for too soon, evaluators may find themselves forced to draw negative conclusions. Given more time, programs that in the short run appear to be deficient may merit a much more favorable judgment from evaluators.

If the purpose of the evaluation is not to provide a summary judgment but rather to provide suggestions for improvement, the evaluator faces a somewhat different set of conditions. In this case, his or her task is to determine satisfactory and unsatisfactory components of the program. The program's continuance is not an issue. Consider the situation presented in Figure 10-3 of evaluating a program under two sets of conditions.

Data-gathering under this set of circumstances is complex, since the task now is to do a detailed analysis of internal program elements. Furthermore, the evaluator typically is challenged to do more than identify problem areas. Specific suggestions for improvement usually accompany the report. Ideas for change have to be practical, and the careful evaluator works closely with teachers and instructors to assure that recommendations will be feasible. Thus the evaluator must maintain good lines of communication with the people responsible for delivering the program.

WHO RECEIVES THE RESULTS OF THE EVALUATION?

A number of individuals and groups have a stake in any instructional program. In public school systems, these people are primarily superintendents, principals, teachers, leaders of parent-teacher organizations, and learners. Each of these groups brings a slightly different perspective to an instructional program. Each has a unique set of needs and priorities. This means the kinds of information wanted from an evaluation of an instructional program will not be the same for each group.

Priorities for teachers might include information about learners' enthusiasm for the program, ease of management of instructional materials and records, and out-of-class preparation time. Principals may be particularly interested in issues such as the impact of an instructional program on standardized test scores. Superintendents, working closely with budgets, may have a need for cost-effectiveness data. (In terms of what it delivers, how does this program's costs compare to that of an alternative?) Depending on the nature of the instructional program, parents may wish to know how well it meshes with requirements for college and university entrance.

Such differences in information needs present evaluation specialists with a real dilemma. One response would be to organize the evaluation effort in such a way that all information needs are accommodated. But, as Cooley has noted, "if the evaluation activity is guided by the information requirements of a variety of stakeholders with a broad range of interests, the evaluation effort tends to try to serve everyone's needs for information and ends up serving no one very effectively" (Cooley, 1983; p. 7).

FIGURE 10-3   Evaluating a Program Under Two Sets of Conditions

Suppose you had an opportunity to lead a team of people charged with evaluating a given instructional program under either one of two sets of conditions, as follows:

Condition A: A positive evaluation will allow the program to continue; a negative evaluation will kill the program.

Condition B: The program's survival is assured. Evaluation results will be directed at program improvement.

First, respond to these questions under the assumption that you have been asked to assume Condition A. Then, respond to them under the assumption that you have been asked to assume Condition B.

1. How much pressure will you feel to avoid negative findings?
2. What will be the nature of your relationships with program developers and with people teaching in the program?
3. How will you personally feel about undertaking the evaluation task? Why do you feel this way?

Another response to this problem has been to identify the needs of one constituency and to design the evaluation primarily with a view to providing information it considers important. Cooley (1983) suggests that, in a school district, the superintendent's information requirements be used as the primary focus for instructional program evaluation. The superintendent, as the chief school officer, has the authority to make the most practical use of evaluation information.

The decision to design evaluations to provide information of relevance to either a single or a very limited number of school program stakeholders does allow for more efficient deployment of the evaluator's resources. The kinds of information needed tend to be limited in scope, and this reduces the complexity of the evaluation design. This approach, however, has the potential to produce an evaluation that will not provide information useful to many who are intimately associated with the day-to-day operation of the instructional program. Teachers may well be disappointed by an evaluation that responds effectively to administrators' concerns but fails to attend well to their own.

There is no simple answer to the dilemmas evaluators face in deciding what individuals and groups are to be served by the results of their work. They must effectively balance the need to husband resources so as to provide information that has some real substance with the desire to respond meaningfully to groups who may have very different information needs.

PROVIDING FOR COMPREHENSIVE EVALUATION: SOME RESPONSES

Responses to the issues raised in the previous section vary tremendously from evaluator to evaluator and from place to place. However, there have been some attempts to lay out general guidelines for responsible practice that are thought to have value in a variety of settings.

A common theme running through the work of many contemporary evaluation specialists is that evaluation ought to be directed at more than making a summary judgment of an instructional program. An evaluation scheme should provide information that can be used to improve programs as they are being delivered. Scriven's idea of formative evaluation introduced earlier has become very central to the field of curriculum evaluation.

DANIEL L. STUFFLEBEAM: THE CIPP MODEL

Stufflebeam has been very much interested in schemes that "lead to evaluations that would aid in managing and improving programs" (Stufflebeam and Shinkfield, 1985; p. 155). Stufflebeam takes a very broad view of evaluation, pointing out a need for the evaluator to become involved at the initial planning stage, even before an instructional program is implemented, as well as at later stages.

Stufflebeam developed a four-part model that has been widely used as a basis for educational evaluation. (See Figure 10-4 for an illustration.) Stufflebeam's model includes what he calls (1) context evaluation, (2) input evaluation, (3) process evaluation, and (4) product evaluation. This is popularly known as the CIPP model for evaluation (Stufflebeam et al., 1971).

Context Evaluation

In the CIPP model, context evaluation has been included out of a recognition that planning decisions that precede implementation of an instructional program have implications for its success or failure. For example, if a program is directed at goals that are inappropriate for the learners to be served, even the best teachers will have difficulty making the program work.

Suppose, for example, that a decision were made to require all grade 9 gifted-and-talented students to study Shakespeare's *Hamlet* as part of their experience in an enriched English program. Several program goals might be developed around this basic idea.

Suppose, further, that a large number of these students, during a special summer course, had engaged in an in-depth study of *Hamlet*. It is

FIGURE 10-4   Stufflebeam's CIPP Model of Evaluation

	Context Evaluation	*Input Evaluation*	*Process Evaluation*	*Product Evaluation*
Objective	To define the institutional context, to identify the target population and assess their needs, to identify opportunities for addressing the needs, to diagnose *problems* underlying the *needs*, and to judge whether proposed objectives are sufficiently responsive to the assessed needs.	To identify and assess *system capabilities*, alternative program *strategies*, procedural *designs* for implementing the strategies, budgets, and schedules.	To identify or predict in process, *defects* in the procedural design or its implementation, to provide information for the programmed decisions, and to record and judge procedural events and activities.	To collect descriptions and judgments of outcomes and to relate them to objectives and to context, input, and process information, and to interpret their worth and merit.
Method	By using such methods as system analysis, survey, document review, hearings, interviews, diagnostic tests, and the Delphi technique.	By inventorying and analyzing available human and material resources, solution strategies, and procedural designs for relevance, feasibility and economy. And by using such methods as literature search, visits to exemplary programs, advocate	By monitoring the activity's potential procedural barriers and remaining alert to unanticipated ones, by obtaining specified information for programmed decisions, by describing the actual process, and by continually interacting with, and	By defining operationally and measuring outcome criteria, by collecting judgments of outcomes from stakeholders, and by performing both qualitative and quantitative analyses.

(Continues)

FIGURE 10-4   *(Continued)*

	Context Evaluation	Input Evaluation	Process Evaluation	Product Evaluation
		teams, and pilot trials.	observing the activities of project staff.	
Relation to decision making in the change process	For deciding upon the *setting* to be served, the *goals* associated with meeting needs or using opportunities, and the *objectives* associated with solving problems, i.e., for *planning* needed changes. And to provide a basis for judging outcomes.	For selecting *sources of support*, solution *strategies*, and procedural *designs*, i.e., for *structuring* change activities. And to provide a basis for judging implementation.	For *implementing and refining the program design and procedure*, i.e., for effecting *process control*. And to provide a log of the actual process for later use in interpreting outcomes.	For deciding to *continue*, *terminate*, *modify*, or *refocus* a change activity. And to present a clear record of effects (intended and unintended, positive and negative).

Source: Reprinted from Stufflebeam and Shinkfield, *Systematic Evaluation* (1985) by permission of Kluwer-Nijhoff Publishing.

conceivable that some of them might well resent being taught what they believe themselves already to know. Attitudes could be negative from the very beginning, and the new program might not be well received at all.

Context evaluation is directed at preventing this sort of error by examining the initial program-planning assumptions. For example, context evaluation might well seek information about students' prior exposure to *Hamlet*. The effort should determine whether a program centering on this play would truly be providing a new and enriching experience for learners.

Context evaluation attempts to look carefully at the nature of the population to be served. This means looking at the specific learners who will be recipients of the program, not the general class of such learners (e.g., all gifted-and-talented ninth graders in the United States).

If proposed programs goals cannot be defended in light of the real needs of the learners, then prospects that the program will succeed are dim. Feedback from context evaluation allows program planners to adjust program goals. It provides a "reality check" that allows instructional designers to ascertain the adequacy of their assumptions about the learners and other features of the context in which the completed program will operate.

Input Evaluation

Once the evaluator is satisfied with the adequacy of basic goals established to guide development of an instructional program, he or she needs to look at the means proposed to meet these goals. This component of evaluation looks at plans for implementation, asking the key question: "Given the options available for meeting established goals, is this the best choice?"

For example, if context evaluation revealed that the goal of familiarizing gifted-and-talented ninth graders with a Shakespearean tragedy was defensible, evaluators might look at specific instructional materials to which, it has been proposed, learners will be exposed. An initial plan might prompt such questions as these:

1. To what extent have students already read and learned about this play?
2. To what extent do features of *Hamlet* exemplify the general character of Shakespeare's tragedies?
3. What specific edition of *Hamlet* will be available for learners? How appropriate is it?
4. What are the advantages of using *Hamlet* as the major focus as opposed to such plays as *King Lear* or *Macbeth*?

In addition to asking questions about the play that is to serve as the major content focus, evaluators at this phase also look at general features of the instructional design. Some relevant questions for input evaluation are:

1. How is content to be sequenced? What is the basis for this decision?
2. What specific instructional techniques are to be employed? Why are these techniques to be preferred over alternatives?
3. What provisions are there for assessing learners' progress? Is this the best arrangement that can be devised?

Input evaluation attempts to validate the adequacy of the instructional design with the goal of helping program developers make the best possible plans before instruction commences.

Process Evaluation

Process evaluation occurs as an instructional program is being implemented. The idea is to monitor instruction so as to assure the program is being delivered as designed. This is an especially critical activity in a large program involving many teachers or instructors.

Process evaluation requires feedback at frequent intervals to those who are teaching the program. Stufflebeam reports on one large-scale evaluation effort where instructors received reports from evaluators once every two weeks (Stufflebeam and Shinkfield, 1985).

However, process evaluation has functions that go beyond providing feedback to teachers and instructors. It also provides insights regarding the adequacy of the preparation of individuals who are delivering a program. Information from process evaluation can suggest needed modifications in the training of teachers who may begin teaching the program at a later date. Finally, the process evaluation record provides a summary of how well, on average, program implementation followed program design.

Product Evaluation

Product evaluation is that component of the evaluation process that answers the question: "Were the goals of the instructional program achieved?" This phase of evaluation occurs at the conclusion of the planned instructional program. Data from product evaluation may be used as a basis for modifying the design of another cycle of the instructional program but not to improve the program being evaluated. That program is viewed as completed once product evaluation begins.

Stufflebeam is an example of a contemporary evaluation specialist who is a strong partisan of the evaluation-for-program-improvement point of view. Two of his major categories, context evaluation and input evaluation, involve the evaluator even before the program is implemented. While he does not dispute the importance of summative or product evaluation, his priority is ongoing program improvement.

ROBERT E. STAKE: THE COUNTENANCE OF EDUCATIONAL EVALUATION AND RESPONSIVE EVALUATION

As with Stufflebeam, Stake's interest in curriculum evaluation goes well beyond a consideration of whether established program objectives are achieved. In 1967 Stake wrote an article entitled, "The Countenance of Educational Evaluation," that continues to be regarded as an important contribution to the field (Stake, 1967). An illustration of the general categories to which Stake believes evaluators should attend is provided in Figure 10-5.

FIGURE 10-5   Stake's Antecedents, Transactions, and Outcomes Framework

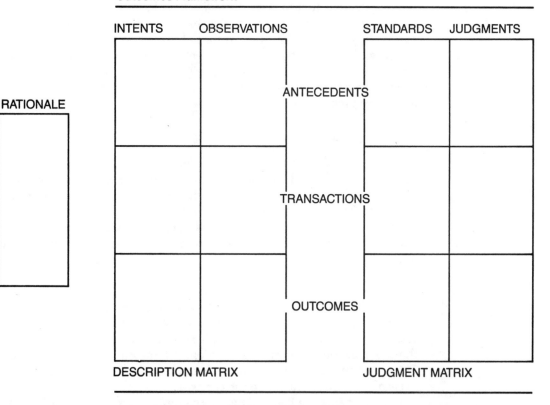

Source: Robert E. Stake. "The Countenance of Educational Evaluation." *Teachers College Record*, *68*, (April 1967), p. 529. Reprinted by permission of Teacher's College Press. Copyright © 1967.

Antecedents

Evaluation related to *antecedents* focuses on information that is available before an actual instructional sequence is implemented. The category includes dimensions of both Stufflebeam's context and input categories. With respect to antecedents, the evaluator is charged with identifying conditions that might have some impact on learners' performance once an instructional sequence begins.

These antecedent conditions can be quite varied. Suppose, for example, that a group of disadvantaged learners lived in poorly heated, substandard housing. During the winter months, such learners might have frequent colds, influenza episodes, and other conditions that could deplete their energies and cause frequent absences from school. Antecedent evaluation is directed toward identifying such circumstances, and data are used to illuminate further the meaning of learners' test scores and performances on other evaluative measures.

Transactions

Evaluation that focuses on *transactions* looks at elements of an instructional program as it is being delivered, similar to Stufflebeam's process evaluation. Among other things, transaction evaluation looks at patterns of interactions among teachers and learners, considering their adequacy. This information, along with antecedent-evaluation data, is used to help explain patterns of learner performance on tests and other assessment measures.

Outcomes

The area of *outcomes* involves judgments in light of the goals and objectives established to guide the instructional program. This component of Stake's scheme is similar to what Stufflebeam has called *product evaluation*. These outcomes relate not only to the impact of a program on learners; data should also be gathered regarding program influences on teachers, administrators, parents, custodians, and any other potentially affected parties.

Along with these categories, Stake proposed a five-step evaluation process. The five parts are illustrated in the diagram in Figure 10–5. First, the purpose or rationale of the program must be identified. Next, it is necessary to identify *intents* (what people want to see occur) for each of the three evaluation categories—antecedents, transactions, and outcomes. Third, *observations* must be made to determine what is actually happening in each of the three evaluation categories.

Once data have been gathered, the next step requires identification and description of some *standards*, or acceptable conditions, for each of the categories. The final step requires *judgments* to be made. Judgments are made in consideration of program intents, observations, and standards. The purpose of these judgments is to provide some indication of the general level of satisfaction with the instructional program.

Stake (1975) has been increasingly concerned with the issue of summary judgments about programs. He suggests that because different people have different views as to what constitutes excellence, evaluators should work hard to learn the priorities of the individuals affected by programs (for example, teachers, administrators, parents). He proposes that evaluators themselves gather data relevant to the interests of these groups, so that the groups can then make summary judgments regarding how well the program is serving their own interests. Consider the perspectives reflected in the situation described in Figure 10-6.

Stake's interests in serving the varying needs of individuals affected by instructional programs have led him to coin the term *responsive evaluation*. Responsive evaluation recognizes that different people apply different quality indicators. It places an obligation on the evaluators to gather and package data in different ways to meet the special needs of groups with individual interests in the instructional program.

FIGURE 10-6   Who Should Make the Judgment?

At a recent symposium, two debaters focused on the pronouncement: "Resolved that consumers of evaluation data, not evaluators, should judge the quality of evaluated programs." Comments of the two sides are briefly summarized here:

Pro Position. No evaluator can be as intimately associated with the true purposes of an instructional program as can be its designers and those who teach in it. These people know what they want. They *do* need data that can be supplied by professional evaluators. What they do *not* require is some outsider making a value judgment about their own programs.

Con Position. Allowing consumers of evaluation data to make judgments about program work assures that the negatives will be overlooked. Program developers and those who teach in programs have too great a personal investment to subject themselves to harsh self-judgments. An outside evaluator brings a fresh perspective, and he or she properly should judge.

1. What are your general reactions to the pro position as presented here?
2. What are your general reactions to the con position?
3. What other arguments might you wish to add to either the pro position or the con position?
4. What is your own position on this issue?

Stake places a very high priority on close relationships between the evaluators and the people who design and deliver instructional programs. He points out, for example, that some program goals develop as a program is being taught (Stake, 1975). The evaluator and the individuals responsible for the program should work together to identify these emerging goals. Data should be gathered regarding these emerging goals as well as information regarding those goals that were originally identified.

Stake's responsive evaluation is heavily oriented toward providing information that those involved with the program will find useful. This implies a great deal of flexibility on the part of the evaluator, as he or she assesses the evaluation effort in terms of its practical value for those who, in the end, will receive the information.

MALCOLM PROVUS: DISCREPANCY EVALUATION

Malcolm Provus developed an approach known as *discrepancy evaluation* when he served as director of research for the Pittsburgh schools. Discrepancy analysis calls for a comparison to be made "between reality and some standard or standards. The comparison often shows differences between standard and reality; this difference is called discrepancy" (Provus, 1971; p. 46). Provus suggested that the following five stages characterize the discrepancy-evaluation process: (1) design, (2) installation, (3) process, (4) product, and (5) cost.

Design

At this stage, the evaluator is charged with working closely with program developers to ascertain exactly what they wish to do. This goes beyond questioning central office administrators and supervisors, to getting information directly from teachers and instructors. Often this phase begins with a series of questions to the instructional staff, such as: "What is it you would like to accomplish?" "How would you describe the nature of students when they first come to you?" "What are your priorities for change?"

Evaluators work with program personnel to focus on these questions and to develop a consensus in support of a preliminary program design. Outside experts and other professionals study this design to contrast it with an ideal design. To the extent possible, the design is reworked so that it meets both the needs of local teaching and administrative staff and the criteria of excellence accepted by experts.

Installation

The program design specifies what is to be done instructionally. The *installation* phase of evaluation is designed to determine the extent to which the program design is being implemented. Provus was especially concerned about the consistency of application of agreed-upon elements of the instructional program. He reported on one case where an innovation labeled as "team teaching" was being taught in 131 different ways in a single school district (Provus, 1971). Installation evaluation provides evaluators with information regarding the extent to which program elements are being implemented as intended. Some curriculum professionals find a consistency-of-program-delivery checklist useful as they try to determine how a planned program is being implemented. An example of such a checklist is provided in Figure 10-7.

If it is determined that there are discrepancies between what the program design calls for and what is being taught in the classrooms, the evaluator has several things to consider. On the one hand, he or she may determine that the basic program design is flawed and that the deficiency does not result from an inconsistent pattern of program delivery. Should this be the case, there is a need to revise the design itself.

On the other hand, the problem might lie not with the design but with some other variable. For example, there may be problems in terms of

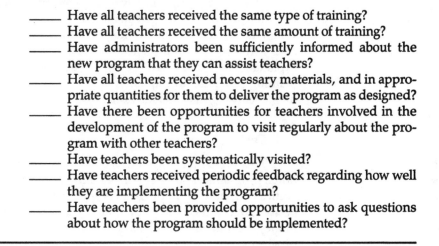

FIGURE 10-7   Consistency-of-Program-Delivery Checklist

When large-scale instructional programs are evaluated, there is an assumption that all teachers have been teaching the program as it was designed. When this is not the case, summary judgments may be meaningless because actual performances of individual teachers may vary tremendously.

The following items are among those that might be found on a consistency-of-program-delivery checklist. You may wish to extend the list by adding other entries.

_____ Have all teachers received the same type of training?
_____ Have all teachers received the same amount of training?
_____ Have administrators been sufficiently informed about the new program that they can assist teachers?
_____ Have all teachers received necessary materials, and in appropriate quantities for them to deliver the program as designed?
_____ Have there been opportunities for teachers involved in the development of the program to visit regularly about the program with other teachers?
_____ Have teachers been systematically visited?
_____ Have teachers received periodic feedback regarding how well they are implementing the program?
_____ Have teachers been provided opportunities to ask questions about how the program should be implemented?

how individuals have been trained to work with the new program. Supplies needed to support the program may not be uniformly available at all school sites. Or there may be still other reasons that account for the inconsistent pattern. The evaluator must study unique characteristics of the program under consideration before making a recommendation.

Process

Process evaluation in the Provus model requires the evaluator to look at some short-term or interim results of the program. Suppose a new program had been developed to increase the rate at which students became familiar with present-tense endings of French verbs. There are three major categories of French verbs: *er* verbs, *ir* verbs, and *re* verbs. Process evaluation might look at the extent to which learners were able to produce correct endings for each of these verb types. Learning these endings is a subordinate component of the larger activity that, it is hoped, will allow students to express present-tense forms of all three major verb types.

The standard of performance for each of the activities should be described in the program design. When there is a discrepancy between standard and actual performance, the evaluator and others responsible for the program must take corrective action. Corrective action could involve, among other things, tinkering with the program design or checking on the adequacy of implementation.

Product

The *product* stage involves an evaluation designed to determine whether standards prescribed in the program design have been met. When there is a discrepancy, the evaluator and other professionals associated with the project are encouraged to consider a number of possible explanations. These might be still-present flaws in the basic design, remaining problems in implementation, or inadequate mastery of subordinate learning that was not noticed during the process evaluation stage.

Cost

This evaluation stage takes place once all other data are in. Instructional programs encumber scarce instructional resources. It is not always sufficient to note that a program is effective. Sometimes programs have to be weighed in terms of "how much good" is delivered for "how much money." Evaluators may be asked to compare relative costs of alternative programs.

ADVERSARY EVALUATION

In recent years, an approach to program evaluation called *adversary evaluation* has attracted attention. Adversary evaluation attempts to apply certain judicial procedures to program evaluation. Specifically, there are attempts to view evaluation issues as two-sided and to charge specific individuals with "making the case" for each contending position.

Adversary evaluation developed out of a concern that evaluators might identify too closely with the interests of program developers. This can be a particular problem when evaluation is thought of as directed toward the end of program improvement. Such evaluations depend very heavily on close working relationships between evaluators and individuals charged with designing and delivering instructional programs. Under these circumstances evaluators may tend to overemphasize strong points and deemphasize weak ones to maintain the supportive relationship that has evolved as the program has been planned and implemented. The issue of evaluator bias is explored in Figure 10-8.

Adversary evaluation proposes to resolve this possible problem by assuring that negatives and positives associated with each issue are aired.

FIGURE 10-8   Can Program Evaluation Be Bias-Free?

The following comments were made by someone interested in evaluation of instructional programs:

> "The basic difficulty with instructional evaluation is that it is almost impossible to get a completely fair judgment. This results because of the nature of the relationship between evaluators and their employers.
>
> "If the evaluator is a member of the school district, he or she faces great pressures to come up with a finding consistent with administrators' wishes. For example, if administrators have committed a great deal of public money to a new program, they are going to be unhappy if an evaluation reveals it to have been a 'failure.'
>
> "Even when outside evaluators are brought in, there still may be problems. These people are employees, even though temporary ones, of the school district. If the evaluation does not turn out 'right,' he or she may not be invited back. If the word gets around to enough districts, this evaluator may find it hard to get other consulting contracts."

Think about these arguments as you answer these questions:

1. How severe is the problem alluded to above?
2. What might be done to reduce the intensity of some of these pressures?
3. Is it possible to get bias-free evaluation?

One model for doing this has been proposed by Wolf (1975). Wolf identified the following four stages in the adversary evaluation process:

> Stage 1. Issue-Generation Stage
> Stage 2. Issue-Selection Stage
> Stage 3. Preparation-of-Arguments Stage
> Stage 4. Hearing Stage

Issue-Generation Stage

At this stage, evaluators work with key individuals responsible for the instructional program to identify issues that might be considered in judging its relative strengths and weaknesses. Sometimes these isuses are developed in question form. (Is the program cost effective? To what extent do learners find it interesting? Does content coverage compare favorably with alternative programs?) Whatever the method, evaluators at this stage generate a long list of potentially relevant issues.

Issue-Selection Stage

At this stage, the evaluators and individuals responsible for the instructional program select a limited number of the issues generated in the previous stage to be used in the evaluation. These are selected on the basis of perceived importance.

Preparation-of-Arguments Stage

At this point, two teams are identified. One team is charged with gathering as much evidence as possible to support an affirmative response to each of the issues identified in the previous stage. The second team is charged with gathering as much evidence as possible to support a negative response to each identified issue. (For example, one team might seek as much information as possible to support the position that a new program *is* cost effective, the other that it was not.) The two teams then go about the task of gathering information as requested.

Hearing Stage

At this point in the evaluation, a panel of responsible experts is gathered together to judge the findings. The panel might include people from the school district, or it could consist of experts brought in from outside who have no personal stake in the program, or it might be a mixture of school district and outside people. Paralleling the number of individuals found on many juries, there might be around twelve panel members. Representatives from each team then argue the case for and against each issue while the panel listens. When all testimony has been given, the panel gathers together and renders a final evaluative judgment about the program under review.

The adversary evaluation approach has both strengths and weaknesses. On the positive side, nearly every scrap of evidence relevant to an issue will be publicly presented to the hearing panel. The procedure assures that arguments that may not represent the thinking of certain school district officials will be made. Also, the competitive nature of the procedure may enhance the quality of arguments. There is an incentive for those presenting the positive and the negative cases for each issue to seek the most compelling evidence they can find to support their positions.

On the other hand, the approach has certain drawbacks. It has been argued that not all relevant issues divide into two clearly opposing positions (Arnstein, 1975). The need to find issues that can be debated in a pro and con fashion may result in some important issues being ignored. It has also been argued that the skill of some presenters may influence panel members to make one decision even though the preponderance of evidence points to another. Finally, the numbers of people involved are great, and, consequently, the cost of adversary evaluations can be high.

SUMMARY

Until the 1930s, evaluation of educational programs often looked at teacher characteristics, numbers of relevant materials in the library, and other variables having somewhat tenuous ties to the instructional program itself. Modern program evaluation dates from the work of Ralph Tyler. Tyler proposed that evaluation should focus on how well program objectives were mastered by learners.

In recent years, several concerns have been raised regarding objectives-based program evaluation. Some have suggested that this approach may lead program developers to select objectives that readily lend themselves to measurement rather than those that are intrinsically good. The widespread availability of standardized tests invites the possibility that objectives appropriate for individual instructional settings will be abandoned in favor of those which can easily be measured by standardized tests.

Some critics have pointed out the difficulty of developing objectives for innovative programs which have no "histories," and, hence, no guidelines for program developers to follow. Finally, objectives-based evaluation tends to presume that all learners will be seeking to accomplish the same objectives. Learners in classrooms today are more mixed than they have ever been. It may be that not all learners should be pursuing a common set of objectives.

In thinking about alternative approaches to evaluation that go beyond an exclusive focus on program objectives, a number of issues have faced evaluation specialists. They have had to confront such questions as: "What constitutes excellence?" "Are instructional programs being delivered as designed?" "What are the implications of an 'unsatisfactory' evaluation?" and "Who receives the results of evaluation?"

A number of proposals for comprehensive evaluation procedures have been suggested, most of which tend to view program improvement as an important evaluation function. Stufflebeam's CIPP model clearly reflects this orientation. Robert Stake's responsive evaluation is particularly concerned with the varying perspectives of different groups who will be consumers of educational evaluation efforts. He prefers to work closely with these groups, provide data responsive to their interests, and allow them to make summary value judgments.

Provus has proposed that evaluators identify a number of relevant dimensions of a program. Evaluators are encouraged to identify "what is" and "what ought to be," and then to make judgments about any "discrepancies" between the two.

Wolf has been one of a number of individuals who have attempted to apply certain judicial procedures to program evaluation. Adversary evaluation is designed to provide a fair hearing for two relevant positions and all supporting data germane to a given program evaluation. Arguments pro and con are made before a hearing panel. Then the panel presents its judgments to those responsible for the program being evaluated.

In summary, educational evaluation has come to be viewed as a complex, multifaceted process. Increasingly, there is attention to the need for evaluation to begin early and to be directed, in part at least, to improving the program as it is being delivered.

EXTENDING AND APPLYING CHAPTER CONTENT

1. Invite someone who has directed curriculum evaluation projects to visit the class. Ask this person to address such questions as these:
   a. To what extent should evaluation be directed at program improvement?
   b. Is it the role of the evaluator to make a summary judgment about a program's worth?
   c. How does the evaluator avoid becoming so personally involved with the program he or she is evaluating that his or her ability to make a reasoned judgment is impaired?
   d. What kinds of evidence should be considered in an evaluation? How should this evidence be gathered?
   e. Who should be the primary beneficiaries of program evaluation?
2. A number of approaches to adversary evaluation are reported in the professional literature. Identify two or three of these and prepare a chart comparing similarities and differences. Present this material to your instructor, and use it as a basis for a class discussion focusing on pros and cons of this approach to program evaluation.
3. Suppose you were charged with evaluating an instructional program in your own area of expertise. If you wished to frame your evaluation effort using Stufflebeam's CIPP model, what kinds of evaluation data would you seek to gather under the respective categories of context, input, process, and product. How would you go about gathering data under each category? When would you be satisfied that you had enough information? Prepare your evaluation plan in the form of a written report and present it to your instructor for review.
4. Think about your own area of instructional expertise. Suppose you were charged with evaluating a new program in this area. Make a complete list of all the groups that might have an interest in this program. What specific information about the program might each like to have? How would you go about gathering this information? Given that your resources are limited, how would you allocate the time of the evaluation staff in seeking information of interest to each group? In other words, how would you establish priorities among these groups? What is your rationale for this decision? Present your findings to the class in the form of an oral report.
5. This chapter introduces only a few program evaluation models. Find

three to five others in the professional literature. Your instructor may be able to suggest some names to look for. Prepare a chart on which you compare perspectives of developers of these approaches to any two of those introduced in the chapter. Comparisons might focus on such issues as (1) position regarding evaluation as more directed toward summary judgment than program improvement, (2) responsibility of the evaluator as the person who makes the summary judgment, (3) the nature of the relationship between the evaluator and the program developers, and (4) the primary audience(s) to be served by the evaluation. Share your chart with others in the class. Your instructor may wish to use these charts as a basis for a classroom discussion.

BIBLIOGRAPHY

Arnstein, George. 1975. "The Outcome." *Phi Delta Kappan, 57,* (November: 188–190.

Bryk, A. S. 1983. *Stakeholder-Based Evaluation.* San Francisco: Jossey-Bass.

Cooley, William W. 1983. "Improving the Performance of an Educational System." *Educational Researcher, 12,* (June/July): 4–12.

Nowakowski, Jeri R. 1983. "On Educational Evaluation: A Conversation with Ralph Tyler." *Educational Leadership, 40,* (May): 24–29.

Provus, Malcolm. 1971. *Discrepancy Evaluation for Educational Program Improvement and Assessment.* Berkeley, Calif.: McCutchan Publishing Corporation.

Scriven, Michael. 1967. "The Methodology of Evaluation." *Perspectives on Curriculum Evaluation.* Edited by Robert W. Stake, et al. AERA Monograph Series on Curriculum Evaluation, No. 1. Chicago: Rand McNally, pp. 39–83.

Stake, Robert E. 1967. "The Countenance of Educational Evaluation." *Teachers College Record, 68,* (April): 523–540.

Stake, Robert E. 1975. "Program Evaluation: Particularly Responsive Evaluation." Kalamazoo, Mich.: Evaluation Center, Western Michigan University, Occasional Paper Number 5, (November).

Stufflebeam, Daniel L., Walter J. Foley, William J. Gephart, Egon G. Guba, Robert L. Hammond, Howard O. Merriman, and Malcolm M. Provus. 1971. *Educational Evaluation and Decision-Making.* Bloomington, Ind.: Phi Delta Kappa.

Stufflebeam, Daniel L. and Anthony J. Shinkfield. 1985. *Systematic Evaluation.* Boston: Kluwer-Nijhoff Publishing, pp. 170–171.

Tuckman, Bruce Wayne. 1985. *Evaluation Instructional Programs,* 2d ed. Boston: Allyn & Bacon.

Tyler, Ralph W. 1949. *Basic Principles of Curriculum and Instruction.* Chicago: University of Chicago Press.

Wolf, Robert L. 1975. "Trial by Jury: A New Evaluation Method." *Phi Delta Kappan, 57,* (November): 185–187.

Author Index

*n: citation or bibliographic reference.

Subject Index